DD 175 GER

New Perspectives in German Studies

General Editors: Professor **Michael Butler**, Head of Department of German Studies, University of Birmingham and Professor **William Paterson**, Director of the Institute of German Studies, University of Birmingham.

Over the last twenty years the concept of German studies has undergone major transformation. The traditional mixture of language and literary studies, related very closely to the discipline as practised in German universities, has expanded to embrace history, politics, economics and cultural studies. The conventional boundaries between all these disciplines have become increasingly blurred, a process which has been accelerated markedly since German unification in 1989/90.

New Perspectives in German Studies, developed in conjunction with the Institute for German Studies at the University of Birmingham, has been designed to respond precisely to this trend of the interdisciplinary approach to the study of German and to cater for the growing interest in Germany in the context of European integration. The books in this series will focus on the modern period, from 1750 to the present day.

Titles include:

Michael Butler and Robert Evans (*editors*)
THE CHALLENGE OF GERMAN CULTURE
Essays Presented to Wilfried van der Will

Michael Butler, Malcolm Pender and Joy Charnley (*editors*)
THE MAKING OF MODERN SWITZERLAND 1848–1998

Wolf-Dieter Eberwein and Karl Kaiser (*editors*)
GERMANY'S NEW FOREIGN POLICY
Decision-Making in an Interdependent World

Jonathan Grix
THE ROLE OF THE MASSES IN THE COLLAPSE OF THE GDR

Henning Tewes
GERMANY'S CIVILIAN POWER POLITICS
The Western Integration of East Central Europe Since 1989

Maiken Umbach
GERMAN FEDERALISM
Past, Present, Future

New Perspectives in German Studies
Series Standing Order ISBN 0–333–92430–4
(*outside North America only*)

You can receive future titles in this series as they are published by placing a standing order. Please contact your bookseller or, in case of difficulty, write to us at the address below with your name and address, the title of the series and the ISBN quoted above.

Customer Services Department, Macmillan Distribution Ltd, Houndmills, Basingstoke, Hampshire RG21 6XS, England

German Federalism

Past, Present, Future

Edited by

Maiken Umbach
Lecturer in Modern European History
University of Manchester

First published 2002 by
PALGRAVE
Houndmills, Basingstoke, Hampshire RG21 6XS and
175 Fifth Avenue, New York, N. Y. 10010
Companies and representatives throughout the world

PALGRAVE is the new global academic imprint of St. Martin's Press LLC
Scholarly and Reference Division and Palgrave Publishers Ltd
(formerly Macmillan Press Ltd).

ISBN 0–333–96860–3

This book is printed on paper suitable for recycling and made from fully
managed and sustained forest sources.

A catalogue record for this book is available from the British Library.

Library of Congress Cataloging-in-Publication Data
German federalism: past, present, future/edited by Maiken Umbach.
        p. cm. – (New perspectives in German studies)
        Includes bibliographical references and index.
        ISBN 0-333-96860-3 (cloth)
        1. Germany–Politics and government–History. 2. Federal
        government–Germany–History. I. Umbach, Maiken. II. Series

JN3221 .G474 2002
320.443′049–dc21
                                                                            2001038905

10   9   8   7   6   5   4   3   2   1
11 10 09 08 07 06 05 04 03 02

Printed and bound in Great Britain by
Antony Rowe Ltd, Chippenham, Wiltshire

Contents

Acknowledgement

The lecture series and symposium on which this volume is based was generously supported by the Anglo-German Foundation, London, and the Goethe Institute, Manchester.

Foreword

Hagen Schulze

Never in history has the political unity of the Germans been something to be taken for granted. After the Middle Ages the world of nations developed that was to determine the history of Europe right up to the present day: England, France, Spain, the Ottoman Empire, Russia, Sweden, and then later the United Netherlands and Denmark – all sitting on the periphery of Europe, blessed with more or less natural borders and fairly similar geographic, political, economic and cultural centres.

In the midst of this lay European no-man's-land, a profusion of 'Germanies' – 'les Allemagnes', as they say in France – a multitude of larger or smaller territories between Maas and Memel, Etsch and Belt, where although German was generally spoken, allegiance was given to the ruler and his religion, and the Kaiser and Empire were perceived at best as a sort of colourful *fata Morgana*: stirring, but very distant and without substance. The weakness of the Empire compared to Western Europe became apparent by the thirteenth century, if not before. The low concentration of centralized power in the Holy Roman Empire can largely be explained by the fact that the German King and Roman Emperor were almost entirely dependent on the agreement of the Empire's great nobles. An elective monarchy is weak by nature and therefore backward in its development into a modern, centrally governed state.

There are a number of reasons why a modern great power did not develop in this area as in the rest of Europe: the absence of a natural centre, the lack of natural boundaries; the country was dispersed, open on all sides, and, what is more, transportation was impeded by a landscape criss-crossed by rivers and mountains. At the beginning of the sixteenth century there was indeed an attempt to form a united German state out of the transnational, somewhat metaphysical structure of the Holy Roman Empire. In the following period, however, German unity fell victim to the Reformation and Counter-Reformation. While the struggle between the confessions was decided one way or the other in every other European state, it remained unsettled in Germany, petrified to a certain degree in the territorial state principle of *cuius regio, eius religio*. The territorial division was arched over by the religious one, with consequences for the political culture of the Germans that remain visible up to the present.

This fragmentation was the abiding constitutional principle of the Holy Roman Empire, a structure without its own statehood, organization or power. All of these had been transferred to the territories and Imperial cities and, furthermore, after the Thirty Years' War, their 'liberties' *(Libertäten)*, their sovereign rights, were guaranteed by an international treaty, the Peace of Westphalia of 1648. Henceforth, the constitution of the Empire – 'an irregular body of state which resembles a monster', as Pufendorf puts it – was considered to be an element of international European law. In other words, the organization, order, and basic principles of the German Empire's internal politics were the business of all the European powers.

This constellation was no accident, but the logical outcome of the European order. It was only the amorphous character of Central Europe that kept the continent in balance, and a glance at the map shows why: whoever possessed this region, be it one of the European great powers or a power that emerged in Central Europe itself, could be the master of Europe. Hence every concentration of power in Germany was seen as a threat to Europe's equilibrium. The inevitable consequence was the formation of hostile coalitions, and these were all the more likely to succeed because any Central European hegemonic power had to assert itself on several fronts at the same time, and had no defensible natural borders.

For this reason, the European neighbours regarded the 'liberties' of the more than three hundred small German states as the guarantee of European freedom, the equilibrium of the states and their survival. The states of Europe as a whole therefore guaranteed the survival and the independence of the minor German principalities and the Imperial cities. Any encroachment by a great power inevitably led to competition. During the earlier period the Habsburgs' attempt to transform the semi-metaphysical Imperial conglomerate into a more or less modernized state power had already failed for this very reason. Subsequently, therefore, Austria-Habsburg oriented itself increasingly towards the European periphery, towards Eastern and South Eastern Europe as well as Italy, and in the same measure lost power in Central Europe. This was Austria's long migration out of German history, which came to an end provisionally in 1866, and definitively in 1945.

Germany's political fragmentation was seldom considered a burden. Even though it had been bemoaned since the days of the humanists, the remedy was certainly not thought to lie in the creation of a single nation-state along the lines of France or England, but rather in a greater degree of solidarity among the princes and more committed support for the Kaiser. It was not the Empire's territorial fragmentation that was seen as the problem, but the egoism of its rulers. The multitude of ruling families, royal capitals and constitutions in the Empire was seen as an advantage because, in the words of Christoph Martin Wieland, it set limits on the despotic exercise of power, and at the same time natural diversity of habits and traditions, and indeed of theatres and universities, fostered culture and tolerance. Furthermore, he noted, wealth was more evenly distributed than in countries whose riches were all concentrated in a single place. According to Friedrich Schiller and Wilhelm v. Humboldt, Germany, with its extraordinary cultural richness, was the new Greece – powerless, but intellectually supreme. The new Rome, on the other hand – politically dominant, centrally organized and civilized, but lacking the kind of culture in which Germans took such great pride – the new Rome was France. Surely, as Metternich's advisor Friedrich v. Gentz believed, a unified German state was a dangerous chimera: 'The union of all German tribes in an undivided state' was 'a dream discredited by the experiences of a thousand years and finally rejected ... [a dream] which no combination of human efforts could fulfil, and the bloodiest revolution could not bring about, and which only the absolutely mad could still follow'. Gentz concluded his observations by stating, not without certain prophetic insight, that should the idea of national state unity in Europe prevail 'the only inheritance left for our progeny would be a wilderness of bloody ruins'.[1]

However, as far as Western Europe was concerned, in the course of the nineteenth century the national centralist state became the European model for the future. In the 1848–49 revolution this was the model that the German National Assembly delegates in Frankfurt had in mind, and it was one of the crucial reasons for the revolution's failure: not only traditional state legitimation but also military and administrative power lay with the states of the German Confederation, and they had no intention of giving these up in favour of the Frankfurt parliament. The revolutionary executive, on the other hand, was utterly powerless; it was completely dependent on the support of the large and medium-sized German states and crumbled as soon as Prussia and Austria withdrew their protection.

The lesson to be learned from this failure was that Germany could not be unified without the cooperation of the German minority states. German unification was only achieved in 1870–71 because Bismarck had learnt this very lesson. The artist Anton v. Werner depicts the result in his famous painting of the Kaiser's proclamation in Versailles on 18 January 1871: the new German state is brought into being by the German princes and the armies of the German minority states; the Prussian King appears as an equal among equals, as president of a princes' confederation and with the title of hereditary German Kaiser. It was not Wilhelm I who was the ruler of the German Empire, but the 18 governing German princes embodied in the Federal Council. It was an oligarchy not a monarchy, a victory for the principle of federalism over the idea of a united state.

The German Länder have never given up their role as a constituent and determining force within the German state. When in 1919, again after a revolution, the constituent German National Assembly in Weimar sought to create a unitary national state and to strip the Länder of power, the attempt was bound to fail, as in 1848. The ability of the traditional Länder to endure so well lay essentially in their bureaucratic and administrative strength. As 'administrative states' with firmly established and confident management and well-rehearsed administrative practices the Länder could not be set aside. Placing them under centralized control would have led to severe disruption of the established administrative system. The dynastic principle, which had disappeared with the November Revolution, was now replaced by the bureaucratic principle as the basis of German federalism. This is why the German Länder were able successfully to oppose the move towards a centralized state.

There was only one occasion in German history when it looked as if the national aversion to federalism as an expression of 'German disunity' might be successful. Hitler declared: 'Divided once and for all into hundreds of small states by the Treaty of Münster after the Thirty Years' War, our people has wasted all its strength in internal conflict. Princes and princelings, kings and religious dignitaries, they have sustained disunity among our people, and then, just when it seemed as if this purely dynastic corrosion of the body of our people would come to an end, the political parties came along, with world-views that perpetuated what had once been started.'[2] The independence of the German Länder, German history's oldest legacy, was brutally swept away within months in the course of the National Socialist seizure of power. In place of Minister-Presidents there were now *Reichsstatthalter* (special Nazi commissioners), and in the 'Third Reich' the dream of a centralized German state became nightmarish reality.

The special traditions of German history meant that a centralized unitary state could only be achieved under a dictatorship. This proved to be the case once again when the German nation-state ceased to be, and one of the two successor states, the GDR, disposed of the Länder after a few years, in order to eliminate any possible obstacles to the implementation of 'actually existing socialism' by the police and the bureaucracy. By contrast, the occupying powers in the Western Zone took great care to launch the West German state along federal lines. On 1 July 1948 the eleven Minister-Presidents of the West German Länder, who saw themselves as the trustees of German politics, received the 'Frankfurt Documents', the birth certificate of the Federal Republic of Germany, from the Military Governors of the Western Allies. This document calls upon them to create for West Germany a democratic constitution of a federal kind, because this type of government was best suited 'to re-establish German unity that is at present torn asunder'.

So it was once again the Länder which came together to found a German state. Just how apt the Military Governors' assumption was that future German unity could only be achieved via a federal system became apparent in 1991. It was the new GDR Länder that re-established German unity by joining the area of the German Basic Law. Even though German federalism is in constant danger of being overruled from the centre when it comes to tax revenue, education policy or cultural autonomy, it has stood the test of time and is in the best of health. The lesson from Germany history, that national state unity can only be achieved with the representatives of the various regional governments and not against them, can certainly also be applied to the next level – Europe. Since the diversity of the German Länder is mirrored in the structure of the German federal state, even in the most testing times in domestic affairs there is always a level at which pressures can be relieved. Germany's federal structure means that problems such as those experienced by the French with the Corsicans or the British with Northern Ireland have not arisen. In some respects the problems faced by European unity are the same as those Germany has been confronting for 200 years in its attempts to achieve unity.

Back to Europe: if there is one lesson that emerges from the numerous setbacks to European unification it is that unity can only be achieved with the nations and their legitimate peculiarities and not without them, just as the nations, for their part, are beginning to realize that they are by no means 'all one and indivisible' but consist of many ethnic, linguistic and geographical entities. As a step towards European unity the nation-state is not yet redundant: we still need it even if it has long-since ceased to be the be-all and end-all where politics is concerned.

The lasting unity that diversity brings cannot be achieved by a centralized unitary state complete with all the modern trappings of power, for which the stage already seems to be set in the present Brussels Commission with its far-reaching authority in matters of economic policy. A European constitution can only last if it takes its nations, their history, languages and states into account. Moreover, the regions and provinces in these countries have likewise developed from long traditions and become homelands, especially dear to their people. And this is where the communities are, where normal everyday life goes on, and where the decisions that affect it are played out. All this can only be combined in one whole structure if the Europe of the future is built in the spirit of subsidiarity, as suggested, for example, by Joseph Rovan: a relatively loose structure of countries on several political levels, 'in which an issue may only be passed up to the next level if it cannot be sorted out at the lower level'.[3] In this respect the history of the German constitution can serve as a good example, from regional autonomy, via the federal principle, and culminating in a state treaty between the Länder. In the case of a united Europe this could be concluded both between the nation-states and between the regions. The European heads of state and government as its joint leadership; a European government made up of a few ministers; a European Federal Council where countries and perhaps even regions are represented, and which would form the legislative counterweight to the pan-European parliament – these are all figures which will be dealt with only briefly here, but which are well-known to those familiar with German constitutional history. They are experiences from Germany's past which could perhaps enrich Europe.

Notes

1. F. Gentz, *Die Fragmente aus der neuesten Geschichte des Politischen Gleichgewichts in Europa* (St Petersburg [=Leipzig] 1806), p. 24.
2. Speech of 10.1.1939, printed in Max Domarus, ed., *Hitler – Reden und Proklamationen 1932–1945* (Munich 1963), ii, p. 1627.
3. Joseph Rovan, 'Wo ist die vierte Etage?', *Rheinischer Merkur/Christ und Welt*, Nr. 25, 23.6.1989.

Notes on the Contributors

Alon Confino, Associate Professor at the History Department, University of Virginia, USA, works on German cultural history of the nineteenth century. His publications include *The Nation as a Local Metaphor: Württemberg, Imperial Germany, and National Memory* (1997) and *The Work of Memory: New Directions in German Culture and Society* (with P. Fritzsche, forthcoming 2002). He is currently completing a book on *Pleasures in Germany: A Study of Travelling in Modern Culture, 1933–1989*.

Mary Fulbrook is Professor of German History at University College London's German Department. Her numerous publications include *A Concise History of Germany* (1990, updated 1992), *The Divided Nation: Germany 1918–1990* (1991), *German History since 1800* (1997), *Anatomy of a Dictatorship: Inside the GDR, 1949–89* (1995), *German National Identity After the Holocaust* (1999) and *Interpreting the Two Germanies, 1945–1990* (2000). She is currently completing *Perfectly Ordinary Lives? A Social History of the GDR*.

Martin Durrell, Henry Simon Professor of German at the University of Manchester, is a specialist of German dialects, and has published on linguistic as well as political aspects of the German language and its historical evolution. Major books include *Using German: A Guide to Contemporary Usage* (1992), *Hammer's German Grammar and Usage* (3rd edn 1996) and *Using German Synonyms* (2000).

Charlie Jeffery is Professor of German Politics and Deputy Director of the Institute for German Studies at the University of Birmingham. His major publications include *German Federalism Today* (with P. Savigear, 1991), *Federalism, Unification and European Integration* (with R. Sturm, 1993), *A Giant with Clay Feet? United Germany in the European Union* (1995), *Recasting German Federalism: The Legacies of Unification* (1999) and *Germany's European Diplomacy: Shaping the Regional Milieu* (with W. Paterson and S. Bulmer, 2000). He is Head of the German Politics Research Group at Birmingham and co-editor of *Regional and Federal Studies*.

Anthony Nicholls is Professor of Modern History at the University of Oxford, Director of the European Studies Centre and Official Fellow at St Antony's College. He is author of *The Bonn Republic. West German Democracy 1945–1990* (1997), *Freedom with Responsibility: The Social Market Economy in Germany, 1918–1963* (1994), *Weimar and the Rise of Hitler* (3rd edn 1991), and has edited numerous collections of essays on German and British history in the twentieth century. He is also general editor of *Perspectives in German History* and *The Post-War World*.

Jeremy Noakes, Professor of History at the University of Exeter, works on twentieth-century Germany, particularly the Weimar and Nazi periods. Major publications include *The Nazi Party in Lower Saxony, 1921–1933* (1971), *Government, Party, and People in Nazi Germany* (1980), *Nazism 1919–1945: A Documentary Reader* (with G. Pridham, latest edn 1998) and *Nazism 1919–1945*, vol. 4, *The German Home Front in World War II* (1998).

Wolfgang Renzsch is Professor of Politics at the Otto-von-Guericke-Universität Magdeburg. His publications include *Finanzverfassung und Finanzausgleich: Die Auseinandersetzungen um ihre politische Gestaltung in der Bundesrepublik Deutschland zwischen Währungsreform und deutscher Vereinigung, 1948–1990* (1991), *Föderalstaatliche Entwicklung in Europa* (with J. J. Hesse 1991), *Die Finanzverfassung der Bundesrepublik Deutschland* (with D. Frey 1995) and *Transformation der politisch-administrativen Strukturen in Ostdeutschland* (with H. Wollmann, H.-U. Derlien, K. König, W. Seibel, 1997), as well as numerous English articles on German party politics, fiscal policy and federalism.

Hagen Schulze is Professor of History at the Free University Berlin and Director of the German Historical Institute in London. Major publications available in English translation include *Nation-Building in Central Europe* (1987), *Is There a German History?* (1988), *The Course of German Nationalism. From Frederick the Great to Bismarck 1763–1867* (2nd edn 1995); *States, Nations and Nationalism. From the Middle Ages to the Present* (1996); *Germany: A New History* (2nd edn 2001). He is currently editing *Deutsche Erinnerungsorte* (3 vols, 2001).

Maiken Umbach is Lecturer in Modern European History at the University of Manchester and currently a visiting fellow at the Minda de Gunzburg Center for European Studies, Harvard. She is author of

Federalism and Enlightenment in Germany, 1740–1806 (2000) and numerous articles on eighteenth- and nineteenth-century German political
and cultural history. She is completing a book on *Regionalism and
Modernity: Cultural Politics in Berlin, Hamburg, Munich and Hagen,
1890–1926.*

Joachim Whaley, Lecturer in the University of Cambridge's German
Department and Fellow of Gonville and Caius College, has principally
published on eighteenth-century German history and culture. He is
author of *Religious Toleration and Social Change in Hamburg, 1529–1819*
(1985). He is currently completing a book on *The German Lands and
The Holy Roman Empire, 1495–1806.*

1

Introduction: German Federalism in Historical Perspective

Maiken Umbach

Federalism is a thorny political issue. On the European level, it refers to what is perhaps the most important legacy of late twentieth-century politics: the gradual dissolution of national sovereignty. Instead, political and economic decision-making increasingly takes place on a supranational level – in pan-European political institutions and courtrooms – as well as on a sub-national level – in the regions. This process has polarized public opinion in Europe. From the time of Adenauer to Schröder, Germany has played a key role in promoting progress towards a federal Europe. Britain, despite recent moves towards devolution for Ireland, Scotland and Wales, remains sceptical about the erosion of national sovereignty, and of Germany's role in promoting it.

The theoretical literature on European federalism is extensive.[1] Yet it has done little to bridge political divides. The language of academic political science is often arcane and abstract. Even when political scientists have tried to address a wider public, however, their influence has remained limited. European federalism is more than an administrative and 'technical' problem that can be solved by experts – it is eminently political. Historical experience, national memory and ideology shape its meaning, and the word federalism means different things in different cultures. In Britain, federalism is often taken as a synonym for the threat of a bureaucratic European super-state. In Germany, the same term is used to describe an ideal of diversity within unity, emphasizing the element of devolution. It seems that the search for political compromises is futile if this difference of perception is not addressed. An 'objective', scientific definition of federalism cannot solve the problem. On the contrary, if a theoretical definition is superimposed upon people's political instincts, 'federalism', promoted to unite Europeans, will continue to divide them.

1

How did German 'federalism' come to acquire such different connotations from those of the English term? To answer this question, scholars from a wide range of academic disciplines collaborated in a seminar series and conference that took place in 2000 at the University of Manchester. This book presents their findings. The approach we adopt is historical. German *Föderalismus* is not, and never has been, an abstract concept. It has no single founding document and no universal definition. Its meaning evolved gradually, over many centuries.[2] And while this process of evolution is by no means complete, history itself plays a central role in defining federalism in German minds. Indeed, federalism has become, for many, the central embodiment of the country's history, or at least of its positive (that is, anti-totalitarian) aspects. In the individual chapters of this volume, experts on the various epochs of modern German history examine the changing meaning and reality of German federalism over many centuries. Their contributions are arranged in chronological order, but they do not 'narrate' German history. Rather, we have used different approaches – cultural, political, linguistic, constitutional – to examine the concept of German federalism at distinct phases of its evolution.

The investigation begins in the eighteenth century. It was then that federalism was first used in the modern, political sense. America led the way. The War of Independence provided the historical backdrop for the publication of the famous 'Federalist Papers' of 1788. America became a federal experiment that excited Europeans as well: for the first time, it seemed, the federal theories of Montesquieu, Rousseau and other leading lights of the Enlightenment were translated into political reality. In the process, the term federalism assumed much more specific connotations. It was no longer one branch of political theory: it became a political movement which faced one important political opposition – and one only. A unitary state was not an option for the diverse set of former colonies. What American politicians disagreed about was merely the degree of independence that individual states should retain. The label 'Federalist' was assumed by those who advocated a relatively high degree of political coherence. The state they envisaged was far removed from the centralizing ambitions of European absolutism. Indeed, Montesquieu's and Rousseau's federalism which had inspired the American Federalists was conceived as a liberal alternative to absolutist centralization. But the American opponents of the Federalists were not defenders of absolutism: conversely, they were those who advocated an even smaller degree of centralization, at best a loose confederation of states, with no supremacy of federal law, and the right of secession for all member states. In the political controversy that ensued, therefore, the label 'federalism' gradually became synonymous with promoting greater integration of the American states, and the original opposition between federalism and centralism faded into oblivion.[3] A 'federal' institution or law was one that asserted a unitary authority over the laws and customs of individual states. The civil war, in which many of the fears which Anti-Federalists voiced in the 1770s came true, seemed to confirm the equation between 'federalism' and the forceful imposition of common policies and standards upon unruly regions. This plot has remained largely unchanged. The same theme features in countless popular US movies of recent years, where FBI agents clash with the spirit of self-reliance and anti-Washington sentiment of their counterparts in remote southern or western states. In popular culture, Waco is emblematic of the authoritarian image of 'federal' America.

In Germany, the development of federalism as a political category started at about the same time – but soon took a different turn. Here, too, the ideas of Montesquieu and Rousseau formed the starting point.[4] And as in America, they were quickly absorbed into a political discourse that was essentially practical. Uninterested in pure speculations about an ideal state, German political and legal writers of the eighteenth century such as Johann Stephan Pütter were concerned to address the pressing problems of the day. The polycentric structure of the Holy Roman Empire, which had shaped German politics for many centuries, provided the background. The War of the Bavarian Succession brought home to observers that this imperial constitution was threatened by the ambitions of 'absolutist' rulers, most notably those of Prussia and Austria. Whaley's chapter in this volume examines the response of the intellectuals of the day. It widens the focus from the specialized legal debate to the broader intellectual consensus that emerged from it, showing how federalism became an – albeit implicit – part of German national consciousness. Whaley takes issue with two myths of German historiography. One is the nationalist myth. For the entire nineteenth and for much of the twentieth centuries, German historians condemned the Holy Roman Empire as weak: its destiny was to be quashed by the modern forces of nationalism, embodied by the state of Prussia. Whaley argues that the decentralized structure of the Old Reich was by no means dysfunctional; in fact, it was highly effective in fulfilling its purposes – above all, the maintenance of peace and the rule of law in the German lands. Political centralization, however, was not its purpose, and the absence of centralizing moves thus not a 'failure'. Instead, the Old Reich was in many ways a federal state – but it was not (yet) defined as such. Whaley is sceptical of the current fashion for portraying the medieval or early modern Reich as a model for EU government. This is the second, contemporary myth he sets out to dismantle.[5] The nature of politics has undergone such a profound transformation since the early modern period that formal constitutional comparisons with the present-day situation are nonsensical. If the Reich was not a model for the twentieth century, however, it left an important intellectual legacy behind. Responding to eighteenth-century territorial absolutism, German intellectuals and political commentators began to redefine imperial devolution in an enlightened vocabulary. This influenced German politics for decades to come, by providing a repository of precedents for smaller German states to invoke when they defended their autonomy vis-à-vis central governments.

None of these arguments became obsolete with the so-called unification of Germany in 1871. The nation state that Bismarck created was little more than a federation of largely sovereign individual states, and even under Wilhelm II, Prussia's dominance in the field of high politics did little to eradicate individual-state consciousness and confidence. The third chapter turns to the theme of continuity, by examining a set of arguments that emerged in the 'federal' debate in Germany in the late eighteenth century, and then tracing the ways in which these arguments were revived and recycled by federalists of the post-unification era. German historians have rarely commented on such continuities. Their reluctance is understandable. A healthy mistrust of teleology belongs in every history book. There was no causal chain of events that links the constitution of the Old Reich with contemporary German federalism. Instead, there were many turning points where German history could have turned in different directions – and indeed several points where it did precisely that, as the later chapters of this volume which deal with the anti-federal nature of the Nazi state and the GDR show.

If contingency is writ large, was there any sense in which German federalism had a *longue durée*? Participants of the Manchester conference converged on the view that to understand German federalism, we need to move beyond the conceptual opposition between contingency and historical determinism. German federalism, we suggest, did produce a continuity of a kind. This is to be found not in an unbroken chain of events, much less in causal links between these events, but in the *lieux de memoire*, the focal points of national memory, that constitute German political culture. Not all German regimes were federal. But federalism never disappeared from the German political imagination. There was little 'federal' resistance to the centralizing impulses of totalitarian governments. Federalism did, however, play an important role in reconstructing democracy after the end of totalitarian regimes. The late 1940s as well as the early 1990s witnessed a truly remarkable process. Rather than being seen as a hostile plot to subdivide the nation, the 'foreign' introduction of federalism soon acquired the status of an 'authentic' expression of German identities – even when, especially after 1945, few of the new Länder directly corresponded to the former states of the Old Reich or the Bismarckian Empire. To be sure, federalism was adopted under considerable pressure from the Western Allies after the Second World War. This provoked some suspicions amongst ordinary Germans, and even more so from some prominent SPD and KPD politicians. Yet given the circumstances, it is not the existence of such opposition, but its relative ineffectiveness and fleetingness which requires explanation. The German states' separate histories were not a direct cause of the successful reinvention of German federalism. But federalism's prominent place in German national memory did facilitate the absorption of what was in fact a new form of federalism into the political culture of the day. Federalism should thus be understood as a continuous sub-current of German history, often inactive and ineffectual, but ready to be revived whenever dramatic political transformations needed to be assimilated.

Federalism's relative vagueness and shifting meaning was an important ingredient in this success story. Federalism can be associated with 'authentic national identity', because both concepts are flexible enough to change with the times. Moreover, federalism, in reconciling a regional and a national sense of belonging in a non-hierarchical order, is predicated on the assumption of a plurality of identities, and thus defies any attempt to equate it with a single political concept or ideology. Many historians have pointed out that federalism has no clear-cut political meaning. To date, however, few have seen this lack of precision as the secret of federalism's success in the German political imagination. This conclusion runs as a guiding thread through most of the chapters of this book. Federalism has survived dramatic historical transformations because it is cloaked in the most successful political rhetoric of the modern age: the rhetoric of pragmatism. It therefore adapts more easily to changing circumstances, and it appeals to people from a wider political spectrum, than classical ideologies.

Notwithstanding their ideological flexibility, federal systems in German history functioned in highly specific ways, and generated complex political mechanisms and institutions. Federalism combines both: a vague sense of cultural belonging, and a sophisticated constitutional mechanism of devolved government. Debating this issue at our conference, we found it helpful to draw upon a categorization proposed by the American sociologist Theda Skocpol. Considering the role of cultural modes of analysis for social and political sciences, Skocpol introduced a distinction between what she called 'cultural idioms' and 'political ideologies'.[6] Cultural idioms are enshrined in popular beliefs and mentalities, a particular register of language, a set of (largely unreflected) stereotypes, a 'habitus'. They provide the framework within which political discourse takes place; they influence what is thinkable in a political culture. They do not, however, determine practical outcomes or 'cause' political decisions. Political ideologies, by contrast, are more conscious, deliberate creations. They tend to be highly specific to a particular time and place, they change rapidly and depend on the agency of individuals or distinct groups.

The Germans' pronounced sense of regional identity is a cultural idiom in Skocpol's sense. It formed a necessary prerequisite for all German federal constitutions. Only if we take into account the way in which Swabian, Bavarian or Hanseatic identities were defined, defended and redefined over long periods of time can we make sense of German federalism. This requires extending the scope of the investigation beyond high politics and constitutional history. The chapters by Confino and Durrell show how regionalism functioned as a part of day-to-day German culture. Durrell examines the role of dialects in the era of German unification. Linguistic theories of the period reflect the interplay of cultural and political factors in German federalism. High German, nineteenth-century linguists argued, was a peripatetic language: it evolved as a result of contact with the shifting intellectual centres of Germany's history. The language absorbed vital impulses in fourteenth-century Prague, sixteenth-century Wittenberg, and so on. In this view, the High German that had emerged at the end of this journey represented an organic synthesis of Germany's regional cultures: it was a truly 'federal' language.

Such academic debates went hand in hand with a powerful popular revival of regionalism. Not all European states that experienced a resurgence of regionalism during the long nineteenth century became federal states. The best example is France, probably the most centralized state in Western Europe at the time. Both here and in Germany, local and regional identities gained momentum in the age of triumphant nationalism. This trend was reinforced by the experience of the First World War. Yet there are few signs of France's political system moving towards a more federal composition – Corsica is an exception rather than indicative of a general trend. The regional revival of the nineteenth century cannot, therefore, provide a sufficient explanation for political federalism. Other, more contingent factors encouraged the adoption of a federal system in Germany. Does this mean we can dismiss the role of the cultural idiom of regionalism for the history of German federalism? Hardly. Federalism is unthinkable without it. This was partly due to the historical precedent of the Holy Roman Empire. Even if we now know that early modern French absolutism was less centralized than historians thought a generation ago, its intellectual legacy allowed for a very different approach to central government in France than in the German lands.[7] The significance of these two different histories was not that they in themselves prescribed federal or centralist styles of government. But the Holy Roman Empire did provide an important argument for the defenders of German federalism that their French counterparts lacked. This was all the more important because the age of nation-state formation in Germany was an age that was intensely historically minded. It witnessed the birth of academic history writing as well as the triumph of 'historicism' as an architectural and artistic style. In this climate, the historicity of federalism was a useful argument for those pushing for a federal constitution. Their motivation in doing so, however, tended to be practical. Bismarck's decision to unify Germany as a federal state in 1871, like the decision of the Allies to recreate at least a semblance of that federal structure after 1945, or indeed the decision of the Kohl government to engineer the German unification of 1990 as federation of the West German and the East German Länder (instead of the unification of two states) – all these have to be accounted for with reference to power politics, international relations, the personal vision of key political actors, and other 'non-cultural' factors. It is not the purpose of this book to invalidate such modes of explanation. It merely suggests that such explanations leave important questions unanswered. The authors of this book draw attention to underlying cultural paradigms which made such decisions possible and feasible in the first place.

If history was one of these underlying paradigms, the fashion for things vernacular that accompanied industrial modernization in Germany was another. As Confino shows, the German *Heimat* movement's reputation as merely conservative is in urgent need of revision.[8] In this book, Confino argues that *Heimat* was a highly dynamic concept. It reinvented local and regional traditions in such a way as to make them compatible with a very modern nationalism. As a half-hearted compromise between the new nationalism and the old particularism, federalism's appeal would have been somewhat limited in an age of 'charismatic politics'. The success story of German federalism in this period relied on the way in which the peculiarity and diversity of the regions could be presented as an asset to the nation as a whole. The *Heimat* movement provided the missing link, which enabled people to project a spontaneous sense of belonging to the locality or region onto the more abstract entity of the nation at large. This cemented the polycentric structure of the German state and made full-scale centralization more difficult – but by strengthening the bonds between the citizens and the state, regionalism benefited the national movement.

Of course, this story requires social differentiation. A positive identification with locality and region strengthened the national allegiance of those who maintained strong ties with their native homelands. The *Heimat* movement thus proved highly effective in mobilizing a broad base of support from German soldiers serving in the First World War, the majority of whom came from rural areas. For those who had recently migrated large distances to find work in the newly industrializing cities, however, the experience was different. Germany's Social Democratic Party opposed regionalism. My own chapter highlights this difference by focusing on the Free Hanseatic City of Hamburg. In defending the city's special privilege to maintain a free-trade harbour, the senators of Hamburg argued that the city's political and economic autonomy was vital for its role as the Germany's 'Gateway to the World' – a core element of Wilhelmine nationalism. In promoting this claim, the senators used historical arguments, alluding to a largely fictitious history of the medieval Hanseatic League. They also drew upon the modern vocabulary of the *Heimat* movement, notably when the new free harbour was constructed in a vernacular North German style. The synthesis between regionalism and nationalism was successful, in that it convinced authorities in Berlin to preserve Hamburg's autonomy after unification. But it excluded the lower classes, whose vision of the nation was more egalitarian, and who, having arrived in the city as a highly mobile industrial workforce, had no personal ties with the city-state's history or its culture of Hanseatic regionalism.

With the emergence of the Nazi dictatorship and of the 'German Democratic Republic', early twentieth-century Germany witnessed a process of political centralization in which federal institutions more or less disappeared. The motivations are complex, and little research has yet been done in this area. The myth of federalism as the anti-totalitarian doctrine *per se* has prevented historians from taking the question why these two regimes set out to eradicate federalism as seriously as we ought to take it. This book offers some preliminary answers, which are suggested by the story of German federalism as we have traced it up to this point. We can distinguish two important factors. One is that both these totalitarian regimes subscribed to the traditional belief that a strong state is a centralized state. In that respect, they relied on the historical model of territorial absolutism. But their centralizing policies also had modern aspects. Especially the GDR could build upon the anti-federal sentiments that had characterized the German working-class movement from the later nineteenth century. This connection is explored in Mary Fulbrook's chapter. She sees the abolition of federalism in East Germany not merely as a repressive measure to assert total political control. Instead, she argues that the cultural sense of regionalism, too, disappeared in East Germany within less than a generation, because the GDR succeeded in portraying it as alien in spirit to the community of all workers. These workers were united by a history in which region had played a subservient role, but more importantly, by a sense of a common fate in the future, for better or worse, given their enforced confinement in the East German state. This interpretation is bound to spark off much debate amongst historians in years to come. Fulbrook does of course concede that the acceptance of 'democratic centralism' was uneven. Regionalism was preserved in some areas, notably by minorities such as the Sorbs, or by the organizational structure of the Church seeking to evade central party control. The association between opposition politics and regionalism in East Germany raises interesting questions about the swift restoration of federalism in East Germany after 1989, and it is hoped that our publication will inspire future research in this area.

Noakes's chapter shows that, by comparison, the Nazi's anti-federal programme was less successful, but also less unequivocal. In *Mein Kampf*, Hitler declared that federalism was a mask that needed to be torn from the face of the German polity. But in practice, federalism was only abolished on paper, and at least partly reinstated when it came to the day-to-day process of political decision-making. The issue of centralization versus federalism was caught up in the dynamic of competing institutions in the Nazi polycracy: if the Interior Ministry pushed for more centralization, rival institutions competing for the support of the Führer were quick to defend devolution as a means of undermining the Ministry's bid for power. At the same time, the anti-federal programme was less radical from the outset: what was attacked was simply administrative federalism – in keeping with the idea that centralization equalled power, and that historical particularism stood in the way of the Nazi social revolution. Cultural regionalism, however, was excepted from this attack; in fact, *Stammesbewusstsein* – German 'tribal' consciousness – was an important part of Nazi propaganda.

With the collapse of the Nazi state, the stage for federalism's success story in West Germany was set. In the current German constitution, important areas of policy-making remain the prerogative of the individual Länder. They include key issues such as education and the control of large parts of the national budget. Indeed, the subdivision of power in the Federal Republic became more rather than less prominent as post-war Germany developed. While some historians referred to the Federal Republic's early days as 'closet centralism',[9] more recently, political observers have tended to criticize the German constitution's development for 'excessive federalism', a degree of decentralization verging on the total fragmentation of political power. In his survey of federalism's role in West German politics, Jeffery examines the dynamic nature of the German model of 'cooperative federalism'. Beginning with the 1969–79 constitutional reforms, he diagnoses a trend towards ever-greater autonomy of the Länder governments – a 'Sinatra' style of federalism. Yet to Jeffery this is no reason to subscribe to the gloomy view prevalent amongst many German political scientists today, who believe that the development of federalism has effectively reached a dead end. Political debates in Germany may be marked by financial squabbles between the Länder and the national government in Berlin, and the controversy is far from resolved. But ultimately, both sides continue to believe that they stand to gain more than they lose from the federal division of powers between the centre and the regions. Renzsch's chapter analyses the ongoing debate about the future of federalism in German political circles. The author combines the perspective of a political scientist with that of an 'insider' of the German political system. Although he agrees with Jeffery's perception of an increasing disentanglement of German federalism, if not formally, then at least de facto, he argues that German federalism still qualifies as largely cooperative: hardly any federation goes as far as the German one when it comes to centralizing legislative but decentralizing executive authority. Recent years have, it is true, seen a modest transfer of legislative powers back to the Länder. Yet many regions have been surprisingly reluctant to demand more regional taxation powers – not least because they do not want to shoulder the responsibility for taxes unlikely to be popular with voters.

Whatever the outcome of these complex negotiations will be, they are affected by, and they affect, the wider European integration process. Not only do the German Länder have to adjust their agenda to European Union policies: unlike the more technical term 'subsidiarity', federalism for many Germans is a political virtue in its own right – and their passport to European civilization. Developments after 1989 reinforced this notion: federalism was invoked to reassure Germany's neighbours in Europe that reunification would not lead to a resurgence of the old German nationalism, and that the new state would pose no threat to others. And if Germany was more Euro-compatible in a federal shape, the same surely applied to the countries. The more 'federalized' Europe as a whole became, so the argument ran, the easier national conflict would be avoided in future. A 'Europe of the regions' may well be a projection of German identity onto Europe. Yet it is a projection intended to counteract forces of German nationalism – quite the opposite of a callous plot to bring other European states under German dominion.[10]

Even in Germany, however, federalism has many critics. Those on the left of the German political spectrum tend to blame federalism for creating social inequalities between the richer and the poorer Länder, and fear for the future of the financial equalisation mechanism. They also argue that federalism has allowed traditionally conservative Länder such as Bavaria to use a regional platform for defying German constitutional law on issues ranging from banning abortion to the presence of crucifixes in the classrooms of state schools. The fact that radical right-wing parties such as the Bavarian-based 'Europäische Föderalistische Partei Deutschlands' use the federalism label to promote their political ends aggravates such concerns.

Critics of a liberal or moderately conservative persuasion tend to focus on other aspects of the federal system, but are often none the less outspoken in their attacks. Typically, they dismiss German federalism on the grounds that it creates unnecessary tiers of bureaucracy and renders political decision-making inefficient. Economics plays an important role in their arguments. One oddity of the German federal system which is often pointed to is the absence of a single national stock exchange. Unlike all its European neighbours, Germany not only has a central exchange, the Frankfurt *Börse*, but also seven additional

Länder-based exchanges in Berlin, Bremen, Hamburg, Hanover, Düsseldorf, Munich and Stuttgart – and that is not counting specialized exchanges for particular products, such as the two derivatives exchanges in Stuttgart and Frankfurt, or the agricultural commodities exchange in Hanover. Federal traditions such as these seem fundamentally at odds with the economic flexibility required by the process of European economic integration and the recent wave of international mergers usually summarized under the heading 'globalization'. In demanding less Länder-based bureaucracy, modern conservatives differ from nineteenth-century critics of federalism. While traditional nationalists attacked federalism on the grounds that it weakened the (central) state unnecessarily, contemporary conservatives make the opposite assertion. Having absorbed the liberal credo that the state governs best that governs least, they attack German federalism for extending the scope of state intervention by multiplying political institutions, where the market should be given a free hand.

These criticisms notwithstanding, the federal nature of Germany continues to be a centrepiece of German national identity. On this, commentators from a broad political spectrum are in agreement. Even the more radical of the reform proposals currently under debate do not envisage the abolition of the Länder's political autonomy. Interestingly, the most adventurous critics who advocate the total abolition of some Länder are often also the ones who make the case for greater sovereign rights for the remaining Länder. In other words, alongside those who warn of excessive federalism, there are those who advocate yet greater decentralization of political power in Germany.

German federalism's viability can certainly be defended in pragmatic terms. Yet its continuing attraction for the Germans is in no small part a result of the country's turbulent history. Not only does German federalism go back a long way. It is associated with epochs in German history that are perceived as relatively unproblematic. After the anti-federal policies of the twentieth-century dictatorships, federalism stands rehabilitated as an idea. The victorious Allies after the Second World War certainly thought so, when they dissolved Germany's most centralizing power, the state of Prussia, and subdivided the nation into individual Länder. What might have seemed like a hostile Allied intervention was embraced by German public opinion. Germans have no 'French Revolution' to invoke in order to lend a sense of historical legitimacy to modern democratic governments. In place of a French-style revolutionary tradition, Germany's federal traditions could be presented as a home-made alternative to authoritarian politics. For many, federalism is an authentically German recipe for protecting political pluralism and cultural diversity (at least amongst Germans themselves). The authors of this book take a critical view of the historical mythology surrounding the idea of federalism as an anti-totalitarian safeguard. Our response, however, cannot be to adopt an ahistorical perspective.[11] To appreciate the real meaning and the ideological significance of German *Föderalismus*, we have to understand the concept historically. Federalism, we conclude, was never an automatic feature of German history, not even in 'non-totalitarian' periods. But since the eighteenth century, it has played a prominent role in the German political imagination. As a focal point of national memory, it was called upon many times to legitimate the creation of federal constitutions throughout the nineteenth and twentieth centuries. Today, the attraction of the federal option is undiminished. For better or worse, Germans and, increasingly, Europeans live in an age of federalism.

Notes

1. Only some exemplary works can be listed here: A. Bosco, *What is Federalism? Towards a General Theory of Federalism. The Theory, the History and its Application to European Unification* (London 1996); J. J. Hesse and V. Wright, eds, *Federalizing Europe: The Costs, Benefits and Preconditions of Federalism in Europe* (Oxford 1996); D. Elazar, *Exploring Federalism* (Tuscaloosa 1988); M. Burgess, *Federalism and European Union: Political Ideas, Influences and Strategies in the European Community, 1972–1987* (London 1989); C. Jeffery, ed., *The Regional Dimension of the European Union: Towards a Third Level in Europe?* (London 1997); M. Keating and J. Loughlin, eds, *The Political Economy of Regionalism* (London 1997); M. Keating and B. Jones, eds, *Regions in the European Community* (Oxford 1985); R. Morgan, ed., *Regionalism in European Politics* (London 1986). In addition, there are a number of important German studies, such as G. Ammon et al., eds, *Föderalismus und Zentralismus: Europas Zukunft zwischen dem deutschen und dem französischen Modell* (Baden-Baden 1996); K. Assmann and T. Goppel, eds, *Föderalismus: Bauprinzip einer freiheitlichen Grundordnung in Europa* (Munich and London 1978).
2. See, for example, Dieter Langewiesche and Georg Schmidt, eds, *Die föderative Nation: Deutschlandkonzepte von der Reformation bis zum Ersten Weltkrieg* (Munich 2000).
3. The controversy is documented in J. R. Pole, ed., *The American Constitution: For and Against. The Federalist and Anti-Federalist Papers* (New York and Toronto 1987). A useful short commentary is Isaac Kramnick's introduction in James Madison, Alexander Hamilton, John Jay, *The Federalist Papers*, ed. by I. Kramnick (Harmondsworth, New York etc. 1987), pp. 11–82.
4. Reinhardt Koselleck, 'Bund, Bündnis, Föderalismus', in Reinhardtkoselleck, Otto Brunner, Werner Conze, eds, *Geschichtliche Grundbegriffe: Historisches*

Lexikon zur politisch-sozialen Sprache in Deutschland, 8 vols (Stuttgart 1972–97), i, 1, pp. 624–35. For a more detailed discussion of the debate about imperial reform in the Enlightenment, see Wolfgang Burgdorf, *Reichskonstitution und Nation: Verfassungsreformprojeckte für das Heilige Römische Reich* (Mainz 1998).

5. This myth dates back to the inter-war period, when intellectuals such as Ernst Robert Curtius (*Europäische Literatur und Lateinisches Mittelalter*, Bern 1948) promoted the idea of a common European culture based on the medieval Catholic heritage to overcome the forces of modern nationalism. In this they were partly inspired by similar attempts one century earlier, when statesmen such as the Austrian Chancellor Metternich and the Romantic philosopher Friedrich Schlegel promoted theses notions in the journal *Europa*. All harked back to the pre-Reformation Holy Roman Empire as a precedent for confessional and political unity. Such ideas were revived by some German conservative politicians after the Second World War, notably Chancellor Adenauer.

6. Theda Skocpol, *Social Revolutions in the Modern World* (Cambridge 1994).

7. For a sceptical reassessment of the limits of absolutist centralization, see Nick Henshall, *The Myth of Absolutism: Change and Continuity in Early Modern European Monarchy* (London and New York 1992). Absolutism's enduring impact on French political culture and the idea of the state is analysed in Chandra Mukerji, *Territorial Ambitions and the Gardens of Versailles* (Cambridge 1997).

8. Apart from Confino's own *The Nation as a Local Metaphor: Württemberg, Imperial Germany and National Memory 1871–1918* (Chapel Hill and London 1997), the other major contribution to this new reassessment is C. Applegate, *A Nation of Provincials: The German Idea of Heimat* (Berkeley 1990). Both books are concerned with cultural regionalism. Confino's chapter in this volume is the first to establish a connection with political federalism. For the older view of the *Heimat* movement as purely reactionary, see, for example, E. Klueting, ed., *Antimodernismus und Reform: Zur Geschichte der deutschen Heimatbewegung* (Darmstadt 1991) and W. Hartung, *Konservative Zivilisationskritik und regionale Identität am Beispiel der nieder-sächsischen Heimatbewegung 1895 bis 1919* (Hanover 1991).

9. For example by H. Abromeit, *Der Verkappte Einheitsstaat* (Opladen 1992).

10. 'On the European dimension of German federalism', C. Jeffery and P. Savigear, eds, *German Federalism Today* (Leicester 1991).

11. On those rare occasions that existing studies on German or European federalism adopt a long-term historical perspective, this tends to focus on the history of political thought. Notable amongst these intellectual histories are A. Bosco, ed., *The Federal Idea*, i, *The History of Federalism from Enlightenment to 1945*, and ii, *The History of Federalism since 1945* (London 1991–2), as well as the older Bernard Voyenne, *Histoire de l'idée fédéraliste* (Nice 1973), and J. Touchard, *Histoire des idées politiques*, esp. ii, *Du XVIIIe à nos jours*, 10th edn (Paris 1988). Unlike the above, this book is concerned with German federalism as constituted by historical practice, rather than political theory. See also J. Huhn, *Lernen aus der Geschichte? Historische Argumente in der west-deutschen Föderalismusdiskussion 1945–1949* (Melsungen 1990).

2
Federal Habits: the Holy Roman Empire and the Continuity of German Federalism

Joachim Whaley

One of the more surprising recent contributions to the debate about the future of Europe was the accusation levelled against the Germans in June 2000 by the then French Minister for the Interior, Jean-Pierre Chevènement, that they were simply unable to stop dreaming about the Holy Roman Empire. The Germans, he meant to say, still diabolized the nation-state. In their relentless flight into a post-national world, they find themselves perennially caught up in 'the nostalgic dream of a kind of federation that will hold differing parts together as regionally as possible, just as the Holy Roman Empire did...'.[1] The occasion for his remark was a speech made by the German Foreign Minister Joschka Fischer at the Humboldt University on 12 May 2000 in which he reiterated his belief that in the final stage of European unity a union of European states would evolve into a true federation.[2] At one level the remarks simply demonstrated once more the underlying Germanophobia of the *souverainisme* of Chevènement's left-wing *Mouvement des Citoyens*.[3] They also testify to a questionable knowledge of history, which led Chevènement to claim even more absurdly that the Habsburg emperor was a 'federator' in the final phase of the Empire's history. At another level, however, Chevènement's remarks reflect a number of genuine uncertainties: about the German attitude to the nation, about the more general relationship between present and past in Germany, and, more specifically, about the significance of the Holy Roman Empire for the subsequent history of Germany.

Few would query the proposition that German federalism has deep historical roots. Indeed discussion of its contemporary manifestation in the Federal Republic routinely refer to the federal traditions of the Holy Roman Empire before detailing the federal forms developed in the nineteenth and twentieth centuries.[4] They say little, however, about the precise nature of those traditions, about the way in which they were transmitted beyond the dissolution of the Holy Roman Empire in 1806 or about the ways in which they may have shaped or predetermined subsequent versions of German federalism. Indeed it is unclear in many cases whether anything more is meant than a simple reference to the lack of a unitary state or nation-state in the German lands before the nineteenth century. Of course this simple geographical fact is the product of political factors. But the tendency to equate pre-modern federalism with fragmentation and particularism implies a record of failure or of absence rather than any more constructive or positive force.

This uncertainty with regard to the long-term significance of the forms developed in the Holy Roman Empire echoes a generally negative view of that institution that still shapes much thinking about the overall structure of German history. It is underlined by the assumptions that inform many of the recent standard accounts of modern German history. In 1983 Thomas Nipperdey opened his magisterial history of Germany in the nineteenth century by declaring that 'In the beginning was Napoleon.'[5] In 1987 Hans-Ulrich Wehler started his history of modern German society with the words 'In the beginning there is no revolution'.[6] Both scholars see the period around 1800 as a crucial watershed. For Nipperdey the modernization of the German states in the Napoleonic period and the emergence of German nationalism in response to Napoleonic hegemony shaped the beginning of German modernity. For Wehler the essential point is that the German states were modernized from above by ruling elites that carried out their own 'revolution from above' in response to the ideas of the French Revolution. For both scholars the Holy Roman Empire is of little relevance to the modern period: a decrepit and archaic system that had become redundant long before it was finally dissolved in 1806.

This view is not much modified by the latest major survey by Heinrich August Winkler. The first volume of his account of Germany's 'path to the West', published in 2000, opens with words that consciously respond to Wehler and Nipperdey: 'In the beginning was the Reich.'[7] That does not mean that Winkler has a more positive view of the Holy Roman Empire. He too seems to regard the modern history of Germany as a process of overcoming the legacy of the Reich, a system which aspired to be 'more than one among many' states in Europe. It failed to achieve this, he argues, and was crippled in the early modern period first by religious divisions and then by the rivalry between Austria and Prussia after 1750. According to Winkler, these developments fostered the establishment of the small absolutist territorial state at the expense of the nation state. German patriotism expressed itself in loyalty to these units rather than to the nation as elsewhere in Western Europe. By the end of the eighteenth century, he concludes, all that really united the Germans was their language.[8] In so far as the Holy Roman Empire had a legacy it took the form of an elusive yet seductive myth. The memory of the old medieval aspirations returned to unsettle Germans when the Second Reich of 1871 was beset by a profound crisis at the end of the First World War.[9]

In some ways the approach of these historians is understandable. All histories have to start somewhere, and the period of the French Revolution is commonly accepted as the beginning of 'modern' history generally. In the case of Germany too the main focus is inevitably on the two twentieth-century world wars and the regimes that generated them. The long pre-modern history of the Holy Roman Empire seems to contribute little to an understanding of these events. The survival of its sclerotic structures to the threshold of the modern era, it is often assumed, merely delayed the development of German society. The enduring fascination of its mythology allegedly merely complicated the evolution both of the nation-state formed in 1871 and of the democratic system instituted in 1919.

Increasingly, however, it is difficult to reconcile these rather dismissive views of the Holy Roman Empire with the image of that system that emerges from the work published over the last few decades by historians of early modern Germany. This has resulted in a much more positive view of the early modern Reich, its institutions and its political culture. For the past decades have seen a systematic reappraisal of the Empire's history. Fundamental to this reappraisal has been the recognition that there were in a sense two Holy Roman Empires: the medieval Empire and the early modern Empire. The foundations for the latter were laid in the late fifteenth century and anchored on the reforms instituted by Emperor Maximilian I between 1495 and 1500. During the sixteenth century its institutions and political and cultural values evolved slowly but steadily. The crisis of the Thirty Years War resulted in the Peace of Westphalia in 1648 that, in addition to setting out the terms of a Europe-wide peace, regulated the relationship between Emperor and Estates. It thus provided the constitutional framework for the development of the German lands until the Empire was dissolved 1806. It is this early modern Empire that is now often referred to as the 'Old Reich' (*Altes Reich*). This was an idiosyncratically German form of political organization that had little in common with the universal medieval Empire: it was a 'German' Empire.

Pioneering work by Karl Otmar von Aretin in the 1960s and subsequently by scholars such as Peter Moraw and Volker Press have by now spawned a mass of detailed research into the Empire's institutions and into the social, political and cultural values that underpinned them.[10] Significantly, these scholars were all in one way or another products of a south German liberal Catholic tradition. It is thus not surprising that their view of the Empire differed sharply from the negative assessments that had been characteristic of the north German/Prussian Protestant historiographical tradition that had been dominant before 1945. While the Prussian tradition criticized the Reich as an obstacle to national unification, the new view appreciated it precisely because it was an alternative to the Prussian-German nation-state that emerged in the nineteenth century. Here was a German state system that was not in any sense a *Machtstaat*, but rather a model of a pre-national (or, perhaps more accurately, non-national) federative union.

While the old Prussian-German nationalist tradition regarded the Reich as a decayed and chaotic institution, corrupt to the core, the new orthodoxy regards it as a system that worked relatively effectively.[11] In its fully articulated form after 1648 it fulfilled a vital role as a *Rechts-, Verteidigungs-, und Friedensordnung*, a system of law, defence and peace in central Europe. As a *Verteidigungsordung* the very existence of the Empire guaranteed both the peace and stability of Europe as a whole. That also ensured the survival of the hundreds of small German territories, most of which would have been incapable of survival as independent units in the competitive world of the European powers. As a *Friedensordnung*, the Empire both provided protection from external threat and served to prevent conflict between the territories. It was thus predicated on the principle of non-aggression and collective self-defence. Finally, as a *Rechtsordnung*, the Empire had developed mechanisms to secure the rights both of rulers and, more extraordinarily of subjects against their rulers.[12] The Reich's institutions, particularly the highest Imperial law courts, the *Reichskammergericht* in Wetzlar and the *Reichshofgericht* in Vienna, offered legal safeguards for many of the inhabitants of the German territories and contributed to the evolution of a legal culture which had no parallel elsewhere in Europe. The 'juridification' of social and political conflicts at all levels, the potential contained in Imperial law and institutions for the resolution of conflicts, marked the German lands apart from their western neighbours in the early modern period.[13]

At the same time other features of the Reich have also increasingly intrigued scholars. Two are of particular significance. First, the old view of Imperial politics as a futile dualism between emperor and princes has been replaced by the view of the Reich as a system characterized by collective-corporate representative and decision-making mechanisms.[14] From the Reichstag down to the Imperial Circles and their numerous sub-committees decisions were made collectively. Where the older nationalist tradition saw a hopelessly sclerotic system that rarely made decisions at all, the new view sees a system in which consensus was regarded as the highest good. Decisions were generally reached painfully slowly, but that was because all the Estates had a voice. Often decisions were never reached, but that was because the agreement of all was a precondition for a binding resolution. In the light of contemporary experiences in the European Union, such procedures seem far from unusual, and even positive. Indeed many have seen the Holy Roman Empire as an institution in which subsidiarity was practised.[15]

Second, in addition to setting a legal framework, the Reich also aspired to set a framework for social and economic policy. In the sixteenth century attempts to regulate currency or to control the activities of the great south German trading companies were unsuccessful. Thereafter, however, the Imperial Circles, especially the Swabian, Franconian and Bavarian circles, played an increasingly active role in regional currency regulation, in regulating customs dues, road construction, food supply in times of shortage, and social policy generally.[16]

Of course all these activities were not always very effective in practice. Nor did the Circles invariably collect Imperial taxes efficiently, raise Imperial troops in sufficient number in the required time, or execute decisions of the Imperial courts effectively. There were also periods in which the system broke down: most spectacularly and disastrously during the Thirty Years War, and again during the Seven Years War. By the end of the eighteenth century furthermore the rivalry between Austria and Prussia so overshadowed the system that it seems possible the Reich could not have survived even had it not been destroyed by the French invasion. On the other hand, for three centuries, and particularly for the hundred and fifty years following the Peace of Westphalia, the Reich served as an effective umbrella for the German Länder. It preserved their regional variety just as it maintained their collective solidarity, despite the profound and often bitter religious divide that plunged so many western European states into civil war in the late sixteenth and seventeenth centuries.

The merits of the system did not go unnoticed by contemporaries. Traditional scholarship seized upon those views that were critical of

the Reich and that expressed exasperation with its long-winded procedures or focused on the ideas of intellectuals such as Schiller concerning the idea of a cultural nation. More positive assessments were often
simply overlooked. Indeed, precisely at the time when the Reich came
under attack from France and when German society was confronted
with the new ideas of the revolutionary state, many commentators
penned elaborate hymns of praise to the German system. Wieland was
not untypical when he eulogized the Reich in 1792 as that system that
had brought the Germans stability and prosperity. There was no need,
he declared, to fear comparisons with France; the only thing the
Germans lacked was sufficient belief in the value of their own institutions.[17] Equally, in this period, as throughout the eighteenth century,
experts in Imperial law and others were busy formulating plans for the
reform and renewal of the Reich. Indeed major works on the subject
were still being published even as the Reich was in the process of being
dissolved between 1803 and 1806. There was widespread recognition of
the problems of the Imperial system and its all too evident weakness in
the international crisis of the 1790s and the first years of the nineteenth century. On the other hand commentators on Imperial law had
no doubt that Germany had long enjoyed a well ordered constitution
that guaranteed freedom and peace, and that consequently the
Germans had no need to fear a revolution.[18] Even during the very last
years of the Reich's existence, after the process of dissolution had
already begun with the secularization of the ecclesiastical territories by
the *Reichsdeputationshauptschluß* of 1803, impressive reform plans continued to appear. Leading commentators such as Leist (1803), Gönner
(1804), Schmalz (1805) and Schnaubert (1806) produced major works
on the public law of the Reich that sought both to describe its present
state and to integrate into its structures the new principles of sovereignty and citizenship.[19]

During the same years the question of the reorganization of the
German Länder also once again became acute, and the most popular
options were those that stressed 'community and liberty'. In the literature devoted to Germany's future between 1806 and 1815 the overwhelming majority of writers formulated schemes that embodied what
they perceived to be the main characteristics, and virtues, of the 'Old
Reich'. A new union of German states had to provide a basis for a
general European *Friedensordnung*. Such a union should be capable of
defending itself and its members from external aggression. It had to
guarantee the independence and peaceful coexistence of its members
internally and provide a legal basis for fundamental rights common to

all Germans. Few espoused the idea of a unitary nation-state at this time.[20] Even Fichte, traditionally viewed as the leading exponent of such a vision of the future, preached something quite different in his *Reden an die deutsche Nation*. He did not argue for the restoration of the traditional framework, but his idea of a national religion represents a radically modernized version of the Christian traditions of the Reich. The princes were to be swept aside in a new Reich or state that he later defined as a 'Bund der Freien' (a 'league of the free').[21]

The traditional scholarly view saw the dissolution of the Holy Roman Empire in 1806 as a dead end, with the Prussian opposition to Napoleon as the new beginning. That is being replaced with a more nuanced assessment of a complex transition from one kind of federal system to another in the German Confederation of 1815. Now too the Confederation of the Rhine, despised by nationalist scholars as an alien French construct, can be seen as part of this 'federal tradition'.[22] Indeed some are beginning to trace lines of continuity beyond 1815. Through the nationalist discussions of the 1820s and 1830s to the debates at the Frankfurt Parliament 1848–9 and beyond, plans for federal solutions continually harked back to the Reich before 1806. *Pace* Heinrich August Winkler, these plans were inspired not so much by the ideal of medieval universal empire as by an early modern system that had been distinguished by an optimal balance between unity and diversity and that should serve as a model for the future.[23] Indeed Wolfgang Burgdorf has recently argued that the tradition of *Reichspublizistik*, writing about the public law of the Reich, both provided the framework for thinking about the organization of the German states until 1871 and largely set the agenda for the theoretical political debates about those states as well.[24]

The rediscovery of lines of continuity from the eighteenth to the nineteenth centuries at the 'national' level has been matched by similar findings at the levels of territory, town and locality. Much of this builds on the fundamental work of Peter Blickle who since the 1960s has dedicated himself to proving that 'German history [has] not been a tale of continuous subjection of subordinate classes'.[25] Blickle's studies of communalism, of both urban and rural communes resisting authority and thus ultimately shaping the development of the state, implicitly pointed to parallels between the habitual patterns of disobedience of early modern communities and citizens' initiative movements of the late 1960s.[26] Others have subsequently elaborated the long early modern prelude to democratization. As Andreas Würgler has shown, for example, the memory of eighteenth-century conflicts lived on in the historiography of the early nineteenth century. The issues at the core of those conflicts – for example, the demand for the publication of constitutions and the like, the assertion of a right to public assembly, the demand for popular participation in government – remained central to the political debates of the new century. Of course the French Revolution shaped the tradition, supplying new vocabulary and concepts, but contemporaries experienced the 'lines of tradition ... more strongly than the undoubtedly important turning points of 1789, 1798, 1806 and 1815'.[27] Just as individuals lived through these turning points to pursue careers begun before them or fight causes that predated them, so ideas, issues and slogans survived through the period of revolutionary upheaval, emerging changed but still recognizable at the end. Again, these rediscovered lines of continuity echo the ideas of earlier scholars in the 1960s and 1970s who sought to establish continuity between early modern Estates and modern parliaments.[28]

Just as fascinating as the emergence of the new view of the Old Reich has been the development of a sense in the West German historiographical tradition of the contemporary relevance of its study. In the GDR, of course, historical study within the Marxist framework was always politically relevant.[29] Moreover the East German interpretation of early modern history also underwent considerable shifts, particularly the renewed interest in the Reformation as an 'early bourgeois revolution' and the re-evaluation of the contribution of eighteenth-century Prussia to the general development of German history. Yet, fundamentally, GDR scholars viewed the Reich as an antiquated feudal system, part of a past rendered utterly redundant by the triumph of socialism. In the West German tradition the sense of the relevance of the history of the Old Reich was quite slow to develop. However, in the last two decades in particular it seems that early modern historians in the Federal Republic have been increasingly interested in emphasizing the wider significance of their research.

In some respects attempts to make links between early modern history and contemporary circumstances are not particularly new. In the aftermath of 1945, for example, some attempted to argue against what were perceived to have been negative Prussian-German traditions. Among others, Elisabeth Schmittmann, widow of the Catholic Rhineland federalist Benedikt Schmittmann, argued in the journal *Neues Abendland* in 1946 that the medieval Reich would be a better model for the Germany of the future than the nation-state of 1871. Traditions of diversity, unity, peaceful integration into the world community and the recognition of a higher moral law were, she argued, characteristic of the Reich and had been undermined in modern times by blinkered nationalism.[30] In a similar vein the Catholic political theorist Hans Maier called in 1966 for a re-evaluation of the political thinking of the early modern Reich.[31] He both drew attention to the continuity between early modern and modern administrative theory and emphasized the relevance to the practice of the Federal Republic of the study of an early modern administrative theory shaped by social and ethical principles based on the notion of the common good. In the second edition of his book Maier was even more insistent on the contemporary relevance of his material and made even wider claims for it in a new concluding excursus entitled 'The older German teaching on the state and western political theory'.[32] Conventionally, he argued, the German tradition had been neglected and viewed as at best second rate compared with the great Western European tradition from Machiavelli to Hume and Rousseau. Apart from Althusius and Pufendorf the Reich produced no major first-rank theorists until the great philosophical revolution initiated by Kant at the end of the eighteenth century. On the other hand, Maier suggested, the numerous minor authors who formed the distinctive German tradition of writing about administration nonetheless deserved recognition. For they contributed fundamentally to the emergence of the modern social welfare state, a state with moral obligations to its citizens in which those who rule and govern are bound by Christian responsibility.[33]

For a long time, however, such attempts to reconnect the (West) German present with historical traditions that long pre-dated the nation-state of 1871 seem to have had only limited impact, even among scholarly circles. In the last ten years or so, however, they seem to have become more frequent and more successful in attracting the attention of a wider audience. The reasons for this renewed sense of the 'relevance' of the history of the Reich are complex. The growing establishment of the new view as the new orthodoxy is undoubtedly important, as is no doubt the need for early modern historians to assert the position of their subject in the curriculum at school and university and in the competition for funding. But it seems likely that factors external to the discipline are also playing their part. Some, largely non-German, observers regard what they see as the 'idealization of the old Reich' as a manifestation of a 'new nationalism' in post-reunification Germany.[34] A common German response to such implied criticisms is that this phenomenon has nothing to do with nationalism or even a reappraisal of Germany's national history, but that it represents a reappraisal of European history. According to Heinz Schilling, for example, the renewed interest in the Holy Roman Empire is part of an attempt to clarify the German contributions to 'European historical, political, legal and social culture' and to identify the (German) 'roots of the modern European constitutional and welfare state'.[35] A significant part of Schilling's own contribution to this exercise has been the recovery of 'republican' traditions in German towns in the early modern period.[36]

The trend is not by any means uniform. The work of Karl Otmar von Aretin, for example, has been fundamental to study of the Old Reich since the late 1960s.[37] To date he has, however, consistently argued that there was a more or less complete break in German history around 1806. For all the virtues of the system and for all the fact that it functioned effectively for much of the period after 1648, Aretin believes that the Reich was an anachronism by the end of the eighteenth century.[38] Its end was inevitable because of the emergence of the idea of state sovereignty in both Prussia and Austria. The sovereign ambitions of each and the rivalry between the two effectively paralysed and undermined the Reich even before it was subject to external assault by France in the 1790s. Once the system began to falter, the only interest of Prussia and Austria, and then of the other larger south German states, was to soak up as much territory as possible. It was a venerable but essentially bankrupt institution that ultimately fell victim to an unseemly scramble for its remaining assets. Furthermore, according to Aretin, the Reich's bankruptcy was not simply a question of its inability to defend itself. Like Nipperdey and Wehler and others, he has argued that the Reich was itself an obstacle to reform and modernization. Only after its dissolution were the modernizing energies that lay in the larger territories unleashed. The nineteenth-century German constitutional state, he argues, was based on the French model.[39] The reforms of the period 1806–15, let alone those of any time thereafter, he suggests, were unthinkable under the 'Old Reich'. In Aretin's view, the Reich was a system dedicated to maintaining an equilibrium that was increasingly at odds with the rapidly modernizing world around it.

In this context another feature of Aretin's work acquires an intriguing significance. His belief that the Italian Imperial feudal nexus remained a meaningful part of the Holy Roman Empire until the end of the eighteenth century also seems to emphasize the older understanding of the Reich as a universal (non-national) institution.[40] While most recent scholars have simply ignored these remnants of the medieval Imperial system as an irrelevant curiosity, Aretin persists in taking them seriously. Indeed he argues that the early modern struggle for influence in Italy between the Reich, Spain and the Papacy led to a 'refeudalization' of Italy in the seventeenth and eighteenth centuries. Aretin himself concedes that Italy never played a central role in the history of the Reich. Yet his inclusion of Italy in his recent major study demonstrates Aretin's affinity with older scholarly traditions rather than with the new history of the Reich since the 1960s.

Finally Aretin and others emphasize what they see as the essentially rather negative implications of the Reich's legal culture for the development of modern Germany.[41] Judged on its own terms the Reich was remarkable in the degree to which it provided judicial mechanisms for groups and individuals to pursue grievances against their lords and rulers. As the Imperial court notary (*Reichskammergerichtsnotar*) Johann Melchior Hoscher pointed out in 1790, there was no need in Germany for subjects to resort to revolution or to self-help, and consequently no need for rulers to fear unruly subjects. For the constitution of the Reich provided for an 'Oberrichter' or supreme judge (the Emperor) to adjudicate between the rights of both.[42] The result of such mediations, however, was almost invariably the maintenance of the status quo. Ultimately this enhanced the prestige, and hence the power, of the state in Germany as the source and guardian of law. The early modern juridification of conflicts, the minute regulation of society and resolution of social tension by law, arguably inhibited thinking about politics and political activity. Particularly after 1789, both became suspect, and the idea of the *Rechtsstaat* became a substitute in the German states for the democratic institutions that developed elsewhere in Western Europe.[43]

In these kinds of argument, traces of the older, negative views of the Holy Roman Empire remain visible. Many other recent studies of the Reich, by contrast, seek to emphasize a more positive assessment. Increasingly many of the scholars involved in the revision of the history of the Old Reich seem to wish to suggest that it influenced modern German society in ways that were more positive than generally allowed by those who have regarded the nation-state as the norm. On the one hand there has been a tendency to emphasize the model nature of the early modern Reich. On the other hand there has been a desire to reassess its role in both German and European history.

It is the European dimension that has perhaps been the most striking. Comparisons between the Reich and the European Union have become almost routine in the scholarly literature, and the suggestion that the pre-national Reich might well serve as a model for a post-national Europe is by no means uncommon. A systematic survey of these comparisons is impossible, but a few randomly selected examples will illustrate the trend.

Michael Stolleis, for example, commented in 1987, in the introduction to a volume of essays devoted to early modern German political thought, that the 'peculiar constitution of the Holy Roman Empire', with its union of diverse ecclesiastical and secular territories, invited comparison with the evolution of the European Union.[44] Significantly, however, he simultaneously argued that the writers featured in his volume made little impact on modern German political culture.[45] On this view the Reich thus provided an example of a pre-modern federation but its political theory contributed nothing to German history in the long term. In 1993 Peter Claus Hartmann declared that the Reich between 1648 and 1806 might serve as a model for Europe today.[46] It was, he suggested, 'a *Mitteleuropa* of the regions'. Those Germans who feared the rapid pace of European integration might be reassured by the example of the Reich, a union in which 'strong regional powers existed in the framework of a loose state structure with a weak centre'. The Reichstag after 1648 performed the functions that today are performed by the European Union, by NATO and by the United Nations. It guaranteed collective security against external attack (for example, against the Turks). It maintained the peace within its frontiers, particularly by eliminating religious conflict and by guaranteeing freedom of conscience and by providing for parity between Catholics and Protestants in all Imperial institutions. It ensured a degree of harmonization between the regions while at the same time allowing each to decide on things that did not necessarily concern the whole. Its regional Circles, the *Reichskreise*, were, according to Hartmann, directly comparable in both scope and functions with the regions of the contemporary European Union. Hartmann's discussion appeared in the official newspaper of the Bundestag and one might perhaps be inclined to class his article as ephemeral, more a flight of journalistic fancy than a serious scholarly contribution. In the previous year, however, he had published a scholarly article in a prestigious academic journal arguing that the Circle assemblies (*Kreistage*) were in essence forerunners of modern parliamentary institutions.[47] Similar arguments then subsequently reappeared in his immensely scholarly study of the Bavarian *Reichskreis*, which emphasized the functioning of the Circle alongside the Swabian and Franconian Circles as 'regions' with serious political, economic and social functions.[48]

In a rather similar vein Reinhart Koselleck has recently characterized the Reich as both pre-national and post-national, as both pre-modern and post-modern.[49] In a review of Helmuth Plessner's study of Germany as the 'delayed nation', he questions the notion of a normative development for European nations. Koselleck draws attention to the fact that Plessner only used the term 'delayed nation' in the title of the 1959 second edition of the work he originally published in 1935 under the title 'The Fate of the German Mind at the End of its Bourgeois Age'.[50] The new title was perhaps more appropriate to the post-1945 context and more suited to stimulate debate in it, but Koselleck argues that it distorted the suggestive brilliance of Plessner's analysis, and generated a misleading debate. Talk of Germany as a 'delayed nation' is, he believes, simply misplaced. The fundamental reason why the Germans were prevented from forming a nation-state until the 1871 was, quite simply, because the long-term structures of German history were never national but rather federal from the start.[51] 'What hindered the development of a German nation-state in the modern democratic sense throughout the centuries,' Koselleck argues, 'were the federal structures.'[52] Originally the term 'Germans' simply denoted the ruling aristocracy who were entitled to participate in Imperial elections. They ruled over a mixed collection of albeit related peoples – Saxons, Bavarians, Hessians and the like – who only became legally defined as 'Germans', members of a single people or race, in the twentieth century. The Holy Roman Empire, the German Confederation, the Reich of 1871 were all technically leagues or unions of princes. Though the Reich remained a hierarchical feudal order, the various Estates organized themselves federally, in 'lateral' unions that ran counter to the 'vertical' hierarchy. According to Koselleck, peasants, knights and townsmen all lost their rights of federation during the sixteenth century. However, the ruling Estates – the princes – defended this federal principle successfully and further developed it. They defended it against successive attempts by the Habsburgs to transform the Reich into a state. The experience of religious division and conflict in the sixteenth and early seventeenth centuries led them to translate the federal principle into one of religious toleration and parity in 1648. Since the ruling noble caste was allied by marriage to the surrounding European nobility, including most of Europe's ruling dynasties, the Reich also held the key to the stability of Europe as a whole.

For Koselleck the important lesson of this longer-term view of German history lies in two principles of politics that he regards as fundamental to the success of any union of European states. Fundamental is the insight that the only unions that retain the capacity to take effective political decisions, and hence remain viable and durable, are those in which all members are willing to compromise: even a minimal willingness to compromise will guarantee a maximum success. Second, only institutions that provide equal rights for all groups, regardless of their relative size and power can guarantee that 'equality of unequals' that is the precondition of peaceful coexistence.[53]

What might be described as the 'Europeanization' of early modern German history has become almost a prevailing tendency among historians concerned with the history of the 'Old Reich'. Many of the parallels drawn and conclusions suggested are undoubtedly stimulating and conceivably even of value in presenting a historical perspective on various forms of federal union being discussed today. On the other hand they have arguably also come to exert a distorting effect on the understanding of the Holy Roman Empire as part of German, as opposed to European, history. One of the reasons why many have found the study of the 'Old Reich' so attractive and rewarding is precisely because it seemed to provide a model for a non-national or pre-national federation. That in turn runs the risk of distorting the past in that it fails to recognize fully the ways in which the Reich was the product of a uniquely German national experience. It also fails to recognize the ways in which that system shaped and was in turn shaped by an emerging sense of German identity in the early modern period. The German Länder cannot simply be equated with Europe; their history cannot simply be subsumed in European history. Like other parts of Europe, both west and east, they have their own national or ethnic history; and European history, like the European present (and future), can surely never be more than the sum of these distinct parts.

A sense of this emerges from the work of a number of scholars who have begun to reassess the significance of the 'Old Reich' in relation of issues of national identity and national tradition. Important surveys by Dieter Langewiesche and Reinhard Stauber have focused attention on the 'national' significance of the Reich and on the ways in which a German national identity can be said to have existed before 1806.[54] The distinctiveness of the German experience of federalism and the distinctiveness of Germany as a 'federative nation' is also investigated in a recent volume of essays edited by Langewiesche and Georg Schmidt.[55] Langewiesche in particular draws attention to the lasting influence of what he calls 'federative nationalism' in German history. This, he argues, was an enduring heritage of the Reich that shaped the experience of the second Reich and that was not extinguished either by the First World War or by any of the other 'national' experiences of the twentieth century.[56] And while Langewiesche traces lines of continuity after 1806, important work by Wolfgang Burgdorf has uncovered origins of the modern 'national' idea in the eighteenth-century Reich.[57] After about 1750 (specifically, after the Sevens Years War) both the larger territories striving against the ground rules of the Reich for sovereignty and, more intriguingly, the Reich itself were variously conceived as nation-states. This did not materially affect the Reich or bring any of the numerous late eighteenth-century plans for its reform and renewal any closer to realization. Most immediately such notions bore fruit in the larger territories that survived the Reich and gained territory as a result of its dismemberment as they sought to integrate new territory and new subjects and to create 'national' (Bavarian, Prussian, Hanoverian, Württemberg, etc) state identities for themselves. Yet the federative national framework did not simply disappear; on the contrary, the 'desire for national unity in Germany after 1815 articulated itself as a desire for a new Reich'.[58]

The most impressive and wide-ranging reassessment so far of this kind is without doubt Georg Schmidt's study of the relationship between state and nation in the early modern period.[59] Perhaps the most novel feature of Schmidt's analysis, and its central challenge to most previous scholarship, is his insistence that the Reich must be regarded as a state: 1495 marked the beginning of German *Gesamtstaatlichkeit*, or the union of the Germans in a single overarching state organization. Of course this was not a state in the nineteenth-century sense, but Schmidt points out that no early modern state should be judged by the impossible standards set by Hegel and subsequent theorists of the modern *Rechtsstaat*. Hegel wrote in 1800 that 'Germany is no longer a state', but his predecessors – and many contemporaries – would have disagreed.[60] As a political system that functioned, even as a kind of republic, it was clearly classifiable as a state. And while it was common to emphasize the uniqueness of this state, the impossibility of comparing it with others, Schmidt suggests, is that it was in reality perhaps not so different from the far from monolithic 'composite monarchies' of France, Spain or Great Britain. The Reich had a much weaker centre; its component parts, the territories and other Estates, exercized many of the functions of the state. Yet they remained parts of an interlocking system that guaranteed individual rights, regulated disputes and implemented decisions, a system that ensured internal peace and protection from external aggression. As the late eighteenth-century theorist Johann Stephan Pütter put it, the Reich was a structure 'composed of many particular states that are yet still subordinate to a common higher power'.[61]

According to Schmidt, the Holy Roman Empire was a 'complementary state'. 'Governments' at varying levels carried out state functions: the Reich dealt with defence and the legal system; the Circles dealt with the implementation of decisions and the management of infrastructure; the territories governed and 'disciplined' the subjects.[62] Schmidt's analysis takes account of the full range of revisionist writing on the Old Reich over the last decades. In addition, however, his analytical narrative of the evolution of the 'Reichs-Staat', as many eighteenth-century writers termed it, has three important strands that, in his combination, are challenging and original.

First, he traces the geographical extension of the Reich from its original Upper German core to the north and north-west and the elaboration of its institutions from the reforms of Maximilian around 1500 to the Peace of Westphalia. This provided a fundamental law or constitution for the whole system that remained in force until 1806.

Second, Schmidt traces the evolution of a German 'national' identification with this state. From the humanist Imperial patriots of the late fifteenth century, the national anti-Roman rhetoric of the early Reformation and the resistance against Charles V in the Schmalkaldic War, Schmidt traces a line through to the seventeenth-century language societies and the patriotic writers of the Seven Years War. Schmidt's analysis of many episodes in this strand of the narrative draws extensively on the work of literary and linguistic scholars, among whom there has been a resurgence of interest in questions of German national identity over the last ten years or so. Schmidt's use of this evidence is in many ways pioneering, for among historians generally the very concept of the 'nation' was long something of a taboo, and they have consequently been slow to make sense of the findings of these scholars in neighbouring disciplines.[63]

Third, Schmidt analyses the genesis of a distinctive political culture within this national and state community: a set of values and norms that were specifically identified with the Reich. In the sixteenth century German freedom was defined as freedom of property and guaranteed by an Imperial judicial system in which even peasants could, and did, appeal against their lords and rulers. The resolution of bitter confessional divisions brought the principle of freedom of conscience in 1648. By the late seventeenth century writers such as Pufendorf were talking about inalienable rights (Schmidt suggests, 'human rights'), not political freedom or freedom from the state but, in Christoph Link's words, a 'freedom within and towards the state', freedom bound into an 'ethics of social duty'.[64]

These developments were not achieved easily or without cost. Profound and protracted conflicts, Imperial 'civil wars' often threatened to tear the Reich apart before the common interest of its members in the survival of the system led to the formulation of principles designed to satisfy the requirements of unequal partners. That this was achieved at all, however, was remarkable, and the variety preserved in the common framework of the Reich was indeed unique in Europe. This was something, Schmidt suggests, that Germans at all levels – from the learned authority on German public law to the peasants who knew they could pursue their rights in the courts – could identify with. And it was this successful history that alone can explain how a writer such as Christian Ulrich Detlev von Eggers could in all seriousness declare in 1808 that notions of 'unconditional freedom and equality in human constitutions are phantoms of a sick mind'.[65] As Peter Krüger has commented, *Verfassungspatriotismus* has a long history in Germany![66]

Schmidt's analysis of the early modern Reich comes close to describing the kind of world that Anthony Smith has defined as an 'ethnie'.[67] For it came to embrace an extended community united by a common historical experience and, for all the differences between regions and above all confessions, sharing in common 'myths, memories, values and symbols'.[68] As Wilhelm von Humboldt wrote to Stein in 1813: '... the sense that Germany is something whole cannot be eradicated from any German heart, and it rests not only on shared manners, language and literature ... but in the memory of rights and freedoms shared in common, honour won together and dangers withstood, on the memory of a closer union that united our fathers and that now [i.e. after the dissolution of the Reich] lives only in the aspirations of their grandchildren'.[69] Much of this is rediscovered in Schmidt's work.

It remains to be seen whether Schmidt's ambitious attempt to recover the (specifically German) political culture of the Old Reich will promote a reassessment of German 'national' history as a whole or of indeed the history of pre-modern German statehood. Certainly those scholars who have for so long shied away from 'national' issues, preferring to pursue their research under the banner of a less sensitive postnational Europeanism, are unlikely to accept his arguments. Heinz Schilling, for example, has accused Schmidt of reverting to the historiographical traditions of the nineteenth century.[70] In particular, Schilling believes that it is fundamentally wrong to describe the Reich as a state (Schilling prefers the term 'system') and that Schmidt is guilty of confusing patriotism with nationalism. This is more than just a

squabble over terminology: Schilling believes that the use of terms has
serious political implications. The Germans, he argues, will merely fuel
the anxieties of their neighbours if they follow Schmidt in regarding
the Reich as their 'proto-nation state'. In his view, the only current
'political' interest of the study of the Reich lies in the analysis of its
'pre- and non-state functions'. On the one hand these 'permit the ...
comparison with the European Union'. On the other hand they may
contribute to the construction of a 'model of a common historical-
political culture of the Europeans based on law and justice, federal
balance between large and small members, and on the purely defensive
use of armed force'.[71]

Schilling's anxieties about Schmidt's work and his conviction that
scholars of the early modern Reich have a duty to anchor their
(correct) understanding of its character in both the German and the
wider European public consciousness prompt two general concluding
questions. First, what impact do such shifts in interpretation in fact
have outside the narrower scholarly community? And second, do they
have any more general meaning as reflections of contemporary political attitudes?

It is difficult to assess the wider impact of scholarly research very precisely. While some scholars enthusiastically proclaim the contemporary relevance of their work, others complain bitterly about public
indifference to it. Several years after Claus Peter Hartmann's comparisons between the Imperial Circles and contemporary European institutions, Winfried Dotzauer lamented in 1997 that neither the Federal
government, nor the Länder, nor local and municipal governments
saw any comparison between any aspect of their work and that of the
Imperial Circles.[72] Around the same time Johannes Burkhardt noted: 'it
is a public scandal just how little of decades of research on the Reich
has yet made an impact on politicians concerned with education, on
organisers of exhibitions and sometimes even on neighbouring disciplines and teachers'.[73] In the popular imagination at least the old
images live on, reinforced by the major narratives of modern German
history by scholars such as Nipperdey, Wehler, and now Winckler.[74]
Exhibitions such as that which celebrated the 500th anniversary of the
Reichskammergericht in 1995 failed to have an impact in any way comparable to that of recent exhibitions devoted to more recent periods of
Germany history.[75] Most recently, Dieter Langewiesche lamented that
the debate about ethnic minorities, multiculturalism, and the notion
of a German *Leitkultur*, was characterized by an exclusive focus on the
supposed traditions of the German nation state since 1871. None of

the protagonists in the debate thought it necessary to consider any traditions that might have derived from the Holy Roman Empire.[76]

Perhaps inevitably the Reich is unlikely to gain the prominence in the popular imagination enjoyed by later periods. The response (albeit by scholars) to Johannes Burkhardt's attempt to make his subject 'politically interesting' illustrates some of the pitfalls and points to some controversial issues.[77] The occasion for his enterprise was the anniversary of the Peace of Westphalia in 1998, celebrated with major exhibitions in Münster, Osnabrück and Nuremberg, and with the opening of a Thirty Years War museum in Wittstock.[78] Significantly, the linked Münster and Osnabrück exhibitions were sponsored by the Council of Europe and accordingly the peace treaty was presented as a European, rather than a purely German, event.[79] Burkhardt's eulogy to the treaty ('a peace of superlatives'), published in the journal of the German association of teachers of history, emphasized three major facets.[80] First, the peace established a pluralistic state system in Europe. Second, the peace treaty, 'completely literally and in the modern sense', provided the Reich with a fundamental law or constitution. In Burkhardt's view it represented a 'Gesamtverfassung' or constitution for the whole Reich, in which the Reichstag figured as Europe's first standing parliament (the British parliament, for example, sat only periodically, whereas the Regensburg Reichstag was 'perpetual' after 1653). Third, the peace treaty marked the end of religious conflict in Germany and the beginning of the period of (modern) religious toleration.

Two scholars immediately objected to Burkhardt's arguments. In detail the points put forward by Martin Tabaczek and Paul Münch were quite similar.[81] The Peace of Westphalia patently did not end all wars. It did not contain a constitution for the Reich in any modern sense, and the Reichstag was by no stretch of the imagination a modern parliament. Equally, the degree of religious toleration in fact guaranteed by the treaty was extremely limited, and religious conflict was a feature of Imperial politics well into the eighteenth century.[82] Tabaczek is particularly keen to stress that Burkhardt endows the Peace of Westphalia with a modernity that it did not in fact have. He also explicitly denies that there is any link at all between the decentralized structures of the Reich and the modern federalism.[83] Münch's prime concern is somewhat different. He argues that it is positively harmful to idealize the Peace of Westphalia as 'foundation of a peaceful European order and of a better German history'. It did not mark the beginning of the modern German *Rechtsstaat*, and the commemoration of its anniversary cannot be ranked alongside the commemoration of 1848 as a commemoration of the democratic history of Germany. Indeed if that were possible, then history would have to be seriously rewritten, for 'Auschwitz would be not a lesser but a greater disgrace'.[84] According to Münch, Burkhardt's 'anachronistic' view of 1648 and its relevance to the Germany of today is just as much a distortion of 'applied history' as the nineteenth-century view of the tragedy of 1648 in German history.

For Burkhardt the main outcome of the debate is that it has prompted questions about the overall perception of German history ('das Geschichtsbild').[85] Granted that the Reich was an early modern system, he wishes to see the new view of its history developed by scholars over the last few decades reflected in the popular view of the past. Tabaczek and Münch, he believes, wish to remain within traditional interpretations for fear of entering into potentially difficult political controversies. This is, in other words, another case of a typically German debate about how to write about and present the German past. It is a dispute about how episodes in that past are evaluated appropriately in an almost moral sense, and with due regard both to the presumed domestic political implications and the image of the Germans in the eyes of their neighbours.

One perennial anxiety seems to be that any positive re-evaluation of virtually any period in the German past might be perceived as evidence of renewed nationalism. While the anxiety is not unjustified, the perception is open to doubt. To interpret such revisionism as evidence of a 'new nationalism' in contemporary Germany seems both extreme and somewhat misplaced. What it reflects rather is surely something of the strident 'post-nationalism' and firm commitment to European integration that has characterized the German political, economic and intellectual elites over the last decades.[86] It reflects a continuing ambivalence about national identity and national history, and a continuing tendency among many intellectuals to avoid talk of the nation in a society that has long regarded itself as post-national.[87] For many the only acceptable way forward lay in a passionate commitment to Europe, though in a Europe that is wary of German dominance and that often – misguidedly – interprets German Europeanism as a disguized form of German nationalism.

Viewed in this perspective attempts to make the Old Reich 'relevant' to the debate about the contemporary European Union are evidence not of 'new nationalism' but rather of a distinctive German approach to Europe, specifically to the question of state sovereignty.[88] British and French politicians baulk at the idea of relinquishing sovereignty to a European parliament. Despite evidence of considerable, and growing, popular euroscepticism in Germany, in particular widespread anxiety about the prospect of the Euro and anxiety about the prospect of immigration from Eastern Europe that might follow EU enlargement, German politicians seem to have few qualms about moving towards a closer union. Consequently they often demonstrate an inability to understand the hesitation of their British and French colleagues. The reason for this mismatch of perceptions may well lie in the *Geschichtsbild*, in a differing historical experience and collective historical memories. On the one hand the German historical experience has been a federal experience for at least the last five hundred years. On the other hand decades of West German 'post-national' thinking have diminished sensitivity to the continuing significance of national issues for many neighbouring countries.

If this is so then a re-evaluation of the national dimension of early modern German history may not only enrich our understanding of the Old Reich but also provide a welcome, fresh perspective on contemporary issues. The Reich was uniquely German and its federal structures never proved transferable. It lost territory with the secession of the Swiss Confederation and the Netherlands, but it never gained territory. It was a part of Europe, but never a microcosm of Europe. Its history was one of many parallel histories in what was, and what looks set to remain a Europe of nations.

Notes

1. 'Streitgespräch Joschka Fischer contra Jean-Pierre Chevènement', *Die Zeit*, 21.6.2000.
2. J. Fischer, 'Vom Staatenbund zur Föderation – 'Gedanken über die Finalität der europäischen Integration', speech delivered on 12.5.2000 at the Humboldt University, Berlin; the text is available on the German government website www.bundesregierung.de
3. 'Souverainisme' argues that sovereignty resides in the people and that since the people also constitute the nation there can be no such thing as the 'European people', even one constituted by direct elections for a European president. The concept combines a recent form of nationalism based on French republican traditions with a suspicious view of German ulterior motives in promoting the process of European integration. See J. Hénard, 'Jean-Pierre Chevènement: Der Souveränist', *Die Zeit*, 26. 6. 2000.
4. See for example, W. Weidenfeld and K.-R. Korte, eds, *Handbuch zur deutschen Einheit* (Frankfurt a.M. and New York 1993), p. 300.
5. T. Nipperdey, *Deutsche Geschichte 1800–1866. Bürgerwelt und starker Staat* (Munich 1983), p. 11. In an early essay on federalism in German history, the most that Nipperdey was prepared to concede was that the 'federal' Reich was 'nicht ein Nichts': idem, 'Der Föderalismus in der deutschen

Geschichte', *Bijdragen en Mededelingen Betreffende de Geschiednis der Nederlande*, 94 (1979), pp. 497–547, on p. 504.

6. H.-U. Wehler, *Deutsche Gesellschaftsgeschichte* Bd 1, *1700–1815* (Munich 1987), p. 35.
7. H. A. Winkler, *Der lange Weg nach Westen. Bd 1 Vom Ende des Alten Reichs bis zum Untergang der Weimarer Republik* (Munich 2000), p. 5.
8. Ibid, p. 39.
9. Ibid, p. 2.
10. P. H. Wilson, *The Holy Roman Empire 1495–1806* (London 1999), pp. 4–8; C. P. Hartmann, *Der Bayerische Reichskreis (1500 bis 1803). Strukturen, Geschichte und Bedeutung im Rahmen der Kreisverfassung und der allgemeinen institutionellen Entwicklung des Heiligen Römischen Reiches*, Schriften zur Verfassungsgeschichte, Bd 52 (Berlin 1997), pp. 17–23; F. Brendle and A. Schindling, 'Volker Press (1939–1993). Ständeforscher und Historiker des Adels im Alten Reich' in V. Press, *Adel im Alten Reich. Gesammelte Vorträge und Aufsätze*, ed. F. Brendle and A. Schindling, Frühneuzeit-Forschungen, Bd 4 (Tübingen 1998), pp. 9–40, esp. pp. 10–14. For the groundbreaking works of Aretin, see note 37 below.
11. W. Schulze, *Einführung in die Neuere Geschichte* (Stuttgart 1987), pp. 279–82; G. Schmidt, *Der Dreissigjährige Krieg* (Munich 1995), pp. 7–8, 94–8; C. Dipper, *Deutsche Geschichte 1648–1789* (Frankfurt a.M. 1991), pp. 252–62. The most recent handbook summary in German is H. Neuhaus, *Das Reich in der Frühen Neuzeit*, Enzyklopädie Deutscher Geschichte, Bd 42 (Munich 1997). Recent works in English that draws on 'revisionist' studies of the Reich include Wilson, *Holy Roman Empire*; M. Hughes, *Early Modern Germany 1477–1806* (Basingstoke 1992); B. Simms, *The Struggle for Mastery in Germany, 1779–1850* (Basingstoke 1998); J. Whaley, 'The German Lands before 1815' in M. Fulbrook, ed., *German History since 1800* (London 1997), pp. 15–37. Early contours of the new view of the Old Reich are discussed by G. Strauss, 'The Holy Roman Empire Revisited', *Central European History*, 11 (1978), pp. 290–301; leading scholars present their work in *Journal of Modern History*, 58 (1986), supplement 'Politics and Society in the Holy Roman Empire 1500–1806'.
12. See R. Sailer, *Untertanenprozesse vor dem Reichskammergericht. Rechtsschutz gegen die Obrigkeit in der zweiten Hälfte des 18. Jahrhunderts*, Quellen und Forschungenn zur höchsten Gerichtsbarkeit im Alten Reich, Bd 33 (Cologne 1999).
13. Illustrated for the north-west of the Reich recently by H. Gabel's excellent study, *Widerstand und Kooperation. Studien zur politischen Kultur rheinischer and maasländischer Kleinterritorien (1648–1794)*, Frühneuzeit-Forschung, Bd 2 (Tübingen 1995). See also W. Schulze, 'Die veränderte Bedeutung sozialer Konflikte im 16. und 17. Jahrhundert', in H.-U. Wehler, ed., *Der deutsche Bauernkrieg 1524–26* (Göttingen 1975), pp. 277–302.
14. Wilson, *Holy Roman Empire*, p. 8. See also H. Neuhaus, 'The federal principle and the Holy Roman Empire', in H. Wellenreuther, ed., *German and American Constitutional Thought. Contexts, Interactions and Historical Realities* (New York, Oxford, Munich 1990), pp. 27–49. For a critical view see H. Lehmann, 'Another Look at Federalism in the Holy Roman Empire', ibid, pp. 80–5.

15. Hartmann, *Bayerischer Reichskreis*, p. 489; see also essays in A. Riklin and G. Batliner, eds, *Subsidiarität. Ein interdisziplinäres Symposium* (Vaduz and Baden-Baden 1994).
16. Hartmann, *Bayerischer Reichskreis*, pp. 48–51.
17. I. Sahmland, 'Ein Weltbürger und seine Nation: Christoph Martin Wieland', in H. Scheuer, ed., *Dichter und ihre Nation* (Frankfurt a. M. 1993), pp. 88–102, at pp. 93–4.
18. M. Stolleis, *Geschichte des öffentlichen Rechts in Deutschland*, 3 vols (Munich 1988–9), ii, p. 53.
19. Ibid, pp. 53–7.
20. H. Angermeier, 'Deutschland zwischen Reichstradition und Nationalstaat. Verfassungspolitische Konzeptionen und nationales Denken zwischen 1801 und 1815', *Zeitschrift der Savigny-Stiftung für Rechtsgeschichte*, 107, Germanistische Abteilung (1990), pp. 19–101.
21. Angermeier, 'Deutschland zwischen Reichsnation und Nationalstaat', pp. 90–3; R. Lauth, *Vernünftige Durchdringung der Wirklichkeit. Fichte und sein Umkreis* (Neuried 1994), pp. 354–5, 450–1.
22. W. Siemann, *Vom Staatenbund zum Nationalstaat. Deutschland 1806–1871* (Munich 1995), pp. 301–4; G. Schmidt, 'Der Rheinbund und die deutsche Nationalbewegung', in *Die Entstehung der Nationalbewegung in Europa 1750–1849*, ed. D. Timmermann, *Dokumente und Schriften der Europäischen Akademie Otzenhausen*, 71 (Berlin 1993), pp. 29–44.
23. D. Langewiesche, 'Reich, Nation und Staat in der jüngeren deutschen Geschichte', *Historische Zeitschrift*, 254 (1992), pp. 314–81 (esp. pp. 347–50); idem, 'Föderativer Nationalismus als Erbe der deutschen Reichsnation: Über Föderalismus und Zentralismus in der deutschen Nationalgeschichte', in D. Langewiesche and G. Schmidt, eds, *Föderative Nation. Deutschlandkonzepte von der Reformation bis zum Ersten Weltkrieg* (Munich 2000), pp. 215–42; W. Burgdorf, '"Reichsnationalismus" gegen "Territorialnationalismus": Phasen der Intensivierung des nationalen Bewußtseins in Deutschland seit dem Siebenjährigen Krieg', ibid, pp. 157–89.
24. W. Burgdorf, *Reichskonstitution und Nation. Verfassungsreformprojekte für das Heilige Römische Reich Deutscher Nation im politischen Schrifttum von 1648 bis 1806*, Veröffentlichungen des Instituts für Europäische Geschichte Mainz Bd 173 (Mainz 1998), pp. 511–12.
25. R. Scribner, 'Communities and the Nature of Power', in R. Scribner, ed., *Germany. A New Social and Economic History Volume 1, 1450–1630* (London 1996), pp. 291–325.
26. See his *Deutsche Untertanen. Ein Widerspruch* (Munich 1981) and most recently contributions in Scribner, ed., *Resistance, Representation and Community* (Oxford 1997). See also Scribner, 'Communities', pp. 293–4, 319–20.
27. A Würgler, *Unruhen und Öffentlichkeit. Städtische und ländliche Protestbewegungen im 18. Jahrhundert*, Frühneuzeit-Forschungen Bd 1 (Tübingen 1995), p. 320.
28. See, for example, essays in D. Gerhard, ed., *Ständische Vertretungen im 17. und 18. Jahrhundert* (Göttingen 1969); H. Rausch, ed., *Zur Theorie und Geschichte der Repräsentation und Repräsentativverfassung* (Darmstadt 1968); K. Bosl, ed., *Der moderne Parlamentarismus und seine Grundlagen in der ständischen Repräsentation* (Berlin 1977).

29. A. Dorpalen, *German History in Marxist Perspective* (London 1985), pp. 99–167.
30. J. Huhn, *Lernen aus der Geschichte? Historische Argumente in der westdeutschen Föderalismusdiskussion 1945–1949* (Melsungen 1990), pp. 56–7, 60, 62–3.
31. H. Maier, *Die ältere deutsche Staats- und Verwaltungslehre (Polizeiwissenschaft). Ein Beitrag zur Geschichte der politischen Wissenschaften in Deutschland* (Neuwied and Berlin 1966), pp. 17–35, 329.
32. Maier, *Die ältere deutsche Staats- und Verwaltungslehre*, 2nd edn (Munich 1980), pp. 278–96.
33. Ibid, pp. 292–6.
34. See, for example M. Hughes, 'Fiat justitia, pereat Germania? The imperial supreme jurisdiction and imperial reform in the later Holy Roman Empire' in J. Breuilly, ed., *The State of Germany. The National Idea in the Making, Unmaking and Remaking of a Modern Nation-State* (London 1992), pp. 29–46, at p. 30.
35. H. Schilling, 'Profiles of a "New Grand Narrative" in Reformation History? Comments on Thomas A. Brady Jr.'s Lecture "The Protestant Reformation in German History"' in *German Historical Institute Washington Occasional Paper*, No. 22 (1995), pp. 35–47, at pp. 40–1. See also his 'Wider den Mytyhos vom Sonderweg – die Bedingungen des deutschen Weges in die Neuzeit', *Reich, Regionen und Europa in Mittelalter und Neuzeit. Festschrift für Peter Moraw*, ed. P.-S. Heinig et al., *Historische Forschungen* Bd 67 (Berlin 2000), pp. 699–714.
36. See his general remarks in *Aufbruch und Krise. Deutschland 1517–1648* (Berlin 1988), pp. 181–3. For a more detailed analysis see H. Schilling, 'Civic Republicanism in Late Medieval and Early Modern German Cities', in H. Schilling, *Religion, Political Culture and the Emergence of Early Modern Society. Essays in German and Dutch History*, Studies in Medieval and Reformation Thought, Vol. 50 (Leiden, New York and Cologne 1992) pp. 3–59.
37. K. O. v. Aretin, *Heiliges Römisches Reich 1776–1806. Reichsverfassung und Staatssouveränität*, Veröffentlichungen des Instituts für Europäische Geschichte Mainz, Bd 38, 2 vols (Wiesbaden 1976); Aretin, *Das Reich. Friedensordnung und europäisches Gleichgewicht 1648–1806* (Stuttgart 1986); Aretin, *Das Alte Reich 1648–1806*, 4 vols (Stuttgart 1993–2000); further comments, especially on the aftermath of the Reich in Aretin, *Vom Deutschen Reich zum Deutschen Bund*, Deutsche Geschichte Bd. 7, 2nd edn (Göttingen 1993).
38. The most recent statement of this view is Aretin, *Das Reich*, iii, p. 529.
39. Aretin, *Das Reich*, p. 13.
40. K. O. v. Aretin, 'Reichsitalien von Karl V. bis zum Ende des Alten Reiches. Die Lehensordnungen in Italien und ihre Auswirkungen auf die europäische Politik', in Aretin, *Das Reich*, pp. 76–163. See also the relevant sections in idem, *Das Alte Reich*, i–iii, passim.
41. Aretin, *Das Reich*, pp. 19–51.
42. Schulze, *Einführung*, p. 282.
43. Hughes, 'Imperial Supreme Jurisdiction', p. 45; Wilson, *Holy Roman Empire*, pp. 48–9; Stolleis, *Öffentliches Recht*, i, pp. 403–4.
44. M. Stolleis, ed., *Staatsdenker im 17. und 18. Jahrhundert. Reichspublizistik – Politik – Naturrecht*, 2nd edn (Frankfurt a. M. 1987), pp. 11–12.
45. Ibid, p. 10.
46. C. P. Hartmann, 'Bereits erprobt: Ein Mitteleuropa der Regionen', *Das Parlament, 3./10.* December 1993, p. 21.

47. C. P. Hartmann, 'Die Kreistage des Heiligen Römischen Reiches – eine Vorform des Parlamentarismus? Das Beispiel des bayerischen Reichskreises (1521–1793)', *Zeitschrift für historische Forschung*, 19 (1992), pp. 29–47.

48. Hartmann, *Bayerischer Reichskreis.*

49. R. Koselleck, *Europäische Umrisse deutscher Geschichte. Zwei Essays* (Heidelberg 1999), pp. 69, 78.

50. H. Plessner, *Das Schicksal deutschen Geistes im Ausgang seiner bürgerlichen Epoche* (Zurich 1935). The work was republished in Stuttgart in 1959 as *Die verspätete Nation. Über die politische Verführbarkeit des bürgerlichen Geistes* (The Delayed Nation. On the Susceptibility of the Bourgeois Mind to Political Seduction).

51. Koselleck, *Umrisse*, pp. 59–60.

52. Ibid, p. 60.

53. Ibid, pp. 68, 78.

54. D. Langewiesche, 'Reich, Staat und Nation in der jüngeren deutschen Geschichte', *Historische Zeitschrift*, 254 (1992), 314–81; R. Stauber, 'Nationalismus vor dem Nationalismus? Eine Bestandsaufnahme der Forschung zu "Nation" und "Nationalismus" in der frühen Neuzeit', *Geschichte in Wissenschaft und Unterricht*, 47 (1996), pp. 139–65.

55. Langewiesche and Schmidt, *Föderative Nation.*

56. D. Langewiesche, 'Föderativer Nationalismus als Erbe der deutschen Reichsnation: Über Föderalismus und Zentralismus in der deutschen Nationalgeschichte', ibid, pp. 215–42.

57. Burgdorf, *Reichskonstitution und Nation.*

58. Burgdorf, '"Reichsnationalismus" gegen "Territorialnationalismus"', p. 189.

59. G. Schmidt, *Geschichte des Alten Reiches. Staat und Nation in der Frühen Neuzeit 1495–1806* (Munich 1999).

60. G. W. F. Hegel, *Political Writings*, ed. L. Dickey and H. B. Nisbet (Cambridge 1999), p. 6.

61. Schmidt, *Geschichte*, p. 44.

62. Ibid.

63. For a discussion of the, predominantly ambivalent, attitudes of West German historians to national issues, see H.-P. Schwarz, 'Mit gestopften Trompeten. Die Wiedervereinigung Deutschlands aus der Sicht westdeutscher Historiker', *Geschichte in Wissenschaft und Unterricht*, 44 (1993), pp. 683–704.

64. Quoted by Schmidt, *Geschichte*, 240. See also G. Schmidt, '"Wo Freiheit ist und Recht ...", da ist der Deutsche Untertan?' in *Jenaer Universitätsreden*, Bd. 2, ed. K. Manger (Jena 1997), pp. 99–117.

65. Schmidt, *Geschichte*, p. 347.

66. P. Krüger, 'Auf der Suche nach Deutschland – Ein historischer Streifzug ins Ungewisse', in P. Krüger, ed., *Deutschland, deutscher Staat, deutsche Nation. Historische Erkundungen eines Spannungsverhältnisses*, Marburger Studien zur Neueren Geschichte, Bd 2 (Marburg 1993), pp. 41–69, here p. 49.

67. A. D. Smith, *The Ethnic Origins of Nations* (Oxford 1986), pp. 13–18.

68. Ibid, p. 15.

69. W. v. Humboldt, *Werke*, ed. A. Flitner and K. Giel, 5 vols (Darmstadt 1960–81), iv, p. 304.

70. H. Schilling, 'Reichs-Staat und frühneuzeitliche Nation der Deutschen oder teilmodernisiertes Reichssystem. Überlegungen zu Charakter und Aktualität des Alten Reiches', *Historische Zeitschrift*, 272 (2001), pp. 377–95.
71. Ibid, p. 394.
72. W. Dotzauer, *Die deutschen Reichskreise (1383–1806). Geschichte und Aktenedition* (Stuttgart 1998), p. 12.
73. J. Burkhardt, 'Der öffentliche Einzug des Reiches in die Geschichtskultur', *Frankfurter Allgemeine Zeitung*, 14.10.1997, Literaturbeilage p. 32.
74. See notes 5–7 above.
75. Even the excellent catalogue has not attracted the notice that it deserves: *Frieden durch Recht. Das Reichskammergericht von 1495 bis 1806*, ed I. Scheurmann (Mainz 1994).
76. D. Langewiesche, 'War da was vor 1871?' *Frankfurter Allgemeine Zeitung*, 12.10.2000, p. 54. On this debate about multiculturalism and the integration of non-German minorities, see B. Tibi, 'Leitkultur als Wertekonsens. Bilanz einer missglückten deutschen Debatte', *Aus Politik und Zeitgeschichte. Beilage zur Wochenzeitung Das Parlament*, 12, i, 2001, pp. 23–6 and D. Oberndörfer, 'Leitkultur und Berliner Republik. Die Herausforderung der multikulturellen Gesellschaft Deutschlands ist das Grundgesetz', ibid, pp. 27–30.
77. J. Burkhardt, 'Über das Recht der Frühen Neuzeit, politisch interessant zu sein. Eine Antwort an Martin Tabaczek und Paul Münch', *Geschichte in Wissenschaft und Unterricht*, 1 (1999), pp. 748–56.
78. There is a useful bibliography in J. Burkhardt, 'Das größte Friedenswerk der Neuzeit. Der Westfälische Frieden in neuer Perspektive', *Geschichte in Wissenschaft und Unterricht*, 49 (1998), pp. 592–612.
79. H. Gabel, '"1648 – Krieg und Frieden in Europa." Die Europaratsausstellung 1998 in Münster und Osnabrück', *Geschichte in Wissenschaft und Unterricht*, 49 (1998), pp. 613–19.
80. Burkhardt, 'Friedenswerk'.
81. M. Tabaczek, 'Wieviel tragen Superlative zum historischen Erkenntnisfortschritt bei? Anmmerkungen zum Beitrag von Johannes Burkhardt "Das größte Friedenswerk der Neuzeit. Der Westfälische Friede in neuer Perspektive"', *Geschichte in Wissenschaft und Unterricht*, 1 (1990), pp. 740–7; P. Münch, '1648 – Notwendige Nachfragen', *Zeitschrift für Geschichtswissenschaft*, 47 (1999), pp. 329–33.
82. The continuing and conflict-generating nature of the confessional divide is also emphasized by J. Luh, *Unheiliges Römisches Reich. Der konfessionelle Gegensatz 1648–1806* (Potsdam 1995). Cf. too J. Whaley, 'A Tolerant Society? Religious Toleration in the Holy Roman Empire, 1648–1806', in O. P. Grell and R. Porter, eds, *Toleration in Enlightenment Europe* (Cambridge 2000), pp. 175–95.
83. Tabaczek, 'Superlative', p. 746.
84. Münch, '1648', p. 333.
85. Burkhardt, 'Recht', p. 748.
86. R. Münch, 'German Nation and German Identity: Continuity and Change from the 1770s to the 1990s', in B. Heurlin, ed., *Germany in Europe in the Nineties* (London 1996), pp. 13–43, esp. 30–3.
87. Cf. P. Alter, 'Der eilige Abschied von der Nation. Zur Bewußtseinslage der Deutschen nach 1945', in H. Klueting, ed., *Nation – Nationalismus –*

Postnation. Beiträge zur Indentitätsfindung der Deutschen im 19. und 20. Jahrhundert (Cologne and Weimar 1992), pp. 185–202. For a recent discussion, see F. Brunssen, 'Das neue Selbstverständnis der Berliner Republik', *Aus Politik und Zeitgeschichte. Beilage zur Wochenzeitung das Parlament*, 12.i.2001, 6–14.

88. H. Schauer, 'Nationale und europäische Identität. Die unterschiedlichen Auffassungen in Deutschland, Frankreich und Großbritannien', *Aus Politik und Zeitgeschichte. Beilage zur Wochenzeitung das Parlament* 28.2.1997, pp. 3–13. For an intriguing study of anti-europeanism in Germany in historical perspective, see W. Burgdorf, *Chimäre Europa. Antieuropäische Diskurse in Deutschland (1649–1999)*, Historisch-politische Analysen Bd 7 (Bochum 1999).

3

History and Federalism in the Age of Nation-State Formation

Maiken Umbach

German history from the French Revolution to the foundation of the first nation-state is usually described as a process of territorial integration: the pre-modern, polycentric 'Holy Roman Empire of the German Nation' was gradually replaced by a modern, centralized and expansive state under Prussian auspices. Yet not all aspects of the constitutional and cultural history of the Old Reich were rendered obsolete when Napoleon abolished the Empire in 1806. This chapter explores the *longue durée* of the imperial idea in the era of German unification. The memory of the Old Reich continued to shape German thinking about the nation. In fact, even before the Empire disappeared as a political structure, it took on a separate intellectual existence. In the eighteenth century, the so-called imperial reform movement sought to reinvent the Old Reich in a new language. What emerged was the vision of a federal state, compatible with the rational constitutionalism and respect for regional individualism that were hallmarks of Enlightenment thought. This idealized Empire of the Enlightenment in turn offered numerous reference points for nineteenth-century German nationalists, who wanted to lend their utopia of a pluralist, federal *Rechtsstaat* a sense of historical legitimacy. Invoked to defend regional privileges against the central state, the imperial idea was nevertheless more popular among liberals than conservatives. History did not only constrain progressive thinking. In nineteenth-century Germany, more often than not, it became the vehicle for a distinctive project of 'federal' modernization.

In recent decades, historians have come to appreciate the Old Reich in a new light. The negative image of an excessively fragmented, corrupt and hence dysfunctional Empire has given way to the idea of a dynamic political system.[1] This perspective makes the search for the Reich's legacy in modern German politics more fruitful. In order fully to understand the role of imperial memories after 1806, however, we need to consider contemporary perceptions of the Empire as well as its objective achievements.

The historiography of this period is dominated by the assumption that the intellectual movements summarized under the heading 'Enlightenment' undermined the idea of Empire, favouring instead the rise of autonomous, centralized, absolutist states, such as Prussia. Natural law theorists such as Pufendorf, French *philosophes* such as Voltaire and indeed Frederick the Great himself used an enlightened rhetoric to suggest that the Holy Roman Empire was corrupt, outmoded and farcical. Yet not all 'modernizers' promoted political centralization, and not all defenders of the imperial order were conservatives. The writings of eighteenth-century imperial reformers, who wanted to see the Empire transformed into a rational mechanism for regulating and preserving Germany's political and cultural diversity, are increasingly recognized as an integral part of a complex Enlightenment discourse. This includes moderate imperial reformers such as the lawyer Johann Stephan Pütter, and, according to the latest studies, even more outspoken particularists such as Justus Möser, whose writings on imperial history used to be classified as 'conservative', but are now more often than not discussed as integral to enlightened debates.[2] From their exchanges of views and arguments, the imperial idea emerged strengthened – and in a new shape. In a process of legal and intellectual abstraction, two aspects of the early modern constitution were singled out as pillars of imperial authority worth preserving or reviving: federalism, and *Rechtsstaatlichkeit*, that is, a conception of political power founded on the rule of law. They in turn became tropes of German political thought for decades to come. Similarities between the reinvented imperial idea of the eighteenth century and the federal *Rechtsstaat* promoted by liberal nationalists of the nineteenth century were no coincidence – contemporaries often pointed to the historical connection. In the pre-March era, the use of imperial history as a political argument was particularly prominent.[3]

Yet the long-term legacy of the Empire transcended legal and constitutional debates conducted by experts. Specialist debates fed into the formation of a cultural memory of the Old Reich which was more widespread and less conceptually precise than the arguments of quasi-professional political writers. To understand the way in which the Empire was remembered, we need to decode the rhetorical stereotypes and symbolic images that came to shape notions of a 'federal' German history. To be sure, these images and tropes form no single, coherent

line of argument. Germans experienced important social transformations and dramatic political ruptures between the final days of the
Empire and the foundation of the first nation state. What emerged in
the final decades of the Old Reich was no political blueprint for the
next century, but rather a repository of political arguments and images
that were recycled in debates about the federal state at various decisive
turning points in modern German history. This repository was attractive for nineteenth- and even twentieth-century nationalists because its
historicity proved the viability of a 'third way' for the new state,
moving beyond the dichotomy of a (Prussian) nationalist and a (small-
state) particularist camp. Federalism was propagated by those who conceived of regional and political diversity as the core of German
identity, but who never adopted an anti-national position. The rule of
law became the necessary precondition for a culture of 'small units',
but the *Rechtsstaat* was by no means the sole content of the federalist
concept of the nation. The cultural vocabulary of federalism carried a
whole host of ideological associations – but typically, they, too, origi-
nated in the eighteenth century.

The history of the German *Fürstenbund* (League of Princes), or more
particularly, the plans to form a union of small states prior to the
Prussian take-over of the scheme in 1785, can serve as an illustration
for how this vocabulary emerged. Since Leopold von Ranke, historians
have regarded the German *Fürstenbund* as a precursor of the Prussian-
led *kleindeutsch* unification of Germany. The same historians typically
regard the seemingly 'prophetic' quality of the scheme as a result of
chance rather than design. The plan to form an alliance between
Prussia and the small German principalities (including English
Hanover) was a defensive move, designed to preserve the existing
balance of power. The need for it arose as a result of Joseph II's policy
of ruthless expansion, and his paralysing the *Fürstenrat* in the
Reichstag.[4] The *Fürstenbund* was a response to this threat, but one that
was conceived entirely within the framework of conventional ancien-
regime style diplomacy. This interpretation can be traced from the
works of historians such as Treitschke and W. A. Schmidt, to very
recent accounts.[5] Such evaluations of the *Fürstenbund* are based on the
assumption that it was not until 1785 that this alliance was conceptu-
alized under Prussian auspices. In fact, its origins pre-date the Prussian
involvement. In the 1770s, some of the smallest principalities of the
Old Reich, notably Anhalt-Dessau and Saxe-Weimar, became the arena
in which the initial *Fürstenbund* scheme was invented. Contemporaries
such as Edelsheim, the reputed minister of Karl Friedrich of Baden,

himself an important proponent of a small-state union, considered Prince Franz of Anhalt-Dessau the true founder of the *Fürstenbund:*

> In our times, the Electors have ceased to be Germany's supports. Who, then, will walk down the new path and invite everyone to the meal? It is the Prince of Dessau who does this ... He, who is perpetually oppressed by his neighbours [the Prussians], will think to himself: What remains to be done? One of us has to expose himself.[6]

While the bulk of Edelsheim's own thinking concerned strategic rather than intellectual problems, Prince Franz of Dessau and his close political ally, Carl August of Weimar, strove for a federalist reform of Germany's political culture in its entirety. Historiography, however, has largely ignored this project, chiefly because the protagonists failed to synthesize their ideas into a conceptually concise and clear formula. Contrary to the philosophy of enlightened absolutism, made intellectually explicit by leading philosophers and politicians of the time, the emergence of a culture of federalism was a 'silent' revolution of late eighteenth-century political discourse, which left few conspicuous marks.[7]

The political thinking of the courts of Saxe-Weimar and Anhalt-Dessau has to be reconstructed through a careful analysis of the political rhetoric associated with the history of the *Fürstenbund* before 1785. This can merely be adumbrated here.[8] With a view to investigating long-term continuities, it is most useful to zoom in on a few paradigmatic examples that illustrate significant discursive patterns and images. These include the following extract of a letter of Carl August of Weimar, written as a retrospective summary in the face of failure due to Prussian intervention. It deserves to be cited in some detail:

> [These events] have raised the hope in me that *ancient German sentiment and beliefs* may yet again be awakened among us ... I hope especially that a close tie of *friendship* among the German princes might unite within the imperial system our disjoined intentions, interests and forces ... The idea of a union appears to be particularly suitable for this purpose ... and could serve as a firm and stable basis, fitting for the *character of our nation* and an *appropriate* monument thereof ... All these schemes, however, only aim at one single goal, namely to achieve for the whole [of Germany] what every prince ought to pursue in his own territory, that is, an *appropriate and wise order of things*, without which no state can exist and no

prince can claim the honour of his century ... One flatters oneself
with the possibility of awakening the *national spirit* in our fatherland ... and one hopes that the German Union will finally crown
itself with this laurel wreath, as a corps for the preservation of
German liberties, customs, and laws.[9] In spite of this I consider it necessary and proper that ... well-meaning [the German term is *gut-
denkend*], judicious and patriotic princes, who care about the general
good, have united to further and support these causes. It is necessary that the effects of these be clearly visible, so that they may
encourage the many disintegrated, weak parts of the Empire ... It is
my wish to prevent the collapse of a building of which the foundation stone has only just been laid, and which should be the hon-
ourable expression of our way of thinking, and of our century.[10]

It is worth highlighting some of the text's key concepts. The first is the
frequent reference to patriotism, and the definition of certain virtues as
specifically German – Carl August even spoke of awakening national
sentiment. Such phrases must, of course, be understood in the specific
context of eighteenth-century patriotism, that is, against the back-
grounds of texts such as Goethe's *Von deutscher Baukunst* of 1771,
Herder's *Fragmente über die neuere deutsche Literatur* of 1767–8 and
Klopstock's *Hermanns Schlacht* of 1769. Their common denominator
was a cosmopolitan patriotism, which associated certain virtues with
German identity, not vice versa. Despite Germanic overtones, these
virtues were still closely linked to the moral universalism of antiquity
or, more specifically, the attempt to synthesize Greek and Roman
models. One of Carl August's *leitmotifs* is friendship, used to define the
envisaged relationship between the princes. Cicero in particular considered this notion of friendship a necessary component of any well-
functioning *res publica*, offering a private model for public
communication.[11]

The other idea derived from the Roman constitution was an emphasis on the legal order, corresponding to Carl August's insistence on the
reform of imperial law. Alongside such Roman pragmatism, two other
key terms in Carl August's text correspond to Greek categories. The first
is the frequently recurring notion of 'appropriateness', which is dissociated from any specific purpose. Appropriateness is used as a virtue in
its own right along the lines of Greek *prepon*: it denoted a balanced
state of mind, not just a useful strategy, and was therefore a moral category.[12] Carl August's use of 'good' or 'well-meaning' corresponded to a
Greek notion, *agathon* (good), originally designating 'what is worthy of

honour or admiration'.[13] As in the Greek concept, goodness for Carl August was associated both with worthy intentions and with the 'practical wisdom' (insight, judiciousness) required for their realization: a well-meaning, judicious and patriotic prince therefore deserves 'the honour of his century'. In Greek, the word *agathon* in a man denotes not just private morality, but also his useful contribution to society. *Agathon* could be used to motivate political action: virtue had to be applied to improve society. His invocation of Greek values did not distract Carl August from more practical Roman orientation towards legal reform. There was no teleological Grecophile *Sonderweg* at work here.[14]

To grasp the specific nature of this reasoning, Carl August's correspondence needs to be placed in the context of previous debates and in the light of Franz of Dessau's pivotal role therein. His letters about the *Fürstenbund* were less explicit and conceptual than Carl August's. Symptomatic for his writing was the substantial element of secrecy that seemingly evades political analysis. Franz was extremely cautious when writing about the *Fürstenbund*, even relatively harmless circumstances were only indirectly addressed and many thematic discussions were reserved for personal meetings. 'What I have to say concerns ideas which, if they are not considered, answered and contemplated together, would be fruitless'.[15]

Such deliberation and contemplation was almost *by definition* a personal affair: traditional diplomatic correspondence in which thematic, let alone personal issues were not discussed, was no adequate substitute. More important than the fear of spies, this was the reason why Franz always insisted on personal discussions: it was a cultural code, later circumscribed with the notion of 'friendship', that established a tone of political intimacy between the princes. Yet these 'friends' also employed a symbolic ranking system with subtle status indicators. This is evident in the hierarchically arranged name codes. In Franz of Anhalt-Dessau's correspondence on the *Fürstenbund*, people of high status – the Crown Prince of Prussia – deserved the privilege of a complete disguise. The second category comprized princes of lesser importance, whose names were merely abbreviated; the third category included subordinate ministers like Hofenfels and Edelsheim, whose identity was not considered worthy of protection.[16] It should therefore come as no surprise that Franz persisted in his secretive style even after it had become clear that the Prussian king knew what was going on.[17] This kind of secrecy fulfilled none of the 'practical' functions of ancien-régime secret diplomacy. It is more instructive to consider analogous phenomena in the social history of the Enlightenment, namely the constitutive role of secret societies, especially the Freemasons, in formulating and practising enlightened creeds. True, many eighteenth-century writers were incensed by the cult of secrecy in Freemasonry, and conspiracies were detected everywhere. Modern historians have criticized masonic lodges and related associations as a major impediment in the development of an open democratic discourse in Germany.[18] More recently, the use of secrecy and metaphors in politics has been seen in a different light, as part of a broader reappraisal of symbolic or non-verbal communication between the absolutist state and the public.[19] Just as in Franz's *Fürstenbund* letters, tactical considerations cannot suffice to explain the role of secrecy, especially because it already provoked hostile reactions at the time. There was an underlying cultural motive. The masonic *arcanum* was closely related to the symbolic importance of friendship in the lodges.[20] It replaced traditional symbols of status such as aristocratic titles and can be considered a necessary precondition for the elaboration of this new discourse. The *arcanum* founded a new type of sociability, facilitating a seemingly 'bourgeois' etiquette in a society largely dominated by the aristocracy. For Franz, too, the secrecy surrounding the *Fürstenbund* activities was inextricably linked to his attempt to form 'friendships' with the other princes involved. Such friendships were not founded on ideological pledges. Rather, they themselves were metaphors for a reforming impetus, to which the renunciation of traditional indicators of status between the German territories was pivotal. Franz's cult of secrecy and subtle difference can thus be defined as the core component of his federal utopia,[21] simultaneously compensating and enabling reform.[22]

The political relationships of the *Fürstenbund* were conceived as analogous to the personal relationships between the princes, especially between Franz and Carl August. Thereby, the recurring rhetoric of 'friendship' – seemingly purely personal – assumed a political relevance. Franz added a specifically modern, sentimental dimension to the Roman concept. His *Fürstenbund* letters were suffused with phrases such as these: 'My dearest [friend], you know, even without me telling you, how much I love to see you, always and as much as you wish';[23] 'Love me, as I love you, I cannot repeat this frequently enough';[24] or 'My desire to see you again is overwhelming, because it is one of my greatest pleasures to live with you, and I have so many things to ask and report which would hardly fit on a piece of paper'.[25] Even negative experiences such as the abortive attempt to win over Zweibrücken to the *Fürstenbund* scheme were conceived of in terms of emotional disappointment. Thus, Franz tried to appease his friend by emphasizing his

sentimental empathy, and envisaged a solution on an equally emotional level, namely through the restoration of friendship.[26] Likewise,
ambivalent reactions of other princes such as Karl Wilhelm Ferdinand
of Braunschweig were described in sentimental terms, evoking a
dichotomy between 'warm' and 'cold' or 'lukewarm' behaviour.[27]
Changes of attitude appeared as changes of mood.

This sentimental interpretative framework was extended to political
concepts as well. Thus, the *Fürstenbund* scheme is prevalently referred
to as 'the good cause'.[28] Those who enthusiastically participated in the
good cause were consequently referred to not just as friends, but also as
members of a kind of inner circle: 'the good'. These included the
Margrave of Baden, who shared many of Franz's ambitions:

> Dearest, much loved Margrave! It is not flattery, but the expression
> of my heartfelt thoughts, and utterly true, when I tell you that it
> would be my most exquisite pleasure if I was to enjoy more fre-
> quently the personal experience of your friendship. ... We hope ...
> that the good among us should gather together much more fre-
> quently.[29]

In his reply, Karl Friedrich took up Franz's proposal in terms which
echoed his terminology:

> How shall we proceed to fulfil your intention that the good among
> us should gather more often, either in person, or at least entirely
> openly and uninhibited in writing? Should it not be possible every
> once in a while to meet on neutral ground, incognito, without
> attracting attention![30]

The trope of 'goodness', too, had classical models.[31] Yet Franz used the
term in a modern, sentimental fashion. In his letters, 'good' usually
appears in conjunction with 'much-loved', 'faithfully-loved', 'heart',
'joy' and the 'pleasure of friendship'.

By contrast, key classical terms such as patriotism fade into the background. Curiously, patriotism was used by all those involved in the
planning of the *Fürstenbund* except Franz of Dessau himself.
Nonetheless, Franz's political associates repeatedly referred to him as
one of the leading German patriotic princes.[32] This can largely be
ascribed to the symbolically charged stylization of his residence at
Wörlitz. Its political iconography was characterized by the same combination of a sentimental cult of friendship and an enlightenment

state iconography so typical for the correspondence between Franz and Carl-August of Saxe-Weimar. Moreover, acting as the meeting point of numerous *Fürstenbund* negotiations, its cultural symbolism supported the political scheme of a federal nation to such an extent that a comparison to the constitutive significance of Versailles for French absolutism does not seem to be far-fetched. While Versailles embodied the territorial claims to power of a central state,[33] Wörlitz invited the visitor to wander through a series of small, sentimental-humanistic garden scenes, appealing to individual improvement through education, virtue and tolerance on the one hand and social progress through small political units on the other.[34] Wörlitz's most important contribution to enlightenment concepts of federalism, however, were the multifaceted visual reference to English landscape design and the culture of English aristocratic patriotism. For English peers, since the time of the anti-Walpole 'Patriot Opposition' of the 1730s, landscape design, and indeed the entire culture associated with political 'retirement' into the countryside, had become the chief medium for the expression of patriotism. Through English gardens such as Lord Cobham's famous Stowe with its 'Temple of Gothic Liberty', anti-absolutist *topoi* such as patriotic virtue and 'ancient gothic liberties' were vested with enlightenment individualism of a highly 'modern' imprint.[35] Taking up these metaphorical expressions, Franz of Dessau was able to combine the idea of corporate liberties of the *Stände* or the principalities of the Old Reich with a specifically enlightened ideal of federalism.[36]

The discourse of patriotism was tied to that of freedom. About 'the good cause', Franz wrote that 'I trust our rights and liberties [the German term, *Freiheiten*, literally translates as freedoms] will not fall, but be preserved'.[37] Despite its brevity, this comment raised two points of vital importance: the collective use of freedom, in the sense of liberties, and the association of freedom with rights. Franz's reference to rights was not to an abstract concept derived from natural law. It moved beyond a traditional interpretation to include a novel patriotic notion of liberty, as repeatedly expressed in Edelsheim: 'it fills a free prince with sorrow to observe the rapid approach of slavery to his fatherland ... will want to risk both life and property for freedom ... the Ansbach attack signifies an incredible infringement of Germany's liberty.'[38] Prussian state expansionism was incompatible with the corporate liberties of the imperial constitution. Prussian appeals to the small princes to help defend German freedom from Joseph II's devious schemes could not conceal this discrepancy.[39] Indeed, to Carl August Prussia represented the very opposite of a free society: 'I shall soon embark on a journey which, however, will not make me freer, but take away from me, for a time, my personal and particularist freedom – I will go to Berlin for eight days. As soon as possible I shall flee the sight of the blue slaves and return home before the end of January.'[40] Carl August was explicit about the sense of failure of the original *Fürstenbund* conception in the new Prussian-led context:

> We have been altogether forgotten ... since we subscribed to the Union ... [In Berlin] one is used to treating things *en gros*, and forget about the Empire out there. ... The purpose of the association had been not to function as an alliance of three powerful courts, but an imperial union in the widest possible sense. All princes who joined ... were supposed to form a single body, to constitute an imperial unity, the purpose of which was the preservation of Germany according to its constitution, and to lend it the power which the German Empire enjoys whenever it is united in a single patriotic purpose ... Now, however, the minor princes can at best be regarded as supplements to the triple alliance.[41]

The *Fürstenbund* scheme as the small-state rulers had envisaged it failed. Not only did the alliance not materialise before the Prussian take-over; in ideological terms, the federal agenda, the revival of 'ancient' corporate liberties vis-à-vis the absolutist state, was not accomplished. Yet the *Fürstenbund's* long-term influence was profound. It created a precedent for an important strand in modern German nationalism which can not be explained in terms of the traditional dichotomy between nineteenth-century supporters and opponents of unification. Of course, there was no simple continuation of federal Enlightenment thought in the post-revolutionary era. The ideological implications of such arguments shifted with the radically changing social, economic and political context – there are no direct causal links between modern and early modern forms of federalism. Notwithstanding, eighteenth-century debates such as that about the *Fürstenbund* created a 'pool' of images, arguments and tropes of the 'imperial nation' that served as a reference point for later federalists. Though subsequent developments were by no means predetermined by this imagery, enlightened federalism constituted an important and novel connection between 'modern' political terminology and elements of early modern imperial constitutionalism that enabled nineteenth-century liberal nationalists to employ these 'memories' in their redefinition of federalism.

Of these memories, the most obvious related to the legal institutions of the Old Reich, most notably the Imperial Cameral Court at Wetzlar, which excercized a decisive influence on the formulation of liberal *Rechtsstaat* philosophy. Rotteck and Welcker's famous *Staatslexicon* went as far as demanding a reinstatement of the imperial judiciary. By historicizing legal discourse in such a way, the liberal understanding of political participation could be dissociated from radical democratic ideas by suggesting that constitutions, not the direct vote, were decisive in guaranteeing civil rights and transforming 'subjects' into 'citizens'. After 1789, this argument allowed liberals to develop a distinctive stance and maintain their opposition to absolutism without being branded French-style revolutionaries. This is not to say that the Empire became a trope for a 'non-political' attitude that prevented a 'proper' German revolution, as some historians have suggested.[42] The law was more than a practical substitute for political conflict resolution. In the context of nineteenth-century power politics and increasing social antagonisms, it was also a way of adding a sense of historical dignity and legitimacy to the liberal notion of the universal *Rechtsstaat*. But in this context, too, the legal or constitutional arguments provided but a framework for a cultural federalism which was inspired by private patterns of sociability. In the hands of pre-March liberals, the aristocratic analogy between friendships and federations was supplanted by a bourgeois analogy between federations and *Vereine*. Karl von Rotteck made this explicit when he wrote that: 'the state is that association [*Verein*], which encompasses all human endeavours as embodied by one particular nation at one particular stage of its historical development'.

This analogy of state and association arose from the practical experience of liberal politics: orderly discussions conducted in small-scale voluntary associations of propertied, educated citizens. Projected onto the national scale, such *Vereins*-politics found its corollary in the idea of the nation as a federation. The nation was conceived as a legal union of individual states which – analogous to members of a typical liberal *Verein* – did not toe a national party line, but maintained their individual identity. This view was particularly popular among southwest German liberals. By contrast, few German liberals believed that the political nation would naturally grow out of an integrated economic sphere under Prussian hegemony, as Friedrich List had argued.

As the century progressed, liberals lost their dominant role in nationalist debates. It is a historiographical truism that the triumph of 'conservative nationalism' after 1866 ushered in the 'decline' of German liberalism. Yet this was not inevitable. True, the liberals' precarious relationship with the lower classes proved a potential stumbling block to electoral success. The liberal parties in the *Reichstag* were relatively unsuccessful in extending their appeal to new voters. At the same time, liberals continued to dominate local and regional politics in Germany. This was partly a result of a more limited franchise in most individual states. But there were also instances when liberals succeeded in bridging the ideological divide. Federalism was no obstacle to such a broadening of the liberal constituency. On the contrary: it could prove highly popular if linked to the defence of regionalism defined as *Heimat*. The proliferation of popular *Heimat* movements in this period has recently become the focus of a lively historiographical debate.[43] Especially in the south and south-west of Germany, the cultivation of folklore customs and regional traditions could help unite the lower classes and liberal elites in their common rejection of a Prussian-dominated, centralized nation-state.

This alliance seemed unproblematic in areas where the economy remained largely agrarian.[44] It was more precarious in rapidly modernizing regions with an immigrant industrial workforce. Members of the new urban 'working classes' typically left their homes in agrarian regions to move to Berlin or Hamburg or the *Ruhrgebiet* as young adults. They had little incentive to regard the city as *Heimat*. Accordingly, the politics of the Social Democratic Party increasingly evolved around the vision of a centralized nation-state, transcending individual state boundaries both in organizational and in ideological terms. To be sure, this was a gradual process. Recent research suggests that in many areas, until the outbreak of the First World War, the SPD continued to recruit its members primarily from the petty bourgeoisie, small-scale producers, artisans and craftsmen rather than industrial workers.[45] Thus, when it came to political practice, there was often more common ground between the democratic wing of the liberal movement and the SPD than their respective manifestos might suggest. The nature of the 1871 unification quashed hopes that such collaboration might be extended to the national level. The emergence of new national mass associations, such as the Navy League, added to the problems. Deliberate or not, in this new political climate, the defence of the particular institutions, customs and laws of individual states was bound to take on a subtext of elitism and social exclusion. Nevertheless, even now, federalists attempted and, in some cases, succeeded in reconciling particularism and modernization. What was required to maintain regional autonomy after 1871 was an effective strategy towards the central Reich government, showing federalism to be an asset to the nation-state as a whole.

The case of Hamburg is a good example. Though Hamburg was an old free imperial city that successfully defended its independence beyond the dissolution of the Holy Roman Empire, it also became a distinctly 'modern' city: the hothouse of transatlantic trade and one of the centres of industrialization and economic growth. Due to this dual role, combining old historical privilege with a modern economy, the political conflicts that were fought out in Germany's 'second city' played a central part in German politics as a whole. It was not only Hamburg's size which placed the city at the centre of attention. As Germany's largest 'free port', Hamburg became the focus of a modernizing project that shaped the Wilhelmine era as a whole: the quest to turn the Second Reich into a 'seagoing nation'. The built-up of Tirpitz's navy was only part of this project; the merchant fleet was at least as important in challenging Britain's rule of the waves. Hamburg, and, to a lesser extent, the Hanseatic city of Bremen, were at the forefront of this new development. The ships built by Ballin's HAPAG in Hamburg, and by the Bremer Lloyd, were presented in political propaganda as emblems of German modernity. They were given patriotic names, evoking German landscapes, heroes of the national movement, and, increasingly, members of the ruling dynasty. In 1873, the names commemorated the cultural heroes of German classicism: Goethe, Herder, Klopstock. Between 1881 and 1891, eleven new high-speed steamships were named after famous German rivers (such as *Elbe*, *Werra*, *Aller*, *Trave*, *Lahn*), investing the landscape with patriotic sentiments. Shortly afterwards, the HAPAG ordered four even grander and faster ships; their names reflected a shift towards a more openly monarchical and imperialist nationalism: *Augusta Victoria* (1889), *Normannia* (1890), *Fürst Bismarck* (1891). In response, Lloyd launched three even bigger ships, *Friedrich der Grosse* (1896), *Barbarossa* (1897), and *Kaiser Wilhelm der Grosse* (1897). The last in the series, constructed in the Stettin dockyard, was christened by Wilhelm II himself, and was awarded the imperial order of the Blue Riband. Though their excessive use of coal rendered four-funnel steamships uneconomical, Ballin decided that it was a matter of prestige to build one, too, and the *Deutschland*, built in 1900, promptly won the next Blue Riband award. The Lloyd's response was swift, with the completion of the *Kaiser Wilhelm II* in 1903. Germany now possessed the largest and fastest merchant fleet in the world.

Aesthetically, these ships combined the cutting edge of technical modernity with a backward-looking, historicist imagery of imperial grandeur. This clash was indicative of a broader dilemma: unlike in Britain, the German bid for naval supremacy had no historical precedent. The Old Reich had been a continental power. Its trading routes linked it to southern and eastern Europe. In the early modern period, German commercial centres tended to be cities such as Nürnberg, Augsburg, Leipzig and Frankfurt am Main, located in the Southern half of the Empire, and trading with Venice, Triest or Prague, rather than London or Amsterdam. The medieval organization of the Hanseatic League was an exception. In the search for historical justifications and reference points, it therefore became a favoured topic of the apologists of Wilhelmine nationalism. The *Hanse* was not only celebrated; it was reinvented. Professional historians wildly exaggerated the role it had played in the early modern economy. The *Hanse* became a national myth in its own right, and one which was propagated to a wider audience through the use of monuments, popular prints and political rhetoric.[46]

It was not until imperial historiography that medieval naval trade and seafaring were discovered as historical subjects. The myth of the Hanseatic League as a powerful seafaring and trading organization at the heart of the medieval Empire was created. Popular publications keenly elaborated on this idea and contributed to its wider circulation. As a result, it was soon so widely known that the architecture and iconography of numerous grand buildings, such as the *Speicherstadt* or the Elb-bridges in Hamburg and a multitude of public monuments elsewhere, alluded to it. It was in the seaports' interest to emphasize their significance for the entire Wilhelmine Empire on the basis of such historical myths. The Reich as an exclusively continental power was all too happy to acquire a seafaring tradition with roots to the early Middle Ages.[47]

The city of Hamburg was transformed into a visual statement of this ideology, using the Hanseatic myth as a link between the traditions of the small states of the Old Reich and the modern, international economy of the present. In 1888, Hamburg's special status as a custom free zone, maintained beyond the national unification of 1871, was converted into the privilege of a free port zone.[48] This arrangement was soon attacked by advocates of political centralization and economic uniformity. They hoped that Bismarck's enforced fiscal inclusion of Hamburg into the nation state was only a first step towards the complete abolition of all the free imperial city's historical privileges.[49] In this political situation, the government of the city-state commissioned architects to design a new warehouse district, the so-called *Speicherstadt*, as part of the free port area. The aim was to devise a carefully balanced political iconography, developing a style which was at once specifically Hanseatic and emphatically imperial. It was to give three-dimensional expression to the 'Hanseatic compromise' between particularism and national unity: by finally joining the customs union, Hamburg now conformed with national regulations, while the new free port zone catered to the particular interests of the city as a site of international trade.

On 29 October 1888, Wilhelm II laid the foundation stone to the entrance gate of the main bridge connecting the city to the *Speicherstadt*. Like the adjoining buildings, this gate emulated the medieval North-German 'red brick gothic' that was associated with the period of the *Hanse's* greatest influence and wealth. In his speech for the occasion, William II pressed home the point that Hanseatic particularism, far from undermining the Empire, provided a precedent for Germany reaching out to the world at large:

> You are the ones who connect our fatherland with invisible ties to distant parts of the globe, trade with our products, and more than that: you are the ones who transmit our ideas and values to the wider world, and for this the fatherland owes you a debt of special gratitude.[50]

An expression of the self-confidence of Hamburg's trading bourgeoisie, the bridge was adorned by two statues of equal size: the figure of 'Germania', and that of 'Hammonia', according to popular belief Hamburg's patron goddess.

The new Hamburg Town Hall, constructed at the same time, became another important emblem for the fusion between nationalism and particularism enshrined in a historical, imperial ideology. In 1889, Alfred Lichtwark, director of the Hamburg art museum, another foundation of the city's patrician classes, noted: 'The town hall does not serve as the site of municipal administration – rather, it represents the government of an independent state'.

The new building was vested with political and historical symbolism. The design that won the competition in 1885 took the Renaissance

Empire as its principal iconographic reference point, resourcefully combining Hanseatic and imperial imagery.[51] This was no isolated incident in Wilhelmine Germany. In the later 1880s and 1890s, a large number of German cities began erecting new town halls that followed the pattern established in Hamburg.[52] Similar neo-Renaissance town halls were built all over Germany, in well over a dozen cities.[53]

The architects were well aware of the political potency of the architectural allegories. As one member of the Hamburg architect team put it: 'As long as the great views of our Imperial Chancellor of the importance of small, vigorous and independent states within the German federal states are respected, so long our project is safe'.[54]

The town hall architects called themselves the 'Rathausbaumeisterbund'. That they should represent themselves as an association, that is a voluntary union of independent architects brought together by shared convictions, is a punch line that is worth noting in passing. The structure of the new building was designed to reflect the city republic's traditional constitution. All administrative functions were relocated to district authority offices. The remaining space was divided between the senate in one wing, the city parliament in the other; between them lay a large shared hallway as a lobby; the room above it was called the 'Hall of the Republics', and represented the city republics of Athens, Rome, Venice and Amsterdam through allegoric wall paintings. Behind it, the entrance to the main chamber was adorned with a quotation from Sallust that captures well the Hamburg particularism: *Concordia parvae res crescunt, Discordia maximae dilabuntur* – concord lets even minor things grow, discord destroys even the greatest things. Initially, the main chamber walls were supposed to be decorated in accordance with the overall iconography of the house, that is, with historical allegories culminating in the apotheosis of the city goddess Hammonia. After the artist's death, however, it was decided to abandon the allegorical theme and adopt a more realistic mode of representation: in 1908, Hugo Vogel created four large wall paintings that depicted Hamburg's historical development from glacial valley to modern seaport with steamboats.

The façade of the building also focused attention on the relationship between the city-state and the nation. On the first floor level, it featured twenty life-size statues of Emperors of the Holy Roman Empire. This demonstration of imperial power was matched by a series of keystones showing the crests of the members of the Hamburg senate of 1892 and sculpted figures carrying the attributes of local crafts and trades. Additionally, there were statues of the patron saints of

Hamburg's seven medieval parishes, and allegories of virtue. The spire, the expressed emblem of bourgeois liberty, was adorned by the coat of arms of the City of Hamburg, but above it towered the imperial eagle.

This synthesis of the imperial and particularist traditions was tailored to the needs of Hamburg's patrician classes. Yet it was by no means an invention of the time. Eighteenth-century federalists had used very similar historicist allegories. In 1765, Prince Franz of Anhalt-Dessau added a Gothic House to his allegorical landscape garden at Wörlitz, which balanced the universalist classical iconography of the Palladian villa with a more historical, patriotic theme. The Gothic House, or as it was originally and more accurately termed, the *Altdeutsches Haus*, combined English Tudor styles with North German red brick gothic. The interior underpinned the historical associations through its décor and an art collection that illustrated the historical role of small states in the development of the German Reich. A collection of Swiss stained glass windows took centre stage, the images celebrating the autonomy of the cantons. As well as episodes from the Swiss struggle against absolutist oppression, such as the famous Tell shoot, the windows typically featured both the imperial eagle and the coats of arms of the Swiss cantons, or the crests of significant Swiss families, offices and communes. The message was clear: the Swiss Confederation was presented as the prototype of a federal state, the crests depict the principle of 'diversity within unity'.

The Hamburg town hall was no copy of the *Altdeutsches Haus* at Wörlitz. Yet a specific, politically motivated historicism unites the two building programmes. In the Wilhelmine period, Hamburg federalists could draw on a pre-established set of historical tropes and memories in defence of their federal agenda which in turn were the product of the late Enlightenment. Two features unite these two historicisms. The first was the notion of the early modern Empire as a *Rechtsstaat*: The historical allusion was not the medieval Empire, but to the political entity that emerged from the great reforms of the late fifteenth century, most notably the foundation of the supreme constitutional law court, the *Reichskammergericht*. Modern German federalists looked towards the Renaissance period as the founding moment of a conception of Empire as a legal order designed to regulate small-state diversity within Germany. Secondly, even now, the federal conception of politics continued to be inspired by patterns of private sociability. The imperial reformers of the Enlightenment, especially the proponents of the *Fürstenbund*, emphasized that the ties between the German states would resemble friendship ties. The small scale of the states involved was defined as a virtue, in opposition to the anonymity of the political process in the bureaucratically organized large states of Prussia and Austria. In this they resembled pre-March liberals defining the nation as a mega-*Verein*. After unification, the shape of the public sphere in Germany changed; political parties operated on a national level, and modern mass associations supplanted the old clubs. Reacting against the rise of mass politics, traditional symbols of burgher sovereignty, such as the free imperial city, became an alternative vehicle for communicating political intimacy and individualism.

It is not surprising, then, that the mechanisms of social exclusion inherent in this political ideology became more apparent in this period. In Hamburg, the ideal of a refined and paternalistic dilettantism was juxtaposed to the interventionist politics of the professional, Prussian administration[55] – but also to the workers' claims to political participation. In 1910, 53.5 per cent of those who lived and worked in Hamburg had migrated into the city, the vast majority being unskilled workers. To these people, regional loyalties and the particularist traditions of the old free imperial cities meant little.[56] Hamburg became the principal centre of the German working-class movement. The unprecedented dock-workers' strike of 1896–7 was but one symptom of this development; the 1890 elections, when the SPD won all direct mandates for the all-German Parliament, another. The workers' politics were national, their thinking was shaped by the ideal of a modern, uniform nation-state. Hamburg's urban notables, its shipowners and traders may have thought internationally in economic terms, yet their self-conception continued to be based on the city republic. The trade unionists, as representatives of labour immigrants, challenged the notion of political legitimacy based on ownership and wealth, and rejected any allusion to Hanseatic traditions as the basis of legitimate power. They regarded the symbolism of the Hamburg Town Hall with open hostility.

In 1891, Hamburg's trade unions formed the so-called 'Hamburg trade union cartel'. In 1900, the cartel began to plan a central Union Hall that was to give physical expression to the anti-particularist spirit of the movement. The union's own guidebook to the building suggested that 'after intense struggle, various trade union umbrella organizations have now been welded together and the leadership of the labour movement, the general commission of the German trade union, has been housed in Hamburg'.[57] Hamburg's having attracted so many working-class immigrants in recent years was cited to explain why this city was an ideal 'breeding ground for the centralist ambitions of the trade union movement'.[58] The Trade Union Hall, which was built in 1900, was conceived as an anti-type to the Town Hall. A property was purchased in the former suburb St Georg, next to Hammerbrook, a district that had been formed as a result of the 1842 fire. Hammerbrook had one of the highest density living quarters in Hamburg – most families displaced by the construction of the Speicherstadt moved here.[59] An architectural alignment with the working quarters of Hammerbrook, however, was never seriously considered. Indeed, the imposing historicist façade of the new hall faced away from Hammerbrook, towards the political centre of Hamburg.[60]

Heinrich Krug's 1905 design was grand. The Hall's symmetrical façade with the baroque hipped roof and the dome emphasizing the middle tract was reminiscent of a castle. The entrance was flanked by grandiose monolithic pillars of deep red granite. The guidebook published in 1914 by the trade union spoke of 'the elegant opulence of a somewhat wild, modern baroque'. The author even criticized that:

> little reference was made to the simple and beautiful thought of the outstanding strength of the working class which ought to have been captured in this building.[61]

The SPD newspaper *Hamburger Echo* raised a similar point:

> The exuberant splendour of a modernized baroque does not seem to be the most adequate monument to the working class struggle for the betterment of social order.[62]

This aesthetic criticism, objectively justified as it may have been, was beside the point. The building's principal function was political: it was designed as an antithetical response to the Town Hall. The challenge needed to be confident and unambiguous. It was thus only logical that the architect should draw an established visual rhetoric of power, even if this was reminiscent of Wilhelmine courtly representation. The Union's guidebook showed pictures of the Town Hall and the Trade Union Hall opposing one another.[63] This stance was matched by the aggressive diction of the German socialist leader, August Bebel, who in his opening address referred to the Trade Union Hall as 'our spiritual armoury workshop'.[64] Yet some socialists complained that the imagery of the Hamburg Trade Union Hall was too traditionalist, mimicking the symbolic language of Prussian-led power politics and autocracy instead of promoting a functional modernism. In 1911, Clara Zetkin made the point that:

> the style of our trade union, popular and commercial buildings differs little from their bourgeois counterparts. ... In other words, if we take style to be the visual expression of inner life, it seems that the working class has thus far failed to find an adequate architecture to correspond to its 'spiritual life'.[65]

Modern architectural historians have agreed with her verdict:

> Artistically the ornate building with its baroque forms and art nouveau decorations was trapped in petty bourgeois notions of respectability and self-representation. ... It was to be another two decades until the unions' self-confidence was expressed in independent architectural designs such as those of Max Taut, Erich Mendelsohn or Hannes Meyer.[66]

The preoccupation with traditional representation also led to practical shortcomings. The Trade Union Hall included a hostel that was supposed to provide lodgings for newly arriving workers; the Hall was also designed as a leisure space for working-class families after working hours. Both ventures proved uneconomical. In 1912–13, the architect Heinrich Schröder added a further building to the hall in the attempt to avert bankruptcy through more attractive facilities and a more economical use of space. These renewed efforts failed to generate any profit. The hotel 'Gewerkschaftshaus' had to be transformed into an office building. The restaurant and café suffered from poor attendance. This was a by-product of the political agenda: close to the Town Hall and Hamburg's political centre, the Trade Union Hall was too far removed from the domestic quarters of most dock-workers to attract them in the evenings: the cost of public transport was prohibitive – workers from Altona and Langenhorn could simply not afford to visit 'their' Trade Union Hall.

This dilemma was symptomatic of the ambiguous relationship between the German working classes and the Empire: the Prussian monarchy and its centralizing bureaucracy represented both their worst enemy and their ally. Given the anti-particularist attitude of the trade unions, their affinity to the centralizing ambitions of the Berlin government was no coincidence. The eventual relocation of the union's headquarters from Hamburg to Berlin confirms this. And just as the Socialist International failed to prevent the SPD's authorization of war loans in the name of nationalism, the Hamburg trade union cartel could not bring itself to foster modernist architecture. They relied instead on the visual vocabulary developed by the imperial monarchy. Alternative architectural styles did exist in the Wilhelmine era, promoted by the *Deutscher Werkbund*. But these early varieties of functionalism had developed out of the *Heimat* movement, and therefore constituted no acceptable option for the trade unions: they were too closely connected to bourgeois particularism.[67]

The conflict between centralists and federalists in Wilhelmine Germany was not one between modernizers and anti-modernists. In arguing out the tensions between regional self-determination, small-state individualism, and the ambitions of the German nation state, centralizers and their opponents both relied on an allegorical vocabulary that contained traditional and backward-looking elements. In both cases, such historical memories also became vehicles for distinctive visions of modernization. Hamburg's patrician particularism was not only harking back to a golden past, but also served as a launch-pad for the creation of a global trading centre. Similarly, the centralizing nationalism of trade unions, seemingly mimicking official Wilhelmine culture, prefigured the progressive project of a democratic nation-state in which special privileges would be swept aside by the equality of all citizens.

Disputes about other national symbols in this period revealed similar patterns. The national flag was a typical example. The present-day German colours, black, red and gold, date back to the nineteenth century. Originally the banner of a volunteer regiment during the anti-Napoleonic wars, they were cultivated as a patriotic symbol by student fraternities. In 1848, these colours became the official flag of the *Deutscher Bund*. With the end of the revolution in 1852, this decision was reversed, but as late as 1866, the Eighth Army Corps under Prince Alexander of Hesse, the so-called imperial army, was still given black-red-gold armlets as identifying marks. The North-German Federation, however, designed a new national flag: it combined the black and white of Prussia with the traditional red and white of the free imperial cities. The resulting black-white-red flag was adopted as the official flag by the Reich in 1870–1, while black-red-gold was scorned as demagogical and revolutionary. Hamburg's inhabitants enthusiastically flew the new flag on their ships, given that it depicted a union of their own colours with those of Prussia. In 1924, the Hamburg Trade Union Hall housed the inauguration festival of a Hamburg working-class association called 'Imperial Banner Black-Red-Gold'. This association had been founded by Social Democrats to counter the growing influence of right-wing parties and mass organizations. Through its name, the 'Imperial Banner Black-Red-Gold' took up the (supposedly) democratic legacy of 1848, but by emphasizing the traditional colours of German nationalism, also exalted the idea of the unitary state over the idea of a symbolic federation between Prussia and the imperial cities.

Whatever its complex political associations then, historicism was no obstacle to progress. Yet to point to the formative role of 'history', and in particular imperial history, in shaping German visions of modern federalism is not to suggest a direct line of development between the early modern Reich and the modern nation-state. The history of German federalism cannot be written as a single narrative. If this chapter introduced some long-term continuities in German federalism, the term 'continuity' has to be defined very specifically. There was a *longue durée* in German federal discourse, in that certain federal stereotypes, images and tropes, once invented, formed a kind of cultural repository which fueled political debates on the subject over a long period. Elements of this repository, such as the reference to the Renaissance Empire as the model of a federal *Rechtsstaat*, remained surprisingly constant between the late eighteenth and early twentieth centuries. Yet this repository of arguments could remain politically 'inactive': there was no continuity of federal politics in German history – two of the following chapters in this volume explore anti-federal regimes in German history. Imperial memories and historical tropes were only revived when it suited particular political actors and interest groups to do so. This was usually the case whenever relations between centre and periphery, or more accurately, been centralizing ambitions and particularist traditions, were resolved in a federal compromise: in the conflict between absolutists and particularists during late Enlightenment, as part of the creation of the first German nation-state in the later nineteenth century, and again – under very different circumstances – after 1945. Did this use of history constitute a German *Sonderweg*? Hardly. There was no teleology at work here. Nevertheless, and in spite of its indebtedness to English and other models, we may ask why this discourse had no direct equivalents in Britain or France. Perhaps it was because modern German history contained so few real historical continuities, that historical memories could become such dynamic political arguments.

Notes

1. A substantial body of historic re-evaluations of the Old Reich from a post-nationalist perspective now exists. Only a few exemplary classics can be listed here to illustrate the trend: Karl Otmar Freiherr von Aretin, *Heiliges Römisches Reich 1776–1806: Reichsverfassung und Staatssouveranität* (Wiesbaden 1967), John G. Gagliardo, *Reich and Nation: The Holy Roman Empire as Idea and Reality, 1763–1806* (Bloomington 1980), Volker Press, 'Das Römisch-Deutsche Reich: ein politisches System in verfassungs- und sozialgeschichtlicher Fragestellung', in Grete Klingenstein and Heinrich Lutz, eds, *Spezialforschung und 'Gesamtgeschichte': Beispiele und Methodenfragen zur Geschichte der frühen Neuzeit* (Vienna 1981), pp. 221–42.

2. On the imperial reform movement of the late Enlightenment, see Wolfgang Burgdorf, *Reichskonstitution und Nation: Verfassungsreformprojekte für das Heilige Römische Reich Deutscher Nation im politischen Schrifttum von 1648 bis 1806* (Mainz 1998) and Karl H. L. Welker, *Rechtsgeschichte als Rechtspolitik. Justus Möser als Jurist und Staatsmann* (Osnabrück 1996).

3. Compare Volker Press, *Altes Reich und Deutscher bund. Kontinuität in der Diskontinuität* (Munich 1995), Georg Schmidt, 'Der napoleonische Rheinbund – ein erneuertes Reich?' in Volker Press and Dieter Stievemann, eds, *Alternativen zur Reichsverfassung in der Frühen Neuzeit?* (Munich 1995), pp. 227–45, Gerhard Schuck, *Rheinbundpatriotismus und politische Öffentlichkeit zwischen Aufklärung und Frühliberalismus: Kontinuitätsdenken und Diskontinuitätserfahrung in den Staatsrechts- und Verfassungsdebatten der Rheinbundpublizistik* (Stuttgart 1994), esp. pp. 215–29, 256–78.

4. Leopold von Ranke, *Die deutschen Mächte und der Fürstenbund: deutsche Geschichte von 1780 bis 1790* (2 vols, Leipzig 1871–2), i, p. 19. During the 1760s and 1770s, an old disagreement between the Catholic and the Protestant members of the *Fürstenrat* had reached new heights, centring on the question of which side could claim the votes of the Count of Westphalia and Franken. In February 1780, this disagreement led to the suspension of all further meetings. As every decision of the *Reichstag* required the sanctioning of all three bodies, the entire *Reichstag* could no longer function properly as a result. As Erdmannsdörffer argued, an important counterweight to the emperor's using *Reichskammergerichts-* and *Reichshof-rathsprocesse* to dominate the smaller principalities had thus disappeared. Bernhard Erdmannsdörffer, *Politische Correspondenz Karl Friedrichs von Baden, 1783–1806*, i, *1783–1792* (Heidelberg 1888), p. 7.

5. W. Adolf Schmidt, *Geschichte der preußisch-deutschen Unionsbestrebungen seit der Zeit Friedrichs des Großen, nach authentischen Quellen im diplomatischen Zusammenhange dargestellt* (Berlin 1851). In present-day historiography, the *Fürstenbund* is usually discussed as a symptom of the decline of absolutism in the eighteenth century, when Prussia relied on the support of minor princes instead of 'proper' allies. It is seen as a conventional example of those 'rivalries which kept the statesmen and diplomats of ancien regime

Europe busy' by Heinz Duchhardt, *Das Zeitalter des Absolutismus*, Oldenbourg Grundriss der Geschichte, 11, ed. by Jochen Bleicken, Lothar Gall, Hermann Jakobs (Munich 1992), pp. 147–53. See also: Dieter Stievermann, 'Der Fürstenbund von 1785', in Press and Stievermann, *Alternativen zur Reichsverfassung*, pp. 209–26, and Elisabeth Fehrenbach, *Vom Ancien Regime zum Wiener Kongreß* (Munich 1993). Relevant case studies include Walter Schleicher, 'Fürst Leopold Friedrich Franz von Anhalt Dessau und der Fürstenbund' (unpublished PhD dissertation, University of Jena 1924); Ulrich Crämer, *Carl August von Weimar und der deutsche Fürstenbund, 1783–1790* (Wiesbaden 1961); Erdmannsdörffer, *Politische Korrespondenz*, i, *Baden und der Fürstenbund;* Willy Andreas and Hans Tümmler, eds, *Politischer Briefwechsel des Herzogs und Großherzogs Carl August von Weimar* (Stuttgart 1954), i, *Von den Anfängen der Regierung bis zum Ende des Fürstenbundes, 1778–1790.*

6. Andreas and Tümmler, *Politischer Briefwechsel*, p. 158.
7. The same applies to archival material about domestic policy reforms of the states involved. Physiocratic theories receded into the background while, inspired by England and closely connected to a small-state reading of federalism, practical, experimental reforms stressing private initiative ushered in a new style of economic governance. But source material testifying to this shift is difficult to locate, and even more difficult to analyse.
8. For further detail see my analysis 'The Politics of Sentimentality and the German Fürstenbund, 1779–1785', *Historical Journal*, 41 (1998), pp. 679–704.
9. Carl August to Otto Ferdinand Freiherr von Loeben, 30 March 1788, in Andreas and Tümmler, *Politischer Briefwechsel*, i, pp. 465–71, my emphasis. To achieve maximum conceptual precision, Carl August first wrote the letter in French and had it translated into German by Knebel, for whom he also summarized what was most important to him in the text in a separate *Punctation* (ibid., pp. 463–4) – key terms are thus of a particular relevance.
10. Ibid., pp. 469–70.
11. J. G. F. Powell, ed., Marcus Tullius Cicero, *Laelius de amiciti:/ Laelius on Friendship* (Warminster 1990; originally 44 BC). Shortly after Caesar's death, this tract was written with the purpose of forging new bonds among the divided Roman aristocracy. Compare Karl Meister, 'Die Freundschaft bei den Griechen und Römern', in H. Oppermann, ed., *Römische Wertbegriffe* (Darmstadt 1974), pp. 323–9.
12. Wieland found the German constitution 'appropriate' in the same sense: 'What was then the German imperial constitution was, irrespective of its shortcomings and weaknesses, appropriate to the nation's character and the development of its culture'. C. M. Wieland, 'Betrachtung über die gegenwärtige Lage des Vaterlandes', in J. G. Gruber, ed., *Wieland, Sämmtliche Werke* (38 vols, Leipzig 1818–23), 31, p. 237.
13. The term was familiar to the eighteenth-century reader above all through Klaus Manger, ed., C. M. Wieland, *Geschichte des Agathon* (Frankfurt am Main 1986; first published in three versions in 1766–7, 1773 and 1794).
14. The most hysterical exponent of this position is E. M. Butler, *The Tyranny of Greece over Germany* (London 1935), who holds Winckelmann's position responsible for the success of National Socialism in the 1930s.

15. Franz to Carl August, 18 December 1783, Thür. Staatsarchiv, Weimar, D 1653, fol. 11.
16. Franz to Karl Friedrich, Dessau, 11 December 1783, in: Erdmannsdörffer, *Politische Correspondenz*, p. 44–5.
17. On 16 April 1784, Edelsheim wrote a memorandum for Weimar and Dessau, reporting Hofenfels' assertion that the French court was fully aware of 'the entire plan of the patriotic estates' and disapproved of Karl Friedrich's involvement in the scheme. In Erdmannsdörffer, pp. 61–6, quotation from p. 64.
18. Michael W. Fischer, *Die Aufklärung und ihr Gegenteil* (Berlin 1982); Reinhart Koselleck, *Critique and Crisis;* Rudolf Vierhaus, 'Aufklärung und Freimaurerei in Deutschland', in R. v. Thadden, G. v. Pistohlkors and H. Weiss, eds, *Das Vergangene und die Geschichte* (Göttingen 1973), pp. 23–41.
19. Andreas Gestrich, *Absolutismus und Öffentlichkeit: politische Kommunikation in Deutschland zu Beginn des 18. Jahrhunderts* (Göttingen 1994), especially pp. 11–33. Gestrich pointed to the importance of international politics and legal discourses in provoking the formation of a responsive public well before the advent of the economic upheavals which Habermas saw as the primary cause for the public sphere's formation. Compare also the editor's introduction in Craig Calhoun, ed., *Habermas and the Public Sphere* (Cambridge, Mass. and London 1992), pp. 1–48.
20. H. B. Nisbet, 'Zur Funktion des Geheimnisses in Lessings Ernst und Falk', in Peter Freimark, Franklin Kopitzsch und Helga Slessarev, eds, *Lessing und die Toleranz: Beiträge der vierten internationalen Konferenz der Lessing Society in Hamburg vom 27. bis 29. Juni 1985* (Munich 1986), pp. 291–309, esp. pp. 301–3.
21. Consider for example a letter of Franz to Carl August, Wörlitz, 13 February 1785, Thür. Staatsarchiv Weimar, D 1654, fol. 46.
22. Compare Aretin: 'If thus far the measure of importance of a prince and his territories had been the hierarchical order, it now was his capability to form a federation. … Two ideas emerged in the *Fürstenbund* debates that would play a significant role in Germany's future development. One was federalism … The capability to form a federation entailed the notion of social equality which was, however, not realized in Frederick's model of a *Fürstenbund*. The other idea is closely related to this, namely the concept of a "third Germany".' Aretin, *Heiliges Römisches Reich*, p. 163.
23. Franz to Carl August, 25 December 1783, Thür. Staatsarchiv, Weimar, D 1653, fol. 15.
24. Franz to Carl August, Dessau 15 June 1784, Thür. Staatsarchiv, Weimar, D 1653, fol. 65.
25. Franz to Carl August, Dessau 22 December 1784, Thür. Staatsarchiv, Weimar, D 1653, fol. 153.
26. Franz to Carl August, Wörlitz, 29 October and 1 November 1784, printed in Andreas and Tümmler, *Politischer Briefwechsel*, i, p. 110. The rhetoric is reminiscent of the sentimental literature of the period, and its visual application at Wörlitz. Wörlitz provided Franz's preferred setting for secret *Fürstenbund* meetings, which were intended to inspire in the participants those sentiments of friendship which formed the core of Franz's political vision. Such cultural references only functioned, however, in communica-

tion with like-minded princes such as Carl August and, less frequently, Karl Friedrich of Baden. Other prospective *Fürstenbund*-members, such as the princes of Palatinate-Zweibrücken and Gotha did not share in this discourse. Franz proved unable to adapt to different political wavelengths.

27. Franz to Karl Friedrich, Dessau 23 November 1782, in Erdmannsdörffer, *Politische Correspondenz*, i, p. 35.
28. Consider for example: Franz to Karl Friedrich, Dessau 11 December 1783, in ibid., pp. 44–5, and Franz to Friedrich Wilhelm, 19 February 1786, Thür. Staatsarchiv Weimar, D 1656, fols 24–5.
29. Franz to Karl Friedrich, undated, after his visit in Karlsruhe which ended on 19 July 1782, in Erdmannsdörffer, *Politische Correspondenz*, i, p. 34.
30. Karl Friedrich to Franz, his personal rough copy, 14 September 1782, ibid.
31. The term *vir bonus* is a central category in Cicero's Laelius, used to describe the virtues recommended to leading aristocrats. Compare Heinrich Roloff, '*Maiores* bei Cicero', in Oppermann, *Römische Wertbegriffe*, pp. 274–322.
32. For example: Hertzberg to Franz, Berlin, 7 February 1786, in Andreas and Tümmler, *Politischer Briefwechsel*, i, p. 216.
33. Chandra Mukerji moves far beyond the traditional political iconography: Chandra Mukerji, *Territorial Ambitions and the Gardens of Versailles* (Cambridge 1997).
34. A succinct example for this is the political instrumentalization of the 'neptunism-vulcanism' controversy in the so-called Wörlitz Stone. It forms the basis of my essay 'Visual Culture, Scientific Images and German Small-State Politics in the Late Enlightenment', *Past and Present*, 158 (1998), pp. 110–45.
35. For an example of the English model, see George Clarke, 'Grecian taste and Gothic virtue: Lord Cobham's gardening programme and its iconography', *Apollo*, 97 (1973), pp. 566–71.
36. A detailed analysis of the state iconography of the Wörlitz Gothic House can be found in Maiken Umbach, *Federalism and Enlightenment in Germany* (London and Rio Grande 2000).
37. Franz to Carl August, Dessau 18 June 1784, in Erdmannsdörffer, *Politische Correspondenz*, i, p. 76.
38. Edelsheim, 24 October 1782, cited in W. Adolf Schmidt, *Geschichte der preußisch-deutschen Unionsbestrebungen*, p. 18.
39. General Schmettau, 15 February 1785, to Carl August, in Andreas and Tümmler, *Politischer Briefwechsel*, i, p. 128.
40. Carl August to Knebel, 26 December 1785, ibid, p. 211.
41. Carl August to Graf Görtz, 20 February 1786, ibid, pp. 223–4.
42. For the sixteenth century, Horst Raabe, *Reich und Glaubensspaltung. Deutschland 1500–1600* (Munich 1989) suggested this approach.
43. An exemplary analysis that considers the cultural construction of regional identity as an integral part of national discourse is Alon Confino, *The Nation as a Local Metaphor: Württemberg, Imperial Germany and National Memory, 1871–1918* (Chapel Hill 1997).
44. An example is the case of the Palatinate, examined in Celia Applegate, *A Nation of Provicials: The German Idea of Heimat* (Berkeley and Oxford 1990).
45. Thomas Welskopp, *Das Banner der Brüderlichkeit. Die deutsche Sozialdemokratie vom Vormärz bis zum Sozialistengesetz* (Bonn 2000).

46. Volker Plagemann, 'Kultur, Wissenschaft, Ideologie', in Plagemann, ed., *Übersee: Seefarhrt und Seemacht im deutschen Kaisserreich* (Munich 1988), pp. 299–308.
47. Volker Plagemann, 'Kultur, Wissenschaft, Ideologie', ibid.
48. Rudolf Kroboth, 'Flottenbau, Finanzkrise und Reichssteuerreform, 1898 bis 1914', in Plagemann, *Übersee*, pp. 37–40.
49. *Vierteljahrschrift für Volkswirtschaft, Politik und Kulturgeschichte*, vol. 100 (Berlin 1888), p. 38.
50. Quoted from Karin Maak, 'Die Freihäfen', in Plagemann, *Übersee*, p. 110.
51. A detailed discussion of the planning of the new Hamburg Town Hall can be found in Joist Grolle, ed., *Das Rathaus der Freien und Hansestadt Hamburg* (Hamburg 1997).
52. An extensive documentation of all these projects is Martin Damus, *Das Rathaus: Architektur- und Sozialgeschichte von der Gründerzeit zur Postmoderne* (Berlin 1988); see also G. Ulrich Großmann, 'Die Renaissance der Renaissance-Baukunst', in G. U. Großmann and Petra Krutisch, eds, *Renaissance der Renaissance: Ein bürgerlicher Kunststil im 19. Jahrhundert*, I (Munich 1992), pp. 201–19.
53. Wiesbaden (1882–7), Elbing (1891–4), Krefeld (extension, 1891–3), Elberfeld/Wuppertal (1895–1900), Dessau (1896–1901), Altona (extension, 1896–8), Stuttgart (competition in 1895, built 1898–1905), Leipzig (1897–1905), Hanover (1901–13), Remscheid (1902–6), Duisburg (1902), Bielefeld (1902–4), Lippstadt (a historicist refurbishment of the baroque town hall in 1904), Karlsruhe (1905–9), Kassel (1905–9), Recklinghausen (1905–8), Dresden (1905–10), and Kiel (1907–11).
54. Wilhelm Hauers, 1885, quoted from Hermann Hipp, 'Das Rathaus der Freien und Hansestadt Hamburg', in Joist Grolle, *Das Rathaus*, pp. 15–35, quote p. 24.
55. Richard Evans, *Death in Hamburg. Society and Politics in the Cholera-Years, 1830–1910* (Oxford 1987).
56. Ilse Möller, *Hamburg* (Stuttgart 1985), p. 71.
57. *Das Hamburger Gewerkschaftshaus. Ein Führer durch das Hamburger Gewerkschaftshaus* (Hamburg 1914), p. 6. Compare also Elisabeth Domansky, 'Das Hamburger Gewerkschaftshaus' in Arno Herzig, D. Langewiesche, Arnold Sywottek, eds, *Arbeiter in Hamburg* (Hamburg 1983), pp. 373–84.
58. *Hamburger Gewerkschaftshaus*, p. 6.
59. See also Hermann Hipp, *Freie und Hansestadt Hamburg: Geschichte, Kultur und Stadtbaukunst an Elbe und Alster* (Cologne 1989), p. 267.
60. The first Trade Union Hall, built by architect Heinrich Krug in 1905–6, was an odd, somewhat failed symbiosis of castle architecture and the *Kontorhaus* style (typical office buildings of Hamburg's shipping companies).
61. *Das Hamburger Gewerkschaftshaus* (1914), pp. 13–14.
62. *Hamburger Echo*, at the inauguration of the Trade Union Hall, 1906, cited in: *75 Jahre Gewerkschaftshaus Hamburg*, ed. by Deutscher Gewerbschaftsbund (Hamburg 1982), p. 14.
63. Heinrich Krug, architect of the Trade Union Hall, was involved in the construction of the neighbouring 'Großeinkaufsgesellschaft Deutscher Konsumverein' (GEG) in 1906, i.e. immediately after the completion of the

Town Hall. The architecture of the GEG-building is far more humble and modern. This is yet another indication that the pompous style of the Trade Union Hall was not a result of the architect's personal taste, but rather an expression of the ideological viewpoint of his employer.

64. August Bebel, Opening Address of 29 December 1906, quoted from Deutscher Gewerkschaftsbund (DGB), Ortsausschuß Hamburg, ed., *Das Haus der Hamburger Gewerkschaften* (Hamburg 1956), p. 23.

65. Clara Zetkin, quoted from Romana Schneider, 'Volkshausgedanke und Volkshausarchitektur', in Vittorio Magnago Lampugnani and R. Schneider, eds, *Moderne Architektur in Deutschland 1900 bis 1950: Reform und Tradition* (Stuttgart 1992), pp. 184–99.

66. Ralf Lange, *Architekturführer Hamburg* (Hamburg 1995), p. 78.

67. For further information on the *Deutsche Werkbund*, its attitude to modernization and on reform architecture in general, see: *Zwischen Kunst und Industrie: Der Deutsche Werkbund*. Austellungskatalog (Munich 1975), pp. 25–84; Joan Campbell, *The German Werkbund: The Politics of Reform in the Applied Arts* (Princeton 1978), pp. 3–81; Frederic J. Schwartz, *The Werkbund: Design Theory and Mass Culture before the First World War* (New Haven, Conn. and London 1996); Hermann Hipp, 'Fritz Schumachers Hamburg: Die reformierte Großstadt', in Lampugnani and Schneider, eds, *Moderne Architektur*, pp. 151–83.

4
Federalism and the *Heimat* Idea in Imperial Germany
Alon Confino

Federalism, as a mainstay of Germany's political and constitutional order, was adopted with enthusiasm in 1871. It has commonly and correctly been analysed by scholars as a governing mechanism to link local and national levels of politics. Consequently, we know quite a lot about how federalism worked in practice, and how it fitted within German constitutional law tradition. In addition, it is often remarked that federalism, as a political system that linked the local with the national, accommodated the historical experiences of the various states that made the German Empire. But on this topic, in fact, we know very little, namely on the ways in which federalism, as a political system, linked with post-1871 values and beliefs about the place of local and regional identity within the nation. It is this link that interests me in this chapter. What were the relations in the German Empire (1871–1918) between federalism as a political idea and federalism as a reflection of local and national identities? By accepting federalism as a political system, how did Germans negotiate the new 1871 realities of localness and nationhood? Differently put, it is often mentioned that federalism in 1871 reflected traditions and values. But, exactly, which values, and how did they connect to the political system? By thinking about these questions I hope to articulate some of the historical problems posed by federalism to scholars of Germany. My attempt is to link federalism, as a political system that reconciled local and national identity, with the *Heimat* idea, as a symbolic representation whose function was similar.

I would like to point out, first, some of the presuppositions of my approach to federalism. In a familiar historical narrative of the Federal Republic of Germany (FRG) federalism is often presented as a fundamental creation of long-standing German political culture. Thus, one scholar, writing about 'historical determinants of the constitutional structure of the FRG', asked, 'Why does Germany have a federal structure? To answer this question one has to go back to history ... to the long sweep of modern German political evolution'.[1] And a long sweep indeed it is, which begins with Brandenburg-Prussia in the mid-seventeenth century. In this narrative there is the danger of teleology, of suppressing contingency, and of reading into the evidence what has already been decided and what one wants to prove. This *longue durée* narrative of a German tradition of federalism runs the danger, in terms of method and interpretative consequences, of emulating the *longue durée* historical narrative of the German tradition of authoritarianism (the *Sonderweg* approach): both historical narratives read in the past the conditions of the present (or, better, they read in the remote past the conditions of the recent past).[2] An embellished version of this narrative views federalism as a German indigenous political safeguard against authoritarian government. A federal constitution is seen as the legal embodiment of political pluralism and cultural diversity, which is diametrically opposed to German autocratic and totalitarian regimes that tended to centralize power. As one scholar argued, the federal elements in the post-1990 German constitution 'demonstrated rather dramatically that there was to be no return to the [authoritarianism of the] Reich, but instead a reinforcement of the federalist tradition [of democracy]'.[3] This statement may not be wrong, but it does contain the danger of being a triumphalist, predetermined narrative that finds in the past comfortable answers to complex questions.

Certainly, federalism as a German political idea and political reality had existed since the late Middle Ages. Thomas Nipperdey begins in that period his overview of federalism in German history. But he views it as a constantly contingent, descriptive concept without normative attributes; his attempt is to describe how it evolved, not to use the federalist past in order to prove a point in the present.[4] Moreover, as an organizational principle, federalism became effective only in the nineteenth century.[5] Federalism was often chosen and implemented based not on long-term traditions, but on short-term experience and power political calculations. Take, for example, West Germany, where politicians and intellectuals, debating the country's future political system, used federalism between 1945 and 1949 to justify different aims and provide different interpretations of Nazism. Federalists viewed the Weimar political system as not federal enough and pointed out the growth of central power in 1930–3. Unitarians (*Unitaristen*), in contrast, saw the main weakness of Weimar in the widening of regional political powers and the lack of strong and stable governments; they pointed out that Bavaria could foster Nazism in the 1920s in spite of the policies of successive Berlin governments. Obviously, each side selectively picked from the history of federalism the evidence that supported its case. And until 1949, when West Germany was established as a federal state, it was not obvious at all that the federalists would have the upper hand.[6]

There is another difficulty with the *longue durée* interpretation: it supposes that federalism is not only, in a sense, inevitable but also solely political. It thus neglects the cultural element of identity and representation that supports, and at times shapes, federalism as a political system. In this respect, viewing federalism as a political system of governance is correct, but incomplete. It ignores the fact that political federalism, as a system that links the local and national levels, was always associated with cultural regionalism, as a set of beliefs about the place of local and regional identity within the nation.

What were the characteristics of federalism in imperial Germany? The institutional and political history of federalism in the period is well known. Federalism was never put in doubt in 1871. Bismarck himself, the unifier who ended the political independence of the small German states, was a Prussian patriot who did not want to see Prussia dissolving within a centralized state. 'Germany is not France', he used to say, 'and Berlin is not Paris' – meaning that his imperial Germany was not to be a centralized state like France. Hermann von Mittnacht, prime minister of Württemberg from the unification until 1895, recalled Bismarck 'likening readily the Empire to an imposing, secured building with many apartments ... where each tenant can establish himself in such a way as to feel at home'.[7] This sentiment was real, but the adoption of federalism in 1871 is better understood by the specific power relations and political considerations of the unification process of the 1860s than by long-standing traditions of federalism. Bismarck – who brought about the single most dramatic change in the experience of nineteenth-century Germans – was not the kind of person to be sentimental over traditions, real or imaginary. His decision to choose federalism reflected a political calculation. For although Bismarck unified Germany by fighting three wars, one of which a civil war, he did not seek revenge against anti-Prussian states such as Bavaria and Württemberg. Cognizant of the fact that German patriotic feelings coexisted in many states with anti-Prussian sentiments, he sought political stability by acknowledging regional identities and political structures. He knew that a union imposed on the South German states would prove unstable and impractical.

As a result, federalism meant that while the regional states lost their sovereignty in 1870–1, they maintained their pre-unification structure including a head of state, symbols, a Landtag (regional parliament), a government, a bureaucracy, and peculiar laws. Of course, slowly in the 1870s and more effectively from the 1880s, institutions were developed on the Reich level that introduced standardization throughout the Empire. One calls to mind the standardization of currency, weights and measures put into effect in 1873, or the more complex and gradual systematization of law and the court system. But in general, standardization in important fields such as education, social policy, economic policy, national symbols, and also courts and jurisdiction, proceeded little by little; the constitution of 1871 left policy in these and other matters largely to the choice of the states.[8] Perhaps the most revealing element of this federal principle was the multitude of political systems in the Empire. In Germany, as in the United States, the Empire had one political system, while every region kept its own traditional one. As a consequence, the Empire had an authoritarian political system based on free male suffrage and a *Reichstag* (national parliament) that had little real power to influence the government and the Emperor; Prussia had a conservative and anti-democratic three-class suffrage system designed to keep the Junkers in power; while Württemberg, for example, enjoyed a more liberal and democratic political system. These incompatible local political systems and cultures coexisted within a broader framework of federalism.

Moreover, federalism was endowed with a higher meaning when the constitution vested Imperial sovereignty not in the people, but in the federal council, or Bundesrat, which was composed of delegates from the various state governments. Bismarck's conservative aim was therefore to safeguard the position of the royal houses and their ruling élites at the historical age of the national populace.[9] But the Bundesrat was not simply a Prussian political tool of domination. While it reflected the obvious dominance of Prussia in the new nation-state (Prussia had 17 out of 58 delegates), it also put limitations on Prussian power. A constitutional amendment gave to any fourteen votes in the Bundesrat power to veto any constitutional change. As a result, not only Prussian, but also a likely coalition of smaller states such as Bavaria, Württemberg and Saxony could oppose a change in the status quo. Moreover, changes to the constitution that concerned a specific state could be approved only with the specific consent of this state.[10] In sum, while the existence of a powerful national chancellor and a national, representative parliament counterbalanced centrifugal forces and regional particularism, federalism was not simply a political charade. In the age of national standardization and unification, it provided regions with real political power to determine essential aspects of local life.

Certainly, many of the concessions that Bismarck made to the South German states were more symbolic than substantial.[11] Thus, Bavaria could keep a separate army in peacetime, Bavaria and Württemberg kept their separate postal and transportation systems, and all southern states could continue to send and receive ambassadors. All this did not limit the power of the Reich authorities, the chancellor and his government. But it did create politically and symbolically the conditions within which federalism and regional identity became respectable, indeed essential, to the nation-state. For Germans in 1871, whether in the South Germans states, Saxony, or Prussia, federalism was a way to preserve local peculiarities at precisely the same time when national unification threatened to obliterate them. What people in Baden used to say – 'Alles was nicht Baden ist, ist Ausland' ('anywhere which is not Baden is a foreign land') – received legitimacy in the political idea of federalism.

Indeed, the only group in German society that, in various shapes and degrees, opposed federalism after unification was the liberals, who advocated a stronger, centralized state. The National Liberal Party, which was Bismarck's main political ally during the Liberal Era (1871–9), saw many of its objectives realized in that period in the founding of the national bank, the creation of a single national market, the unification of weights, measures and currency, the reforms in the penal code, the national press law, and the freedom of movement for individuals. The liberals opposed in the 1870s what they viewed as the extra-national identifications of Catholics to the Pope in Rome, of socialists to the class idea, and of particularists to the regional states. They therefore saw some elements of federalism as concessions to particularism, although this attitude changed as time passed.[12] While the liberals' hostility to political Catholicism remained a mainstay of German politics for decades, the opposition to particularism subsided when it became clear in the 1880s that particularism lost its political and cultural significance as an antithesis to German national feelings. In sum, apart from liberals, Germans supported federalism as a vehicle to safeguard regional and political identity. Certainly, there were disagreements between the regional states and the Reich authorities over areas of competence, but as a whole federalism itself, as a political system, was not challenged by contemporaries.

Scholars of federalism have essentially emulated this vision. Since federalism was largely accepted, the historical question they have often asked has been how it was implemented in reality, rather than questioning what were its unspoken assumptions in the first place.[13] I do not mean assumptions that go back to the seventeenth century, but instead those that are time-bounded and connected to the unification era and its problems. Thus, there is a distinguished and illuminating tradition of studies on German federalism after 1871, but, in the most part, it saw its task as exploring the relations between Bismarck and the Reich authorities on the one hand, and the federal states on the other. In the case of Württemberg, for example, Mittnacht sought to maintain a whole range of legal, social and economic areas within the authority of the Württemberg state; Württemberg controlled the education system, postal services, railway transportation, and several taxation rights. Bismarck, for his part, wished to encroach upon these privileges.[14] The focus of many studies on federalism has thus been on how federalism influenced areas of trade, education, law and local autonomy, as well as local and national identities. This is an important view, but it is only partially revealing. For it treats federalism, on a fundamental level, as unproblematic, as a political principle that existed, waiting to be used, and needed only to be satisfactorily implemented. This approach explores the political, economic and legal problems of federalism's implementation, but does not problematize the presuppositions of its very existence and adoption in 1871.

These propositions, in and around 1871, were linked to the nation-state. While federalism, as we have said, was never put in doubt as the political system of the German Empire, the new nation-state, like all nation-states, was allergic to competing sources of authority and legitimacy within its territory.[15] Federalism, as a system of governance in which regions and states retain residual powers of government, could have been perceived as a threat to the one, only, and indivisible nation. This was the challenge federalism faced in the age of the nation-state. To adopt federalism as a political system in that age meant to assume certain relationships between the locality, the region, and the nation. Differently put, federalism had a meaning only within a framework that presupposed concepts of nationhood and localness, for these concepts were the building blocks of federalism. To understand how and why federalism was accepted, and indeed sought after, in the age of the nation-state, we should explore the tensions, commingling, and reconciliation between nationhood and localness. In this respect, federalism in imperial Germany was a problem of nationalism.[16]

Right from the beginning in 1871 federalism was linked to the attempts to solve the tensions between local and national identity, between centre and periphery, in imperial Germany. The 1871 unification was the greatest departure from previous experience for Germans in the nineteenth century. Before 1871 there was a history of the Germans and German history, but no history of Germany; only thereafter did German history proceed as a single development. The unification of 1871, therefore, joining the German nation, German society, and a German state within a single territory, redefined the spatial and historical dimensions of the nation. At the same time, in spite of the unification of the nation-state, German nationhood remained a patchwork of regions and states, a mosaic of divergent historical and cultural heritages. The patchwork character of German nationhood was sanctioned by the nation-state's federal system. Federalism thus corresponded not only to the high degree of regional political diversity, but also to a certain idea about German identity, an idea that respected the diversity of regional identities without challenging the oneness of the nation. But, exactly, which idea?

Federalism, therefore, should be explored not only as a political question, but also as an interlocking idea that commingled politics with a certain notion of localness and nationhood. Federalism agreed in 1871 with the political division of Germany into regional and city-states. What then, was the notion of localness and nationhood with which it agreed?

Several years ago I wrote a study on the *Heimat* idea in imperial Germany in which I attempted to articulate the history of a certain German national sentiment, and how Germans internalized the nation through it.[17] The idea of *Heimat*, or homeland, I argued, represented in the German Empire the ultimate German community – real and imagined, tangible and symbolic, local and national – of people who had a particular relationship to one another, sharing a past and a future. It represented interchangeably the locality, the region, and the nation through an interlocking network of symbols and representations in which the nation appeared local and the locality national.

Recent studies of the *Heimat* idea (mine included) viewed the political valence of *Heimat* in terms of how parties and political groups used, manipulated, and appropriated it.[18] This approach is helpful; it contributes to our understanding of the link between identity and politics, and between culture and power, by asking who could appropriate the *Heimat* idea for which political purpose, why, and what did it mean? But this approach is also limited by its straightforward understanding of politics as belonging within the realm of political groupings and agendas. It neglects the field of symbolic representation of political ideas, and, more importantly, of the worldviews that make political systems possible in the first place. I would like to suggest a different association between *Heimat* and politics, the link between *Heimat* and federalism. The *Heimat* idea, as an identity system that linked localness and nationhood, and federalism, as a political system that linked localness and nationhood, seem to have been closely associated. But these associations were not evident before the recent interpretative changes of the role of the *Heimat* idea in German culture and society.

The relations between the *Heimat* idea and politics have been until recently mistakenly viewed in terms of *Heimat's* reactionary anti-modernism, as a conservative idea that idealized the rural past and ignored modern reality.[19] The perceived contradiction between the *Heimat* idea and modernity is a result of the putative dichotomy between modern and anti-modern. But this dichotomy fails to take into account the ambiguity of modernity and of Heimatlers who simultaneously mourned the past while applauding the material progress and cultural opportunities promised by modernity. Instead of viewing modernity and the *Heimat* idea as oppositional, Heimatlers commonly attempted to strike a modus vivendi between the preservation of national roots and the continuation of modernity and the prosperity it promised. The working programme of the Regional Committee for Nature Conservation and *Heimat* Protection in Württemberg (Württembergischer Landesausschuß für Natur- und Heimatschutz) thus declared at the beginning of the twentieth century:

> *Heimat* protection and nature conservation does not mean to restore and maintain retrogressively, artificially, and under every circumstances the old at the expense of the new. It does not mean to impede the progress and achievements of the new age in agriculture, architecture, transportation, industry, commerce, technology, and the like. Instead, *Heimat* protection and nature conservation want to prevent, with a spirit of moderation, harmful side-effects of a rapid economic development. ... *Heimat* protection and nature conservation mean to harmonize the challenges of progress and the preservation of *Heimat's* individuality, beauty, remarkableness, and venerableness.[20]

Heimat thus both glorified the past and celebrated modernity. While taking into account *Heimat's* appropriation by anti-modern reactionaries, we should emphasize the appropriation of the *Heimat* idea by all sections of German politics and society. The *Heimat* idea, more than an anti-modern attack, was a child of modernity, an attempt to reconcile and negotiate between traditions and a fast-changing technological world.[21]

This view opens new interpretative possibilities. As long as the *Heimat* idea was interpreted as reactionary and anti-modern, its relations to politics was narrowly defined as a vehicle of manipulation and irrationalism. The *Heimat* idea was connected with presumed reactions to the modern world (anti-urbanism, bucolic national identity, and the like), not with serious, solid, and less dramatic political systems such as federalism. Furthermore, my interpretation that viewed the *Heimat* idea as a system of diverse local, regional and national representations that were independent yet interconnected enables us to link *Heimat* not only to specific political groups and agendas, but also to abstract political systems and notions that – in order to function and be accepted – demanded abstract symbolic representations. In what follows I would like to think about the connections between *Heimat* and federalism. My discussion, by way of hypothesis, is suggestive, not comprehensive. It aims to articulate new links between politics and identity, to propose new connections, to rephrase old questions.

The *Heimat* idea represented German identity as a network of interconnected local, regional and national affiliations, becoming in imperial Germany an actual representation of the nation. It represented interchangeably the locality, the region and the nation, thus creating an 'imagined community', linking or claiming to link all Germans together.[22] By allowing localities and regions to emphasize their historical, natural, and ethnographic uniqueness and, at the same time, by integrating them all, the *Heimat* idea was a common denominator of variousness. It balanced the plurality of local identities and the restrictions imposed by the imperatives of a single national identity. A thousand *Heimats* dotted Germany, each claiming uniqueness and particularity. And yet, together, the *Heimats* informed the ideal of a unique, transcendent nationality. The national *Heimat* idea was not simply an aggregation of discrete local *Heimats*; rather, it was a new symbolic representation that, while uniting all the German local *Heimats*, was more than the sum of its parts. The *Heimat* idea, that is, localness, became an actual representation of the nation.

While the meaning of the *Heimat* idea was fluid, *Heimat* was – as a value and a belief – an organized and structured social reality. Composed of three elements – history, nature, and folklore, or ethnography – the *Heimat* idea was carried in German society by diverse cultural artefacts. *Heimat* books (*Heimatbücher*), for example, were published by communities to make public to natives and foreigners their singularity in national and local history. These were well-written and well-illustrated publications destined for the family and the school. The books described the locality and the area according to three fields of knowledge: the history from the times of the Germanic tribes to the present; the nature, geography, fauna and flora; and the ways of life and thought of the inhabitants, their character and traditional customs. *Heimat* books appeared everywhere in Germany, from metropoles such as Berlin and Stuttgart to provincial towns such as Giengen an der Brenz in Württemberg, where there were 3459 inhabitants in 1914, when a *Heimat* book was published. In the 1880s and 90s schools introduced *Heimat* studies (*Heimatkunde*) to the curriculum, making the local, regional and national a topic of study according to the formula of history, nature and ethnography studies.

Moreover, 400 *Heimat* museums were founded between 1871 and 1918 across Germany, from big cities to provincial small towns. *Heimat* museums displayed everyday life objects from the community and told the story of local origins. Collectively, Heimatlers created in the museums a visual lexicon of local past, common denominators with which to understand every local history. Part of the larger development of the *Heimat* idea in imperial Germany, *Heimat* museums were a mode of communication to reconcile localness and nationhood, the past and the present, tradition and modernity. As a national phenomenon, *Heimat* museums constructed a particular local *Heimat* identity that could be placed within the national *Heimat*. The fundamental factor of *Heimat* museums was that although they represented hundreds of different local pasts, their representation shared basic common denominators in terms of objects displayed, content, and meaning. The museum activists in Oettingen, for example, who believed that even their small locality possessed 'plenty of historical objects', were true to their words and collected the following items: coats of arms and heraldic figures; documents, deeds, and indentures; drawings, engravings and oil paintings; objects of guilds; all kinds of arms; stoves, tiles, pottery and kitchenware; plaques, photographs, old games, local maps; folk dresses and pictures of them; all kinds of furniture; ornaments; genealogical albums, epitaphs, and pictures of ancestors; prehistoric and archaeological findings; coins, medals, seals and stamps; 'miscellaneous such as' locks, shoes buckles, spoons, knives, rings, boxes, and natural science materials.[23] These objects, representative of *Heimat* museums across Germany, emanated from people's life in the community – the private and the public spheres, the home, the work, and the family. Behind this museum-conception of displaying simple and seemingly unimportant objects lay a self-conscious intention to represent the past, and the community, as an everyday-life experience.

Heimatlers, by displaying everyday life instead of big historical events, ordinary people instead of the élites, and the historical origins of the community, constructed a pattern to understand national history, a national narrative. By reclaiming the local pasts, they in essence represented the locality as the location of the origins of the nation. Local *Heimat* museums represented local history and also the nation as a whole, constructing a narrative of everyday life of origins with which to imagine the nation. *Heimat* museums were thus part of the *Heimat* idea that emphasized local uniqueness only to reinstate this uniqueness into a larger national whole.

Like federalism, the *Heimat* idea reflected a local-national organization and representation of society. Germans organized the *Heimat* idea in a network of associations. Local associations, such as Beautification Societies, historical, folklore and nature associations, were organized in regional bodies: the Schwarzwald Association of Württemberg (württembergischer Schwarzwaldverein) or the League for *Heimat* Protection in Württemberg and Hohenzollern (Bund für Heimatschutz in Württemberg und Hohenzollern). These in turn were organized into national bodies, notably the Deutscher Bund *Heimat*schutz, or the German League of *Heimat* Protection, founded in 1904. This network corresponded to the constitutive metaphor of the *Heimat* ideas – the metaphor of the whole and its parts – which was, of course, also the constitutive metaphor of federalism. Thus, *Heimatschutz*, the periodical of the Deutscher Bund Heimatschutz, explicitly drew in 1915 relations of sameness between the *Heimat* and the federal ideas: 'Unity is the aim of the Deutscher Bund Heimatschutz. Its regional associations and chapters correspond to the federal states in the German Empire. The Bund should integrate their individual achievements, for this is the only way in which the Bund, like the Empire of 1871, can fulfil its work.'[24] The *Heimat* and the federal ideas thus shared an image of the nation. The interlocking structure of national and regional associations, in which the national Deutscher Bund Heimatschutz was comprised of the independent local *Heimat* organizations, represented the relationship between the oneness of the German *Heimat* and the multitude of local *Heimat*s. This resembled the relationship between the oneness of the German political nation and the variousness of the federal states.[25]

As a result, we need to look at the agreements as well as tensions between the Reich authorities and the federal states not only in terms of constitutional law, finance, or political power, but also as a way to negotiate localness and nationhood. Let me give an example. According to the 1871 constitution of the German Reich, Württemberg kept an autonomous railroad administration. In December 1875, Bismarck proposed to transfer the railroads to the Reich's authority, thus absorbing this important transportation sector. The suggestion was starkly opposed in Württemberg, and in 1876 the Landtag debated the issue. Now, trains are not the first object that comes to mind when we think of federalism, and while they are no doubt important, we do not often associate them with a sense of belonging either. But in the debate, grown-up men, who valued practicality and derided frivolity, men who took themselves very seriously, spoke in the Württemberg Landtag about trains in precisely such a language of possession. On the face of it, this was an economic debate over an attempt to rationalize a fragmented railroad system into a single, more efficient agency. But in reality it was about federalism as an expression of localness and nationhood.

Member of the Landtag, Schmid, articulated the stakes of the debate in these words: 'A pain will pierce the heart of the land when it has to cede its railways, this child of attentive care, like the pain that pierces the chest of a father who must bid farewell forever from his child. Gentlemen, I do not need to explain myself further.'[26] Schmid's proposal to the Landtag to support general Reich railroad legislation (*Reichseisenbahngesetz*), but to reject Bismarck's proposal, was approved by a majority of 80 votes to 6. His words expressed a widely shared sentiment among members of the Landtag, namely that, while the national idea and the nation-state were a necessary political reality, local identity remained a mainstay of German identity. Reading the proceedings of the Landtag debate in March 1876, one is struck by the ways in which a rather technical discussion on a legal and economic transportation issue pertaining the federal system transformed into describing political federalism as the guarantor of the integrity of local identity in the age of the nation-state.

A clear demonstration of this sentiment was provided by Moritz Mohl: 'In Berlin one will never get to know well the conditions of the other German states. It is obvious that each person by preference is interested in the land where he lives and where he was born and educated. It is only to be expected, and is only human and natural, that one in Berlin cannot have the same interests in the other German states.'[27] Of course, Moritz Mohl was an opponent of Prussia and the 1870–71 unification, but his words seem to reflect a condition deeper than simply political antagonism. The nation-state existed as a political reality, but local and regional identities were not simply subordinates. Rather, they, as well as the federal system, were the building blocks of the post-unification German political and identity order.

The *Heimat* idea, developed from the 1880s, reflected a cultural and social link between localness and nationhood in the Empire. As such, the *Heimat* idea seems to share important attributes with the German principle of federalism. Post-unification federalism and the *Heimat* idea were a result of a tradition of regional diversity and a condition of pre-1871 political fragmentation. Federalism was for the German political system what the *Heimat* idea was for the German identity system. Federalism elevated diverse regional centres that coexisted with a strong Reich authority, while the *Heimat* idea elevated diverse local identities that coexisted with the overall national identity. In spite of the inbuilt tensions, federalism succeeded in reconciling various regional political systems and traditions within a global national polity, much as the *Heimat* idea succeeded in reconciling the multitude of local identities with the oneness of German identity. The two systems – one belonging mainly to the realm of politics, the other to the realm of culture, one a political practice, the other a symbolic representation – seem to have complemented each other.

Federalism was not dependent on the existence of the *Heimat* idea or vice versa. The two were not causally related, but they did enhance each other, and together they tell us something about localness and nationhood. In the age of the nation-state, both federalism and the *Heimat* idea functioned to alleviate the tensions between localness and nationhood, between the tangible experience of the locality and the abstract experience of the nation. This functional equivalence between federalism, a concept from the realm of politics, and *Heimat*, a concept from the realm of culture, makes their relations fundamental and illuminating. It shows the need after 1871 to find a solution to reconcile localness and nationhood. The connection between federalism and the *Heimat* idea thus seems to be more than accidental. Both federalism and the *Heimat* idea have been central concepts in German society and culture before 1871, both needed a readjustment following the unification, and both ended up representing the relations between localness and nationhood in similar ways. Contingency is important in history, but it seems inconceivable that all this was pure coincidence. The ideas of *Heimat* as well as federalism answered a real concern in German society, culture and politics, namely how to reconcile regional and national traditions, political practices, and identities.

It may be argued that the congruity between federalism and the *Heimat* idea was tenuous at best because federalism, as a political principle, organized the Empire into clearly defined, bounded autonomous territories, while *Heimat* sentiments were by definition ambiguous and interchangeable. Thus Württemberg, as a federal state, included notions of *Heimat*, such as Swabia, that did not correspond to its political boundaries. The problem with this argument is that it assumes that identities must reflect reality accurately, as if the *Heimat* idea was a political blueprint by a social scientist that promised to construct an objective view of the world. The *Heimat* idea was never about reproducing reality, but rather about negotiating with it, a negotiation that necessarily included, as with all identities, distortions, wishful thinking, and even lies. It is irrelevant whether the political borders of German federalism agreed perfectly with *Heimat* sentiments: they did not, and we should not expect them to do so. The significant point is that German politics as well as German culture produced in the Empire systems to negotiate the relations between localness and nationhood that were, in terms of function, strikingly similar.

The success of the *Heimat* idea and federalism rested on their ability to connect the realm of experience on the local level with the realm of expectation on the national one, the transcendent world of the nation with the seemingly banal one of the locality, of everyday life. The locality could not simply be discarded as an item of German identity: it was older than the nation, and a site of tangible social relations and cultural traditions. The *Heimat* idea, in museums, books and images, and federalism, in political practice, found a way to connect the locality to the transcendental nation. In this sense, *Heimat* was a symbolic representation reconciling localness and nationhood, which corresponded to federalism as a political practice that reconciled localness and nationhood.

This way of putting the relations between the *Heimat* idea and federalism, and between identity and politics, opens new interpretative links. There is, first, the topic of local and national identities. Studies on German federalism certainly put, implicitly or explicitly, the issue of local and national identity at the centre. But, while the local and national identities in question are seen as essential they are also, on a fundamental level, taken as uncomplicated categories, for they are viewed as a reflexive result of federalism – as a given that need not be explained. Instead, the relations between local and national identities should be viewed as constitutive elements of federalism in imperial Germany. They were not the only and most important elements, but significant ones nonetheless. Furthermore, scholars tend to treat local, regional and national identities as overlapping but unconnected layers of sentiment, while in fact we need to emphasize the connections among, and interchangeability of, these identities. When we view localness and nationhood as contingent, their boundaries uncertain, and their positions shifting, we can also draw connections, which are not evident at first sight, between *Heimat* and federalism.

Federalism, therefore, always tells us something fundamental about German localness and nationhood, whether it existed as a political system or was abolished. Whether in the nineteenth or in the twentieth century, an interesting question is not only about federalism's implementation, but also about its representation: What did federalism signify for the relations between the local and the national? How did these identities position themselves over time in relation to federalism, and why? These are questions that have not received the attention they deserve. While federalism links multiple representations of identity, these links and representations – is it really necessary to say? – were not fixed. They changed over time, acquiring new meanings, shedding old ones. In West Germany, to take one example, federalism existed, but the *Heimat* idea in the sense of imperial Germany did not. After the Nazi dictatorship and the bankruptcy of German nationalism, *Heimat* could not possibly be used as a metaphor for the nation, only for the locality.[28] The relation of *Heimat* and federalism obtained a new meaning, whereby the locality and by extension German federal tradition were seen as repositories of good German heritages in contrast to the pernicious influence of nation, *Volk*, and race.[29] A different situation existed in the Third Reich and East Germany which abolished federalism.[30] In these cases, the investigation of the relations between federalism, localness and nationhood becomes, in a sense, even more intriguing because the political decision taken at the top by Nazi and Communist officials cannot be viewed as standing for the popular view about federalism and about the autonomy of local politics. With the absence of a federal system, people had to find alternative political outlets to reconcile sentiments and practices of localness and nationhood.

Some two decades ago Thomas Nipperdey described federalism in his characteristically balanced and thoughtful way: 'Federalism is not a static but a dynamic notion: it does not describe primarily a legal, fixed situation, but a process, a movement, in which constantly changing [relations] of integration, disintegration, and positions of equilibrium are created between unity and diversity.'[31] Is this not a fitting definition of the *Heimat* idea as well, an idea that negotiated between the unity of the nation and the diversity of local and regional identities? Federalism and the *Heimat* idea shared, it seems, functional and representational similarities.

It is interesting to compare the association between federalism and the *Heimat* idea in imperial Germany with the arguments raised in this volume by Charlie Jeffery and Wolfgang Renzsch about federalism in West Germany and (after the 1990 unification) in Germany. Jeffery emphasizes the move from cooperative federalism, when federation and Länder cooperated until the 1970s to maintain a uniform and high standard of living, to competitive federalism, when Länder seek to maximize their own interests at the expense of the federation or other Länder. Renzsch, in contrast, argues for the continued vitality of the cooperative model into the post-unification period. These are important models to understand the political operation of federalism. How can one classify the federalism of the Empire? The historian may feel wary of imposing a model on human affairs that are always messy and ambiguous, and often unpredictable; there may be something too neat in the division between cooperative and competitive federalism. Be that as it may, the German Empire did not have, in terms such as technology, communication, transportation and media, the level of integration that West Germany has possessed since 1949. The states in the Empire did not face the same hard choices that federal states in Germany have, namely to make tangible financial sacrifices (say, Baden-Württemberg) for weaker states (say, in north and east Germany). There was cooperation under the loose umbrella of the Empire, for the nation-state between 1871 and 1918 was much more federal and less tightly knit together than the Germany of the late twentieth century. It would be interesting to know, however, what kind of local-national identity West German and post-unification federalism did reflect. Here the issue is not so much about an operational model of federalism (say, cooperative or competitive federalism), but about the cultural foundation of the very existence of federalism. The relations we posit between politics and culture should not be mechanical (for example, the *Heimat* idea agreed with cooperative federalism but not with a competitive one). The point is to find broader links between cultural and political beliefs, which make the polity legitimate in the first place.

A comparison between the unifications of 1871 and 1990 is instructive. Bismarck achieved unification from above and through a civil war, but, all in all, except for a small minority, national unification in 1870–1 was accomplished by accession and greeted with enthusiasm. The unification of 1990, in contrast, was bloodless and from below, the result of a people's revolution in East Germany in the fall of 1989. But what started with chants of *Wir sind ein Volk* quickly turned sour, as deep differences emerged between East and West Germans. Not accession but colonization described the feeling of many east Germans. After 1871, local life changed very little in spite of the national unification; Württembergers, say, needed to make few adjustments at the first years of the empire. The unification of 1990, in comparison, was characterized by a fundamental asymmetry: virtually all adjustments had to be made by easterners. In 1871, federalism, which was not used by Bismarck to foster democracy, was viewed by all Germans as a political symbol of regional diversity. In 1990, federalism, which was based on the democratic principles of the 1949 West German Basic Law, was viewed by many East Germans as insufficient to alleviate sentiments of discrimination and loss of meaning.[32]

The common denominator among federalism, the *Heimat* idea and nationalism is that all signify social experiences and representations where the individual and the collectivity, the locality, region and nation coexist. In this respect the successful commingling of local and national identity in imperial Germany is relevant to present-day politics in Europe. The essential topics of the European union, the relations of the nation-state to a united Europe, and the talk in some circles of making a 'Europe of the regions' – these are all fundamentally topics about how to reconcile different levels of social existence.[33] But there is a certain irony to the story of how federalism and the *Heimat* idea successfully reconciled local and national identities in imperial Germany. German national identity served in the last century, with good reasons, as a model of barbarism and inhumanity. And yet the success story of federalism and the *Heimat* idea may serve as an example for other histories, in other times, perhaps even in the present. So there may be something to learn from federalism and the *Heimat* idea, though what, exactly, is for each of us to decide.

Today, when some countries in Europe are on the threshold of a new federal idea, namely the European Union, the nation-state is to the European Union what the region was to the nation-state after 1871, namely the component part of the whole. Then and now, some members of these component parts (the Moritz Mohls of the situation) feared their distinctive identity would disappear in the big political entity. But just as the nation-state in 1871 could not subordinate regional identity, so, I believe, the EU will not eradicate the particularity of the individual nations. Some identities hold fast quite well in our world, the talk of imminent globalization notwithstanding. In 1871 many believed that, under the standardizing assault of the nation, of Prussia, and of modernity, regional peculiarity would soon be a thing of the past. So, it is not without interest that one notes the recent popularity of the idea of Europe of the regions. Who would have imagined that in 1871?

Germany's federal legacy is often presented as the single most important indigenous safeguard against authoritarian government. A federal constitution is seen as the legal embodiment of political pluralism and cultural diversity. Conversely, autocratic and totalitarian regimes in Germany's past have tended to centralize power and aimed at abolishing Germany's federal character. This may be true, but it is not the whole truth. History is not made by systems of governing, constitutions, or election systems. Weimar was a federal state, and it did produce Nazism. West Germany, and, after the *Wende*, Germany, are stable with but not because of federalism. In the end, people, not abstract political concepts, make their own history, for good or bad. And therefore, perhaps, just as Germans (West Germans in particular), cannot blame the Weimar constitution for the rise of Nazism, they can take some credit for building a democratic society after 1945 – with or without federalism.

Notes

1. Nevil Johnson, 'Territory and Power: Some Historical Determinants of the Constitutional Structure of the Federal Republic of Germany', in Charlie Jeffery, ed., *Recasting German Federalism: The Legacies of Unification* (London 1999), p. 25.
2. For an excellent introduction to the debate on Germany's special historical path (the *Sonderweg* debate), see Jürgen Kocka, 'German History before Hitler: The Debate about the German *Sonderweg*', *Journal of Contemporary History*, 23 (January 1988), pp. 3–16.
3. Johnson, 'Territory and Power', p. 38.
4. Thomas Nipperdey, 'Der Föderalismus in der deutschen Geschichte', in Nipperdey, *Nachdenken über die deutsche Geschichte* (Munich 1991), pp. 71–131.
5. David Dorondo, 'Federalism', in Dieter Buse and Jürgen Doerr, eds, *Modern Germany: An Encyclopedia of History, People, and Culture, 1871–1990* (New York 1998) , p. 317.
6. See Jochen Huhn, *Lernen aus der Geschichte? Historische Argumente in der westdeutschen Föderalismusdiskussion 1945–1949* (Melsungen 1990), p. 249.

And also Jochen Huhn, 'Die Aktualität der Geschichte: Die westdeutsche Föderalismusdiskussion 1945–1949', in Jochen Huhn and Peter-Christian Witt, eds, *Föderalismus in Deutschland: Traditionen und gegenwärtige Probleme* (Baden-Baden 1992), pp. 31–53.

7. Georg Kleine, *Der württembergische Minister-Presidänt Frhr. Hermann von Mittnacht, 1825–1909* (Stuttgart 1969), p. 83.

8. Richard Evans, *Death in Hamburg: Society and Politics in the Cholera Years 1830–1910* (Oxford 1987), pp. 1–2. See also Hans Mommsen, 'History and National Identity: The Case of Germany', *German Studies Review*, 6 (October 1983), p. 575.

9. For an overview of the Bismarckian political system see Katherine Lerman, 'Bismarckian Germany and the Structure of the German Empire', in Mary Fulbrook, ed., *German History since 1800* (London 1997), pp. 147–67.

10. George Windell, 'The Bismarckian Empire as a Federal State, 1866–1880: A Chronicle of Failure', *Central European History* 11 (December 1969), p. 300.

11. Windell, 'The Bismarckian Empire', pp. 299–300.

12. Windell, 'The Bismarckian Empire', p. 301.

13. There are excellent studies, mainly by historians and political scientists, on the financial, legal, economical, and political implementation and functioning of federalism in modern German history. See, for example, Jeffery, *Recasting German Federalism*, Heinz Laufer and Ursula Münch, *Das föderative System der Bundesrepublik Deutschland* (Opladen 1998), Huhn and Witt, *Föderalismus in Deutschland*. On the problems of German federalism after the reunification and the Treaty of Maastricht, see Charlie Jeffery and Ronald Sturm, eds, *Federalism, Unification and European Integration* (London 1993).

14. On the relations between the federal states and the Reich authorities see, Hans-Otto Binder, *Reich und Einzelstaaten während der Kanzlerschaft Bismarcks 1871–1890* (Tübingen 1971). On the unification negotiations between Bismarck and the small German states in 1870–1 see Karl Bosl, 'Die Verhandlungen über den Eintritt der süddeutschen Staaten in den Norddeutschen Bund und die Entstehung der Reichsverfassung', in Theodor Schieder and Ernst Deuerlein, eds, *Reichsgründung 1870/71* (Stuttgart 1970), pp. 148–63.

15. An interesting idea is contained in the study of Rudolf Ullner about the German idea of federalism in the 1860s and how it was influenced by federalism in the United States. Both countries fought a civil war and both faced challenges to national unity. The study, in the tradition of social science studies of the 1960s, takes the political development of the United States not only as a sociological model but, implicitly, also as normative. Rudolf Ullner, *Die Idee des Föderalismus im Jahrzehnt der deutschen Einigungskriege. Dargestellt unter besonderer Berücksichtigung des Modells der amerikanischen Verfassung für das deutsche politische Denken* (Lübeck 1965). See also Ursula Hicks, *Federalism: Failure and Success. A Comparative Study* (New York 1978) and K. C. Wheare, *Federal Government* (New York 1947).

16. See the illuminating volume of Dieter Langewiesche and George Schmidt, eds, *Föderative Nation: Deutschlandkonzepte von der Reformation bis zum Ersten Weltkrieg* (Munich 2000), and Dieter Langewiesche, 'Nation, Nationalismus, Nationalstaat: Forschungsstand und Forschungsperspektiven', *Neue Politische Literatur*, 40 (1995), pp. 190–236.

17. Alon Confino, *The Nation as a Local Metaphor: Württemberg, Imperial Germany and National Memory, 1871–1918* (Chapel Hill 1997).
18. I discussed the connections between *Heimat* and politics in 'The Nation as a Local Metaphor: Heimat, National Memory and the German Empire, 1871–1918', *History and Memory*, 5 (1993), pp. 74–8.
19. Some of the works that interpret *Heimat* as a conservative idealization of the rural past ignoring modern realities are Klaus Bergmann, *Agrarromantik und Großstadtfeindschaft* (Meisenheim am Glan 1970), Hermann Glaser, *The Cultural Roots of National Socialism [Spießer-Ideologie]* (London 1978), Anton Kaes, *From Hitler to Heimat. The Return of History as Film* (Cambridge, Mass. 1989), pp. 163–6, Dieter Kramer, 'Die politische und ökonomische Funktionalisierung von Heimat im deutschen Imperialismus und Faschismus', *Diskurs* 6/7 (3/4 1973), pp. 3–22. Werner Hartung, *Konservative Zivilisationskritik und regionale Identität. Am Beispiel der niedersächsischen Heimatbewegung 1895 bis 1919* (Hanover 1991), pp. 56–7, and Projektgruppe Deutscher Heimatfilm, *Der deutsche Heimatfilm. Bildwelten und Weltbilder: Bilder, Texte, Analysen zu 70 Jahren deutscher Filmgeschichte* (Tübingen 1989), p. 16, an otherwise excellent book resulting from a project guided by Wofgang Kaschuba in the Ludwig-Uhland-Institut für Empirische Kulturwissenschaft at the University of Tübingen.
20. *Arbeitsplan des Württembergischen Landesausschußes für Natur- und Heimatschutz* (Stuttgart n.d.), pp. 1–2.
21. For this interpretation compare Confino, *The Nation as a Local Metaphor*, chapter 5; Celia Applegate, *A Nation of Provincials: The German Idea of Heimat* (Berkeley 1990), pp. 103–7; William Rollins, *A Greener Vision of Home: Cultural Politics and Environmental Reform in the German Heimatschutz Movement, 1904–1918* (Ann Arbor 1997), who convincingly shows the tendentiousness of the anti-modern interpretation of the Deutscher Bund Heimatschutz's environmental activities; Matthew Jefferies, *Politics and Culture in Wilhelmine Germany: The Case of Industrial Architecture* (Oxford and Washington, DC 1995), chapter two; Rudy Koshar, *Germany's Transient Pasts: Preservation and National Memory in the Twentieth Century* (Chapel Hill 1998), chapter one. Other opinions are discussed in Thomas Lekan, 'Regionalism and the Politics of Landscape Preservation in the Third Reich', *Environmental History*, 4 (July 1999), pp. 384–404; and John Williams, 'The Chords of the German Soul are Tuned to Nature: The Movement to Preserve the Natural Heimat from the Kaiserreich to the Third Reich', *Central European History*, 29 (1996), pp. 339–84.
22. Benedict Anderson, *Imagined Communities: Reflections on the Origin and Spread of Nationalism* (London 1990).
23. *Oettinger Amts- und Wochenblatt*, 1.7.1908.
24. *Heimatschutz. Herausgegeben vom Geschäftsführenden Vorstand des Deutschen Bundes Heimatschutz*, 10 (1915), p. 2.
25. On the eve of the First World War, the geographical diffusion of the *Heimat* idea extended to every corner of Germany. By 1915, all important German regions prided themselves on having their own *Heimat* organization. The following Prussian regions and provinces founded *Heimat* organizations between 1906 and 1910: Lower Saxony (1906), Mecklenburg (1906), Cologne and the Rhine (1906), Brandenburg (1907), Schleswig-Holstein (1908), Pomerania (1910), Silesia (1910), Hessen-Nassau, and Westphalia

(1915). They joined *Heimat* organizations in Bavaria (1902), Lippe (1907), Saxony (1908), Württemberg and Hohenzollern (1909), Baden (1909), Hamburg (1910), Eisenach (for Thuringia, 1911). For detailed information about the regional associations and the Deutscher Bund Heimatschutz see *50 Jahre deutscher Heimatbund. Deutscher Bund Heimatschutz*, edited by the Deutscher Heimatschutz (Neuß am Rhine 1954) and *75 Jahre Deutscher Heimatbund* (Siegburg 1979).

26. *Verhandlungen der Württembergischen Kammer der Abgeordneten*, Bd 117, 30. 3.1876, p. 1060.

27. Ibid, pp. 1080–1.

28. On the transformation of the *Heimat* idea from imperial Germany to the 1980s, see Alon Confino, 'Edgar Reitz's *Heimat* and German Nationhood: Film, Memory, and Understandings of the Past', *German History* (June 1998), pp. 185–208.

29. Following the establishment of West Germany, and the end of the debate on whether to adopt federalism, this view was almost universally accepted.

30. One result of the Nazi policy of *Gleichschaltung* was the abolition of Germany's federal system that existed since 1871. Aiming to create a fully unified Germany, the Nazis abolished autonomous political centres, such as the federal states. In March 1933, the Nazis reduced the powers of the federal states. On 7 April 1933 they appointed ten *Reichstatthalter* (Reich Governors), most often the leading *Gauleiter* of each state (with the exception of Bavaria – Ritter von Epp – and Prussia: Adolf Hitler). The policy was taken to its logical conclusion in January 1934, when the Landtag was everywhere abolished and the federal governments and governors were strictly subordinated to the ministry of the interior. Mary Fulbrook, *The Divided Nation: A History of Germany, 1918–1990* (New York 1992), p. 67. In the Russian occupation zone, five regional states were established between 1945 and 1947; these were transformed into 14 administrative districts in 1952 under the SED policy of centralization. They remained in place for 38 years, until the establishment of five new regional states in July 1990 as a precondition to the unification. See Hartmut Klatt, 'German Unification and the Federal System', in Jeffery and Sturm, eds, *Federalism, Unification*, p. 2.

31. Nipperdey, 'Der Föderalismus in der deutschen Geschichte', p. 71. The essay was first published in 1980.

32. See Andreas Glaser, *Divided in Unity: Identity, Germany, and the Berlin Police* (Chicago 2000) which recounts well how East and West Germans, living through the unification, constructed notions of otherness and sameness.

33. On 'Europe of the regions', see, for example, Joachim Bauer, *Europa der Regionen. Aktuelle Dokumente zur Rolle und Zukunft der deutschen Länder im europäischen Integrationsprozeß* (Berlin 1991).

5
Political Unity and Linguistic Diversity in Nineteenth-Century Germany

Martin Durrell

A central theme of the present volume is the interplay of centralizing and divergent tendencies in 'Germany', the problem of unity and diversity which is introduced in Maiken Umbach's chapter. One of the crucial problems within this is the question of national identity – effectively 'who is a German?' and how can 'a German' be defined? What binds together those groups which constitute the political entity 'Germany' in a contemporary and a historical context? And how is this perception of unity related to the feelings of local or regional identity encapsulated in the untranslatable German word *Stammesbewusstsein* which are clearly real within present-day Germany and have clear historical roots? Although 'federalism' is not a necessary consequence of such regionalism, the connections are clear and can be ultimately perceived by a significant proportion of the population as forming part of the justification for the federal structure of the present German state.

The question of German identity has bedevilled German and European politics over the past two centuries, with notoriously tragic consequences in the Third Reich. At the present time, from the standpoint of a British outsider, the answer seems clear: a 'German' is a citizen of the Federal Republic of Germany. But German reunification is barely ten years old, and as recently as 1982 the writer Peter Schneider expressed a rather different, and not uncommon view in his book *Der Mauerspringer* ('The Wall Jumper'):

> If my fatherland has an existence, then it is not as a state, and the state of which I am a citizen, is not a fatherland. If on being asked my nationality I answer without hesitation that I am a German, then I am clearly not declaring my allegiance to a state but to a people which no longer has any political identity. ... If the

Germans' fatherland has survived and continued to exist in any way, then perhaps only through the common mother tongue ... . After all, the word *deutsch* originally designated neither a people nor a state, but simply meant 'of our people' as a term for the common language of a number of tribal groups, ... This linguistic unity existed centuries before the foundation of the Holy Roman Empire of the German Nation, and it has survived the rise and fall of all subsequent unholy empires. In a certain sense the Germans seem to have returned to the starting-point of their history: the word *deutsch* can now only be used unambiguously as an adjective, and even then, if we are talking of the present moment, not with reference to a particular state or a fatherland, but only with reference to a single noun: the 'language'.[1]

The emphasis Schneider is here putting on a linguistic rather than a political basis for nationhood identifies the core of the problem: are 'Germans' to be defined linguistically as those who speak German, or politically as those who are citizens of the German state? The unification of 1990 has barely simplified this problem, any more than did that of 1871. Even if there are no longer two states claiming to be 'German', there are many speakers of German who are not citizens of that state. Within present-day Germany, too, the problem of nationality is still an immensely controversial issue, with second-generation Turks who were born in Germany and are native speakers of German not possessing a constitutional right to German citizenship, whereas resettlers from Russia (so-called *Aussiedler*) do have this right, even though they may speak imperfect German, or a type of 'German' which few Germans can understand.[2] Nevertheless, the situation of German and Germany is not unusual in central and eastern Europe, although it is quite different from the situation in Britain, in that it is characterized by what has been called a 'vertical ethnic community', with the majority defined on linguistic (in other places on religious) grounds and which typically has 'chronic difficulty in defining and maintaining a clear national territory'.[3]

In a popular view, the course of German history in the nineteenth century led to the *Reichsgründung* of 1871 as the fulfilment of an ultimately unstoppable popular demand among the German people for a nation-state which represented their inevitable historical destiny. In the short term this was the culmination of a movement which had begun in the Napoleonic wars, but in fact it reflected the fulfilment of a national destiny which had been thwarted in the later Middle Ages by the breakdown of the Holy Roman Empire after Barbarossa's reign. The ultimate result of this was the wholly unjustified delay in the formation of a German nation-state, for which foreign interference had been largely responsible, but this had been overcome and the German people at last had the state which had always been their due. The justification for this state was essentially ethnic-linguistic: the peoples of the new *Reich* were linked by a common language, and they had been conscious of the unity of this language called *deutsch* for over a thousand years – in effect back to the first written records of this language and the Carolingian empire, which itself had been the first unified German state.[4]

This grossly simplified presentation would be challenged by most historians nowadays,[5] but its teleology is superficially plausible and aspects of it are remarkably persistent. We have already seen how Peter Schneider, despite his scepticism about a German fatherland as a state, accepts the notion of German linguistic unity going back to the earliest records of a language which might be called *deutsch*. This acceptance of linguistic unity since time immemorial has, as we shall see, crucial significance in notions of German nationhood. Aspirations towards national unity in nineteenth-century Germany were commonly justified by reference to ethnic-linguistic criteria, i.e. that the speakers of German constituted a distinct ethnic group and this was taken to legitimize demands for an independent political entity which would include all 'Germans', defined in terms of the common language which they spoke. As E. J. Hobsbawm writes:

> For Germans ... , their national language was not merely an administrative convenience or a means of unifying state-wide communication ... . It was the *only* thing that made them Germans ... and consequently carried a far heavier charge of national identity than, say, English did for those who wrote and read that language. ... for the German ... liberal middle classes language ... provided a central argument for the creation of a unified national state.[6]

Essentially, the membership of the 'nation' was defined on linguistic terms, and such a 'nation' came to be seen as the self-evident basis for a distinct state.

But this brings us immediately up against an even more intractable question than defining what is a German, i.e. 'what is the German language?' The question is difficult to answer clearly even today,[7] but it is well-nigh impossible in respect of the first quarter of the nineteenth century, when aspirations to national unity based on ethnic-linguistic criteria began to be voiced. There had arisen, by 1800, a relatively standardized literary language, commonly referred to as 'High German' (*Hochdeutsch*). This was a highly stylized variety which existed almost exclusively in the written form, being known and used only by a middle-class cultural elite (not the aristocracy, which preferred French) which acquired it through the process of education.[8] Its origin was not in any spoken form of German (unlike standard English, which had at least a partial base in the spoken language of the upper classes and the court in London), but it had arisen through a long process of selection from regional written forms of the language. It is difficult to obtain reliable information about actual language use at this time, but a crucial factor is that scarcely anyone in the late eighteenth century will have acquired any form of *Hochdeutsch* as their first language.[9] It is indicative that it was commonly referred to as *Schriftdeutsch* throughout the nineteenth century, as it still is in German-speaking Switzerland, and we might best envisage the linguistic situation in Germany around 1800 as comparable to that of modern Switzerland, with dialect as the first language of the whole population and *Hochdeutsch* being acquired (if at all) through education and used only in writing and for formal public speech.[10]

In this context it is important to be fully aware of what is meant by a 'German dialect', particularly from an English perspective. In terms of the autochthonous language forms, the 'dialects', the German speech area is not only the largest in Europe (and it was even larger before the mass expulsions after 1945), it is also the most varied. As Barbour says, 'probably no other European language is so diverse, and groups of dialects elsewhere which show a similar diversity are considered to be several languages'.[11] It is scarcely an exaggeration to say that the variation found within German is as great as that within the whole of the Slavonic area. Certainly, distant dialects are not mutually comprehensible. Monolingual speakers of standard German can only understand Swiss German or Luxembourgish with immense difficulty, and it is a common topos that a farmer from, say, East Friesland or Holstein could barely understand a farmer from Swabia or Carinthia if both only had command of their own native dialect. There is no inherent reason why, given different political developments, three or four standard languages should not have arisen in this area, say on the basis of the main written dialects of the early modern period.[12] Dutch, after all, did break away from the dialect continuum and develop independently after the establishment of the Republic of the United Provinces.[13] And Luxembourgish has effectively broken away in the present century, indeed since 1945 – a classic example of an emergent national identity forming the trigger for the establishment of a new national language as a symbol of that identity and the state with which it is associated.[14]

Given this diversity in the language actually used every day by the bulk of the population, what needs to be explained is how a linguistic unity came to be perceived such that it could be adduced as a justification for political unification on ethnic-linguistic grounds in the nineteenth century. It is certainly not the case that there was a recognized unity of a people speaking *deutsch* going back into Carolingian times, as Schneider asserts, although this idea is widespread in both academic and popular writing.[15] The origin of the word *deutsch*, which is unique among European designations for ethnic groups in referring initially exclusively to language, not to a tribal group, is one of the most controversial issues in the linguistic historiography of German. However, the word is actually first attested, in the guise of a Late Latin form *theodiscus*, in the year 786, to refer to Old English, and its original use seems to have been in the learned language of the period to designate any of the Germanic dialects of western Europe rather than specifically those of what was to become Germany; significantly, it is only used in its Latin form in Old High German times, not in German.[16] The breakaway of Dutch, too, would seem to belie the notion of a universally perceived unity of people speaking *deutsch* since Carolingian times. Indeed, this notion, though often propounded, clearly arose as a history of the 'national language' was being established in the nineteenth century to provide a historically based legitimation for aspirations towards political unity. At best, what was expressed in earlier centuries through the word *deutsch* was a relatively weak and negative sense of identity, as is shown by the antonym of *deutsch*, which is *welsch*, an adjective which is applied by all the early west Germanic peoples to their nearest non-west Germanic speaking neighbours, whether Celtic (as in Great Britain), or Romance (as in western Europe). Polenz considers that 'a general, vague consciousness of common linguistic features (not "unity"!) already existed centuries before the development of the pre-national standard language ... . However, it was linked right into the 17th and 18th centuries with a strong consciousness of the (oral and written) independence of the regional languages'.[17] It is characteristic that the adjective *deutsch* was most often used into the late Middle Ages with a plural noun, e.g. *in den deutschen Landen* 'in the German lands', *die deutschen Zungen* 'the German languages'. In effect, *Deutsche* were simply people who did not speak Celtic, Romance, Slavonic, Magyar or Danish, and this fits in with late medieval notions of 'nation', for instance at the medieval universities, and with the designation of the *Holy Roman Empire of the German Nation*, which itself only dates from the fifteenth century (as does the term *Deutschland*).[18] Barbour's view that 'Germans are simply those Europeans who are not anything else' summarizes the situation succinctly; the supposed centuries-old unity of peoples speaking *deutsch* is, in fact, a myth created by nationalist linguistic historiography in the nineteenth century as a retrospective justification for political unity.[19]

However, although the notion of an underlying unity to the German language dating back to the early Middle Ages cannot be sustained, neither is it the case that linguistic unity arose subsequently to political unification in 1871 – in effect that the language used to legitimize the establishment of the state in ethnic-linguistic terms was created after its foundation. It would by no means be an unusual sequence of events for a national standard language to have been devised subsequent to the formation of a national state,[20] and some contemporaries even considered that this was true of German, too, i.e. that the national language was a product of national unification. The historian Heinrich Grimm wrote in 1890 that 'the present-day language has emerged from the coming together of North and South Germany in 1870'.[21] Indeed, after 1871 standard *Hochdeutsch* did become a national language, the language of the newly unified state, and this state clearly regarded it as a vital symbol of the new national unity, since, as Polenz writes 'for the as yet not fully established and as yet not very popular idea of "imperial nationalism" additional symbols of unity were required in order to create a sense of solidarity'.[22] An important indicator of this was that significant steps were undertaken at this time to complete the codification of standard *Hochdeutsch*. A uniform spelling system for the whole Empire was only finally achieved in 1901 after the so-called 'Second Orthographic Conference' in Berlin, but the first initiatives occurred immediately after unification in 1871, and the First Orthographic Conference had already met (although without producing a result) in 1876.[23] These moves were clearly motivated by unification. Konrad Duden, the schoolteacher whose proposals for a uniform spelling system were eventually accepted, was quite explicit, in the preface to his first dictionary in 1872, that a single German orthography should be created to reflect the new political unity.[24] Similarly, a uniform formal pronunciation of the language, particularly for the stage and public use, was codified by a commission chaired by Professor Theodor Siebs in 1902. This was intended to be free of any trace of regionalism, but it was in effect wholly artificial, relying on each letter of the written form being articulated fully.[25] In this way, after 1871, there were significant developments in the process of codifying the standard language, *Hochdeutsch*, the unity of which was regarded as highly significant as a symbol of the new political unity of the *Reich*. Indeed, this codification was particularly rigorous, characterized by what Polenz refers to as 'extremely strict norms in orthography and pronunciation with an idealized supraregional unity, especially within Bismarck's Empire, with the typical syntax of the formal written language even used for official speech'.[26] Essentially, a model of invariant formal correctness was established for standard *Hochdeutsch* which represented the linguistic ideal of the educated middle classes and which they saw as an appropriate reflection of the new nation-state.

Recent studies of the course of German nationalism in the nineteenth century have suggested that nationalism was rather a consequence than a cause of unification.[27] Given the diversity of German, particularly in the spoken medium, and the fact that, as we have just seen, the final stages in the codification of the language took place after 1871 with the explicit intent of confirming the national language as a symbol of national unity, it would appear at least a plausible hypothesis that linguistic unity, like widespread national feeling, was a consequence of political unification rather than one of the factors contributing towards it. A view similar to this is put forward by Stephen Barbour, who states that:

> From a non-German point of view the notion of a uniform German language is questionable right into the twentieth century; into the nineteenth century only a numerically small educated class had a command of the spoken standard language and the fact that the speakers of the extremely diverse German dialects perceived their speech forms as dialects of a single language is, in my view, not self-evident.[28]

However, Barbour's opinion is immediately countered by Polenz in the same volume, who points out that even if variation in the written language was only finally eliminated through the final codification of orthography in the late nineteenth century, this is effectively merely a final stage in the process of the creation of a standard form of the written language which had been going on for several centuries.[29] In effect, it is the relative uniformity of this written language, used throughout the German-speaking lands of the Holy Roman Empire and outside it, which provided the basis for assumptions of ethnic-linguistic unity in the course of the nineteenth century. The fact that it was the language of literacy throughout these territories gives the answer to Barbour's question as to how or why these diverse dialects were perceived as dialects of a single language. Over a period of time people had come to accept the authority of *Hochdeutsch* as the language of educated literacy throughout the Empire, and if it might be rather different from the native dialects, it was still quite obviously related to them.

In fact, by 1800, if there was, as we have seen, still great diversity in the spoken medium, the written language had achieved a considerable measure of standardization. In the early sixteenth century there had been at least three major regional varieties of written German, but over the following two hundred years a process of levelling and selection occurred which eventually eliminated competing regional variants in orthography, grammar and vocabulary.[30] In this, Luther's Bible translation was an important, if not the only, model because of the inherent prestige of the text and the fact that it was used and known over wide areas of Germany. In the seventeenth and eighteenth centuries a number of grammarians took upon themselves the task of codifying this written language. One of their guiding assumptions, which was very typical of the time, was that there was a single 'correct' form of the language which they were attempting to establish. This assumption derived from a commonly accepted view of linguistic diversity from ancient times into the present century, maintaining and maintained by the 'ideology of standard', that there exist fixed entities called 'languages' from which 'dialects' are deviations, and these increasingly come to be seen as corruptions of the 'language' by the uneducated.[31] In the seventeenth and eighteenth centuries it was a common rationalist assumption that the form of this 'real' language could and should be established and fixed, and its rules and lexis prescriptively codified.[32] This notion, which Stevenson refers to from the perspective of modern sociolinguistics as the 'common misconception that the "standard" form of any language is its "original, uncorrupted state", from which all other forms have subsequently deviated',[33] is based in part at least on the perception of the (dead) classical languages, especially Latin, as models and the idea that what needed to be set down and fixed was the true and correct language as created at Babel. Such notions clearly underly the principle of 'inherent correctness' (*Grundrichtigkeit*) which Schottelius, the leading grammarian of the late seventeenth century, posits as the guiding principle behind his work.[34] In the course of the eighteenth century this *Hochdeutsch* was then codified in large measure, especially in respect of morphology, syntax and lexis. Of particular note is the role played by the immensely

influential writer and publicist Gottsched, who unceasingly prosely-
tized his prescriptions for what should be regarded as correct
Hochdeutsch and his view that all persons of quality should use it and
be recognized as educated through their use of it. In this he was motivated in large measure by cultural patriotism, since he was also explicitly aiming to encourage the use of German rather than French and
establish a classical German literature.[35] Another important figure in
this development is Johann Christoph Adelung, who compiled the first
large comprehensive dictionary of *Hochdeutsch* and the first grammar
book designed for use in schools.[36] Ultimately, the prescriptions of
Gottsched, Adelung and others became accepted throughout the Holy
Roman Empire, even in the south of Germany, in Austria and in
Switzerland, which had been slow to accept the pre-eminence of Saxon
and north German models.[37] In this way, rationalist assumptions about
'languages' and 'dialects' prevailed, i.e. that the spoken dialects of the
Holy Roman Empire were simply deviations from the 'pure' or 'correct'
language which was to be established by a cultural elite. It was this
Hochdeutsch which was then used, on the basis of the codifications of
the seventeenth and eighteenth centuries, by the major writers of
German Classicism, notably Goethe and Schiller, who further endowed
it with their cultural prestige. It was this uniform written variety
which, although essentially a cultural artefact, in effect provided a
focus for nationalist aspirations in the nineteenth century, rather than
any spoken form of the language.

By 1800, the characteristic stages of linguistic standardization had
been completed in large measure in respect of the written form of
German: selection of variants, codification, acceptance and elaboration
of function.[38] The important, and in many ways puzzling aspect, is precisely that it was accepted throughout the Empire. After all, Germany
was not a centralized monarchy. It is quite plausible that standard
English, French or Castillian should arise on the basis of usage, written
and spoken, in the courts of London, Paris or Madrid. The crucial question is how and why this standard German was 'able to arise in the
face ... of dialect diversity but also of political fragmentation', as
Barbour puts it.[39] He suggests that a possible cause was precisely the
fragmentation of the Empire. Had powerful independent states
emerged which could have developed into separate nations (as happened, in effect, in the Netherlands), the story might have been different, and three or four distinct standard languages might have emerged
from what we now call the German speech-area. In practice, though,
we could stand Barbour's argument on its head and suggest that it was

precisely the existence of the Holy Roman Empire, which, despite its internal fragmentation, acted as a focus for the possibly vague perception that the all the regional dialects (the so-called *lantsprachen*) were related 'dialects' of the single language of that Empire. This could be identified in part with the emerging *Hochdeutsch*, deriving from the language of Luther's Bible translation, and the grammarians of the seventeenth and eighteenth centuries saw it as their task to establish what the 'real' form of this language was, in order to establish it as a language within the Empire which could compete with Latin and French in terms of prestige.[40]

After the Empire was dissolved in 1806, it was this prestige *Hochdeutsch* which, not least since it was now the language of literary classics, became a focus for emergent nationalist ideas, even though it was, ultimately, an artificial creation, like all standard languages, and divorced from any spoken form of the language, existing almost exclusively in the written medium and with scarcely anyone speaking it as their native variety.[41] The diversity of the forms actually spoken was, in fact, irrelevant, since, as we have seen, these could be conceived of as deviants from this form of the language which stood above the dialects as their most correct form. It is also the case, as Hobsbawn has observed, that it is precisely the '*written* language, or the language spoken for *public purposes* which is crucial'.[42] Elsewhere, he writes perceptively that 'linguistic nationalism was the creation of people who wrote and read, not of people who spoke'.[43] After 1800 in Germany it was precisely these people, the established cultural elite formed by the educated middle classes which developed into the characteristic German *Bildungsbürgertum* of the nineteenth century who took over ideas from Herder and Humboldt about the cultural distinctiveness of linguistic 'peoples',[44] and the perceived ethnic-linguistic unity on the basis of *Hochdeutsch* was identified as a possible basis for political modernization in terms of the creation of a nation-state where the people would be sovereign. What had been a cultural unity in the eighteenth century was politicized in stages, following the classic steps in the development of nationalism,[45] and the cultural and linguistic unity embodied in the standard language came to justify aspirations to political unity. In the course of the nineteenth century, *Hochdeutsch* became a social symbol of the *Bildungsbürgertum*,[46] and, especially in the centre and the north, they increasingly adopted it in speech as well as in writing. Mastery of *Hochdeutsch* became a badge of education, and deviations from it in the public arena were heavily stigmatized,[47] as, in the course of the nineteenth century, it came to be explicitly associated with desires for national unity and the importance of maintaining its unity was stressed.[48] Jacob Grimm's is a characteristic voice here, writing in 1822 that 'only through our written language do we Germans feel the vital bond of our origins and our community, and no people can think to have bought this advantage too dearly or to dispense with it at any price',[49] and in 1848 that 'now all Germans make a concerted effort to cultivate a single language which, like the Attic, should strive to stand above the dialects'.[50] Grimm's own philological and lexicographical work has a very clear ideological motivation, and his stance is that of a very characteristic 'Romantic nationalism'.[51]

Effectively, in the course of the nineteenth century, what had been a pre-political *Kulturnation* was politicized and developed into an ethnic-linguistically based nationalism, on the basis of which a *Staatsnation* was formed out of the larger part of that *Kulturnation* (what became the 'little German' *Reich*), which could then abrogate to itself the right to exclusive representation of the *Kulturnation*.[52] Knowledge of the standard language had originally had the same narrow base in the educated middle classes as political nationalism (and was not necessarily universal within it, especially in south), but after 1871, as we have seen, as nationalism itself was transformed into a popular movement, the unified language was associated with the new state and increasingly mythologized as the *Muttersprache* of all Germans.[53] A final, notably rigid and prescriptive codification was established, as we have seen, and this was propounded as a symbol of the nation. Inculcating it, with all its prescriptions, as the obligatory written form became a major aim of the educational system in Germany. In 1872 H. Weber emphasized the need for 'the cultivation of national education through teaching in the mother-tongue',[54] and Otto Ludwig writes of this period, 'All Germans were to speak a common language. As, however, there was a uniform German language only in the written form, the schools in which this was taught came to be agencies of the state, in which the written language was to be acquired.'[55]

The question then arises of how the observable fact of linguistic diversity, notably in the spoken language, was reconciled with the ideology of a standard national language. One possibility was to ignore it entirely, because speaking did not matter, and this happened in a number of countries, where, as Hobsbawm writes, 'the language(s) spoken within the private sphere of communication raise no serious problems'[56] because they can be seen as occupying a distinct, and subordinate domain of usage. But, in actual fact, contemporaries voiced considerable concern about the use of spoken German. One possibility was to transfer the ideology of standard to the spoken medium, too, and declare that there was a 'proper' form of spoken German – in effect this was identified with the letter-by-letter pronunciation of the written standard language which had in practice arisen in north Germany, especially for use in church.[57] The origin of this as an artificial attempt by native Low German speakers to realize written High German was not recognized. Ludwig points out that it was widely assumed that the *Schriftsprache* must, logically, have arisen from a spoken idiom, since 'it was generally assumed that this language [i.e. written *Hochdeutsch*] could only have arisen on the basis of a spoken form of language. This produced a difficult situation, since the written form had to be explained in terms of something which did not yet exist or which at best was just coming into existence'.[58] Some contemporaries were, however, rather more perceptive, and expressed regret that cultivated speaking was still not widespread in Germany. A writer known only as J. F. identified the German language in 1846 as the one unifying bond of the German people, and bemoans the fact that 'the lack of a common speech of the educated classes is a gap in our linguistic nationhood, and thus a lacuna in our nationhood in general, which we must be ashamed of'.[59] This was eventually rectified, as we have seen, by the prescriptive codification of precisely the north German literal pronunciation in the commission chaired by Siebs in 1902.

One possible consequence of the transfer of the ideology of standard to the spoken medium is the stigmatization of the dialects. Typically they can be discriminated against as 'incorrect', if the underlying reason may eventually be that they present a potential challenge to the hegemony and symbolic authority of the national language. This is a common phenomenon, with France providing a prime example, where, after the Revolution, standard French was rigorously imposed as the national language, and a systematic campaign was undertaken to eliminate *patois* and the regional languages.[60] In Germany, though, there have been conflicting and contradictory attitudes to linguistic variation from the eighteenth century to the present day. Explicit stigmatization of dialect was widespread in the eighteenth century as the standard language was undergoing codification, although at this time it was largely justified in terms of eliminating 'coarseness' or 'provincialism' from the written language of the educated elite.[61] At the same time, though, there was even at this time the beginning of scholarly interest in dialect as the repository of ancient culture and the original language of the people.[62] Features of both these dichotomous attitudes have persisted to the present day.

In practice, stigmatization of dialect appears earliest in the north, and it is here that it has been most intensive, most prolonged, and ultimately most successful. Low German, the autochthonous language of the northern third of Germany, had been a widespread written language in the late Middle Ages, and it had completed early stages in the process of standardization on the basis of the language of Lübeck, being used as the language of administration of the Hanseatic League.[63] After 1600, though, it is actively suppressed in public use, especially by the local princes and the Lutheran church authorities; it is seen as socially inferior and effectively re-dialectized. The reasons why this happened (and with such speed) are still not fully explained, but the effect was to block the codification and development of the one language form which could have provided effective competition to High German as an alternative standard language within the Empire, and to establish *Hochdeutsch* as the public language of the North, too, which was thereby confirmed as part of the territory of 'Germany' and its inhabitants as 'Germans' using the 'German language'.[64] This stigmatization of Low German and its systematic elimination from the public sphere continued into the nineteenth century although the explicit rationale could be different. The notorious pamphlet of 1834 by the radical publicist Ludolf Wienbarg, entitled 'Soll die plattdeutsche Sprache gepflegt oder ausgerottet werden? Gegen Ersteres und für Letzteres' ('Should the Low German language be cultivated or eradicated? Against the former and for the latter'), is motivated by notions of progress and democracy, the idea that the common people of north Germany could only join fully in the political process and become full citizens if they abandon this old language which is a bar to culture and education.[65] In effect, *Hochdeutsch* was successfully imposed on the north, despite protests right into the mid-nineteenth century and pleas to reintroduce the use of Low German so that the common people could understand the Bible and church services.[66] In practice, the bourgeoisie had given it up entirely by the middle of the nineteenth century at the latest, and even the urban working class by the end of the century, so that it is reported for the period immediately before the First World War that 'anyone who can speak it, seems to be ashamed of this',[67] and by the end of the twentieth century Low German had been largely eradicated as an everyday spoken language except in intimate circles in relatively remote rural areas.[68]

It is likely that the crucial factor in the intense degree of stigmatization to which Low German was subjected from such an early stage was that it could be regarded as a different language to *Hochdeutsch* and thus provide a challenge to the hegemony of the latter. In practice this constitutes an exception within Germany, where, elsewhere, active discrimination against dialects, and contempt of them are relatively atypical (certainly compared to France or England),[69] possibly because of the potential contradictions inherent in stigmatizing linguistic varieties which were, even in the later nineteenth century, still the first idiom of the majority of 'Germans' of all classes. Even in the north there have always been conflicting tendencies, and there and elsewhere alternative views of linguistic variation are attested at a quite early stage. From the eighteenth century onwards, these give rise to considerable scholarly and educated interest in the spoken dialects, and this developed rapidly in the nineteenth century.[70] In this view, the dialects are not seen as a challenge to the supremacy of *Hochdeutsch*, but as an integral part of the German language as a whole, whose strength derives in large part from this diversity. The dialects can thus be considered as enriching the language which is ultimately constituted, as an entity, by the totality of its dialects. Such views can be attested from the seventeenth century on.[71] Even Gottsched wrote: 'How many peoples, how many dialects are contained over this large part of the earth!'[72] In 1783, J. C. C. Rüdiger, who was one of Adelung's sharpest critics, saw the dialects not as a hindrance for the standard, but as providing its very foundation, 'Rather did the dialects flow together in this fashion, so that in the formation of our language and literature all provinces played a part, now this one, now that one, each used its own dialect and each took something from the others'.[73] This view of the dialects as enriching and forming the language comes to be expressed frequently in the second half of the eighteenth century by many leading poets and writers, e.g. Klopstock, Lessing, Wieland and Herder.[74] Jacob Grimm wrote in similar vein, 'the result will therefore be as follows: one dialect is as ancient and equal as another, in former times the common man spoke like the nobleman, and in these present times the common language which has come about through the fusing together of the peoples is the possession of the educated part and thus can be acquired by all'.[75] His brother Wilhelm put the idea even more clearly in 1847, 'Our written language hovers over this diversity ... it draws sustenance from the dialects and has an effect back on them, if a slow-acting one ... this relationship is old ... the written language is thus the common element linking all the German peoples.'[76]

By the later nineteenth century this view has become dominant and linguistic diversity is not seen as in any way in conflict with the symbolically important unity of the standard language. The latter can be understood as embracing all the dialects and thus plausibly regarded as the *Muttersprache* of all Germans, as nationalist ideology required. It also forms the basis for a clear view of the development of the national language, whereby it is envisaged that there had always been a prestige form of German in the imperial courts and among the educated, and over the course of the centuries all the German regions had made a contribution to this. Karl Müllenhoff, in particular, tried to show how German developed as a succession of prestige court languages, beginning with the Frankish court of Charlemagne in the ninth century, passing through the court of the Hohenstaufen dynasty in the late twelfth century, the Prague chancery under the Luxemburgers and the south-eastern 'Common German' at the Habsburg court under Maximilian to reach the immediate predecessor of the modern standard language, as used by Luther in his Bible translation, in the Saxon and imperial courts in the early sixteenth century.[77] In this way, practically the whole of the German area is visualized as having made a contribution, at some stage, to the development of *Hochdeutsch*. This is an immensely potent concept in the way it uses the past to legitimize the present and reconciles the fact of a long history of linguistic diversity to the contemporary ideological requirement of linguistic unity. It is useful in presenting a history for the national language in terms of nationalist ideology, with all the diverse German peoples having played a part in the creation of what is truly a 'national' language. Standard *Hochdeutsch*, which has been taken as the basis for aspirations to national unity, may be quite different from the spoken variety of any region and not the native form of any significant group within the German lands in the nineteenth century. But it can be seen as having arisen through a process of blending all the diverse dialects by the leaders of German society over the centuries. The details of Müllenhoff's account are no longer accepted,[78] but at the time it provided an interpretation of the historical developments which corresponded closely to nationalist ideas, and the fact of linguistic diversity no longer constitutes a problem for the unity of the language which is such a crucial symbol of the nation. There is a unified national language, rigorously codified, with very strict norms of usage which are vigorously defended. As long as they do not provide any serious competition in terms of the possibility of another standardization, such as Low German did, the dialects can be encompassed within this unity and contributing to it, especially historically, and providing strength through diversity. They can be tolerated and incorporated within the body of the German language as a whole because they can symbolize those strong regional identities which are themselves perceived as an essential ingredient of German national identity.[79]

Notes

1. Peter Schneider, *Der Mauerspringer. Erzählung*, (Hamburg 1995, originally published 1982) pp. 116–17. [Translation by MD, as in the case of all originally German-language texts in this chapter].
2. See Erica Carter, 'Culture, History and National Identity in the Two Germanies since 1945', in Mary Fulbrook, ed., *German History since 1800* (London 1997), pp. 432–53. Recent changes in the nationality laws mean that people born in Germany of non-German parents will be able to retain dual citizenship up to the age of 23.
3. Stephen Barbour, 'Language and Nationalism: Britain and Ireland, and the German-speaking Area' in M. M. Parry, W. V. Davies, R. A. M. Temple, eds, *The Changing Voices of Europe. Social and Political Changes and their Linguistic Repercussions, Past, Present and Future. Papers in Honour of Glanville Price* (Cardiff 1994), p. 331.
4. This so-called 'Borussian' version of the course of German history along the lines given here was put forward by Treitschke in his *Deutsche Geschichte* of 1879. It is described by Michael Hughes, *Nationalism and Society: Germany 1800–1945* (London 1988), p. 150, as 'a deliberate perversion of Germany's history designed to present it as unbroken progress towards the Prussian-led creation of *Kleindeutschland* in 1871'.
5. For example by David Blackbourn, *Fontana History of Germany 1780–1918. The Long Nineteenth Century*, (London 1997), p. 249, Mary Fulbrook, *A Concise History of Germany*, (Cambridge 1990), pp. 125–9, or Hughes, op. cit., who points out that it 'has lingered on in the popular consciousness'.
6. E. J. Hobsbawm, *Nations and Nationalism since 1780. Programme, Myth, Reality*, 2nd edn (Cambridge 1992), pp. 102–3. See also Ulrich Ammon, *Die Deutsche Sprache in Deutschland, Österreich und der Schweiz. Das Problem der nationalen Varietäten* (Berlin and New York 1995), pp. 18–34, and Florian Coulmas, *Sprache und Staat. Studien zu Sprachplanung und Sprachpolitik* (Berlin and New York 1985), pp. 41–75, who gives a full account of the role of language in the development of the national idea in Germany and other European countries.
7. Compare Stephen Barbour and Patrick Stevenson, *Variation in German. A Critical Approach to German Sociolinguistics* (Cambridge 1990), pp. 1–14.
8. The development and standardization of literary German to 1800 is documented in Eric A. Blackall, *The Emergence of German as a Literary Language 1700–1775* (Cambridge 1959) and Peter von Polenz, *Deutsche Sprachgeschichte vom Spätmittelalter bis zur Gegenwart. Band II: 17. und 18. Jahrhundert* (Berlin and New York 1994).
9. Compare Peter von Polenz, *Deutsche Sprachgeschichte vom Spätmittelalter bis zur Gegenwart. Band III: 19. und 20. Jahrhundert* (Berlin and New York 1999), p. 454, who points out that 'the spoken language at this period was in principle still almost as strongly differentiated regionally as in the 17th and 18th centuries'.

10. Werner Besch, 'Standardisierungsprozesse im deutschen Sprachraum', *Sociolinguistica*, 2 (1988), pp. 186–208, distinguishes between the almost exclusively written *Schriftsprache* which *Hochdeutsch* was in the seventeenth and eighteenth centuries, and the fully fledged *Standardsprache* – a modern standard language used in all registers – which emerged by the end of the nineteenth century. The linguistic situation in German-speaking Switzerland is described in Felicity Rash, *The German Language in Switzerland. Multilingualism, Diglossia and Variation* (Berne 1998), see also Barbour and Stevenson, op. cit., pp. 204–14.

11. Stephen Barbour, 'Language and Nationalism', p. 332. See also Stephen Barbour, 'The Role of Language in European Nationalisms: A Comparative Study with Particular Reference to the German-speaking Area', in R. Lippi-Green, ed., *Recent Developments in Germanic Linguistics*, (Amsterdam and Philadelphia 1992), pp. 7–8.

12. Stephen Barbour, '"Uns knüpft der Sprache heilig Band". Reflections on the role of language in German nationalism' in J. L. Flood et al., eds, *Das unsichtbare Band der Sprache. Studies in German Language and Linguistic History in Memory of Leslie Seiffert* (Stuttgart 1993), p. 323. The main written regional dialects of the early modern period are outlined in Werner Besch, 'Schriftsprache und Landschaftssprachen im Deutschen. Zur Geschichte ihres Verhältnisses vom 16.–19. Jahrhundert', *Rheinische Vierteljahresblätter*, 43 (1979), p. 332.

13. Barbour, '"Uns knüpft der Sprache heilig Band"', p. 324. However, this view of the relationship of Dutch and German is not uncontroversial, compare Peter von Polenz, *Deutsche Sprachgeschichte vom Spätmittelalter bis zur Gegenwart. Band I: Einführung. Grundbegriffe. 14. bis 16. Jahrhundert* (Berlin and New York 2000), p. 84.

14. Gerald Newton, 'Lëtzebuergesch and the Establishment of National Identity' in G. Newton, ed., *Luxembourg and Lëtzebuergesch. Language and Identity at the Crossroads of Europe*, (Oxford 1996), pp. 67–95.

15. Thus, *Meyers Taschenlexikon in 12 Bänden* (Mannheim 1996), p. 734, maintains that Charlemagne founded the German language. Ulrike Haß-Zumkehr, 'Die gesellschaftlichen Interessen an der Sprachgeschichtsforschung im 19. und 20. Jahrhundert' in W. Besch et al., eds, *Sprachgeschichte. Ein Handbuch zur Geschichte der deutschen Sprache und ihrer Erforschung*, 2nd edn (Berlin and New York 1998), i, p. 351, shows clearly how the notion of the historical unity of the German language was a creation of the nineteenth-century middle class to underpin their aspirations towards a national state. Polenz, *Deutsche Sprachgeschichte. Band I*, op. cit., p. 18, is equally clear that there can be no question of German linguistic unity before the eighteenth century.

16. Cf. the articles and material in Hans Eggers, ed., *Der Volksname Deutsch* (Darmstadt 1970).

17. Polenz, *Deutsche Sprachgeschichte. Band I*, p. 83. See also Barbour 'Language and Nationalism', pp. 332–3. Even in the early nineteenth century, Jacob Grimm was still using *deutsch* to designate all the Germanic languages, compare C. J. Wells, *German. A Linguistic History to 1945* (Oxford 1985), p. 32.

18. Polenz, loc. cit. See also Barbour, '"Uns knüpft der Sprache heilig Band"', p. 325.

19. Barbour, 'Language and Nationalism', p. 332. See also Polenz, *Deutsche Sprachgeschichte. Band I*, p. 18. The development of the myth of the existence of German as a separate language since the earliest times is treated in depth by Claus Ahlzweig, *Muttersprache – Vaterland. Die deutsche Nation und ihre Sprache* (Opladen 1994).

20. Coulmas, *Sprache und Staat*, pp. 40–58 and Peter Trudgill, *Sociolinguistics: An Introduction* (Harmondsworth 1974), pp. 149–56.

21. Quoted in Gabriele Schieb, 'Zu Stand und Wirkungsbereich der kodifizierten grammatischen Norm Ende des 19. Jahrhunderts', *Beiträge zur Erforschung der deutschen Sprache*, 1 (1981), p. 137.

22. Polenz, *Deutsche Sprachgeschichte. Band III*, p. 233. Hughes, *Nationalism and Society*, p. 133, shows how the new government was at pains to 'create German national feeling by artificial means'.

23. Polenz, *Deutsche Sprachgeschichte. Band III*, pp. 236–41 summarizes the moves to a uniform orthography. Before 1901 (and especially before 1871) a number of the German states had prescribed different orthographic norms for use in schools.

24. Konrad Duden, *Die deutsche Rechtschreibung. Abhandlung, Regeln und Wörterverzeichnis mit etymologischen Angaben. Für die oberen Klassen höherer Lehranstalten und zur Selbstbelehrung für Gebildete* (Leipzig 1872).

25. The history of this standard pronunciation is outlined by Polenz, *Deutsche Sprachgeschichte. Band III*, pp. 255–62, who correctly points out that it represents an unrealizable ideal which is incompatible with actual linguistic usage. See also Martin Durrell, 'Standardsprache in England und Deutschland', *Zeitschrift für germanistische Linguistik*, 27 (1999), pp. 285–308.

26. Polenz, *Deutsche Sprachgeschichte. Band III*, p. 59.

27. Cf. John Breuilly, 'The National Idea in Modern German History' in John Breuilly, ed., *The State of Germany: The National Idea in the Making. Unmaking and Remaking of a Modern Nation-State* (London and New York 1992), p. 22, and Michael Hughes, *Nationalism and Society*, p. 101.

28. Stephen Barbour, 'Sprache und Nation im deutschsprachigen Raum aus der Sicht der englischsprachigen Wissenschaft' in D. Cherubim, S. Grosse and K.-J. Mattheier, eds, *Sprache und bürgerliche Nation. Beiträge zur deutschen und europäischen Sprachgeschichte des 19. Jahrhunderts* (Berlin and New York 1998), p. 50.

29. Peter von Polenz, 'Zwischen "Staatsnation" und "Kulturnation". Deutsche Begriffsbesetzungen um 1800', in Cherubim et al., *Sprache und bürgerliche Nation*, pp. 55–70.

30. The process of linguistic standardization in German is complex and still not fully understood. A detailed recent survey is to be found in Polenz, *Deutsche Sprachgeschichte. Band I*, pp. 159–83. See also Werner Besch, 'Standardisierungsprozesse', and Werner Besch, *Die Rolle Luthers in der deutschen Sprachgeschichte* (Heidelberg 1999).

31. The assumptions underlying the processes of linguistic standardization in early modern Europe are discussed in depth in James Milroy and Lesley Milroy, *Authority in Language. Investigating Language Prescription and Standardisation*, 2nd edn (London 1991). The term 'ideology of standard' is a key concept in this work.

32. The process of codification of German is traced in detail in Polenz, *Deutsche Sprachgeschichte, Band II*, pp. 107–238. Compare also Martin Durrell, 'Pygmalion Deutsch. Attitudes to Language in England and Germany', *London German Studies*, 4 (1992), pp. 1–26.

33. Patrick Stevenson, *The German-speaking World: A Practical Introduction to Sociolinguistic Issues* (London 1997), p. 10.

34. Cf. Polenz, *Deutsche Sprachgeschichte. Band II*, pp. 152–5. Schottelius was the first to insist that *Hochdeutsch* was quite distinct from any dialect, and indeed stood above all the spoken dialects.

35. Cf. Polenz, *Deutsche Sprachgeschichte. Band II*, pp. 157–61.

36. Cf. Polenz, *Deutsche Sprachgeschichte. Band II*, pp. 163–8 and 189–91 and Irene Schmidt-Regener, 'Normbewußtsein im 18./19. Jahrhundert. Zeitgenössische Sprachwissenschaftler über die Herausbildung und Funktion einer national verbindlichen Sprachnorm des Deutschen', *Beiträge zur Erforschung der deutschen Sprache*, 9 (1989), pp. 164–80.

37. Cf. Polenz, *Deutsche Sprachgeschichte. Band II*, pp. 170–6 and (with particular reference to Austria) Peter Wiesinger, 'Die sprachlichen Verhältnisse und der Weg zur allgemeinen deutschen Schriftsprache in Österreich im 18. und frühen 19. Jahrhundert' in A. Gardt, K.-J. Mattheier and O. Reichmann, eds, *Sprachgeschichte des Neuhochdeutschen. Gegenstände, Methoden, Theorien* (Tübingen 1995), pp. 319–68.

38. These four characteristic factors involved in linguistic standardization were originally identified by Einar Haugen, 'Dialect, Language, Nation', *American Anthropologist*, 68 (1966), pp. 922–35 and have subsequently been widely accepted by sociolinguists, such as R. A. Hudson, *Sociolinguistics*, 2nd edn (Cambridge 1996), pp. 32–4.

39. Barbour, 'Uns knüpft der Sprache heilig Band', p. 323.

40. Cf. Besch, *Die Rolle Luthers*, op. cit., Polenz, *Deutsche Sprachgeschichte. Band II*, p. 136, and Oskar Reichmann, 'Deutsche Nationalsprache', *Germanistische Linguistik*, 2–5 (1978), pp. 389–423.

41. In effect, what arose was a diglossic situation, as in present-day Switzerland, with a standardized written language divorced from any spoken language and only acquired through the process of education. In this way, Werner Besch, 'Entstehung und Ausprägung der binnensprachlichen Diglossie im Deutschen' in W. Besch et al., *Dialektologie: Ein Handbuch zur deutschen und allgemeinen Dialektforschung* (Berlin and New York 1982–83), ii, p. 1404 says that 'the whole nation became bilingual', and Helmut Henne, 'Innere Mehrsprachigkeit im späten 18. Jahrhundert. Argumente für eine pragmatische Sprachgeschichte', in D. Kimpel, ed., *Mehrsprachigkeit in der deutschen Aufklärung* (Hamburg 1985), pp. 14–27, refers to the 'internal multilingualism' typical of this period.

42. Hobsbawm, *Nations and Nationalism*, p. 113. See also p. 111, where he shows on the example of India that, contrary to nationalist myth, a 'people's language' is often not the basis of national consciousness, but the 'cultural artefact' of a literary standard divorced from the spoken varieties.

43. E. J. Hobsbawm, *The Age of Empire* (London 1994), p. 147.

44. See John Breuilly, 'The National Idea in Modern German History' in M. Fulbrook, ed., *German History*, pp. 558–59.

45. As identified by Miroslav Hroch, *Social Preconditions of National Revival in Europe* (Cambridge 1985); compare Hughes, *Nationalism and Society*, pp.12–24.
46. Compare Klaus J. Mattheier, 'Standardsprache als Sozialsymbol. Über kommunikative Folgen gesellschaftlichen Wandels', in R. Wimmer, ed., *Das 19. Jahrhundert. Sprachgeschichtliche Wurzeln des heutigen Deutsch* (Berlin and New York 1991), pp. 41–72.
47. Examples are given in Arend Mihm, 'Arbeitersprache und gesprochene Sprache im 19. Jahrhundert' in D. Cherubim et al., *Sprache und bürgerliche Nation*, pp. 282–316.
48. Compare Klaus J. Mattheier, 'Kommunikationsgeschichte des 19. Jahrhunderts. Überlegungen zum Forschungsstand und zu Perspektiven der Forschungsentwicklung' in Cherubim et al., *Sprache und bürgerliche Nation*, op. cit., p. 3, who shows clearly that the central concern in the course of the nineteenth century was that the standard national language should be disseminated as widely as possible, first in writing, and increasingly in speech.
49. Jacob Grimm, *Deutsche Grammatik*, 2nd edn (Göttingen 1822), i, p. xiii.
50. Jacob Grimm, *Geschichte der deutschen Sprache* (Leipzig 1848), ii, p. 579.
51. The important role of Jacob Grimm in the development of linguistic nationalism is treated in Klaus v. See, 'Politisch-soziale Interessen in der Sprachgeschichtsforschung des 19. und 20. Jahrhunderts', in W. Besch et al., eds, *Sprachgeschichte. Ein Handbuch zur Geschichte der deutschen Sprache und ihrer Erforschung*, 1st edn (Berlin and New York 1984–5), ii, pp. 242–57 and Michael Townson, *Mother-tongue and Fatherland: Language and Politics in German* (Manchester 1992), pp. 92–6. The term 'Romantic nationalism', as a stage in the development of nationalism in nineteenth-century Germany, is discussed and justified by Hughes, *Nationalism and Society*, pp. 23–4.
52. Cf. Polenz, 'Zwischen "Staatsnation" und "Kulturnation"', p. 57 and Patrick Stevenson, 'The German Language and the Creation of Nation Identities' in J. L. Flood et al., eds, *Das unsichtbare Band der Sprache*, pp. 339–40. The terms 'Staatsnation' and 'Kulturnation' are subjected to principled criticism by Ammon, *Die deutsche Sprache*, pp. 31–3.
53. The development of this ideology is traced in detail in Ahlzweig, *Muttersprache-Vaterland*, cf. also Polenz, *Deutsche Sprachgeschichte. Band III*, p. 233.
54. Cited in Schieb, 'Zu Stand und Wirkungsbereich', p. 137. A number of more perceptive individuals pointed out at the time that this standard language was actually some way removed from the actual 'mother-tongue' of most pupils, which was still predominantly dialect; compare Ahlzweig, *Muttersprache-Vaterland*, p. 161 and Hobsbawm, *Nations and Nationalism*, p. 38.
55. Compare Otto Ludwig, 'Alphabetisierung und Volksschulunterricht im 19. Jahrhundert. Der Beitrag der Schreib- und Stilübungen' in Cherubim et al., *Sprache und bürgerliche Nation*, p. 161.
56. Hobsbawm, *Nations and Nationalism*, p. 113.
57. This is in fact the origin of the prescribed pronunciation of standard German, which effectively came to be spoken as it is written. The history of

these pronunciation norms are traced by Polenz, *Deutsche Sprachgeschichte. Band I*, pp. 176–7, *Band II*, pp. 140–5, and *Band III*, pp. 255–62.

58. Ludwig, 'Alphabetisierung und Volksschulunterricht', p. 162.
59. Cited in Stevenson, 'The German Language', p. 338.
60. Cf. Coulmas, *Sprache und Staat*, pp. 30–31.
61. Ulrich Knoop, 'Zur Begrifflichkeit der Sprachgeschichtsschreibung. Der "Dialekt" als Sprache des "gemeinen Mannes" und die Kodifikation der Sprache im 18. Jahrhundert' in H. H. Munske et al., eds, *Deutscher Wortschatz. Lexikologische Studien. Ludwig Erich Schmitt zum 80. Geburtstag von seinen Marburger Schülern* (Berlin and New York 1998), pp. 336–50, gives an account of the stigmatization of dialect in eighteenth-century Germany and its motivation.
62. Cf. Knoop, 'Zur Begrifflichkeit', and Polenz, *Deutsche Sprachgeschichte. Band II*, p. 226.
63. For the history of Low German, see Willy Sanders, *Sachsensprache, Hansesprache, Plattdeutsch. Sprachgeschichtliche Grundzüge des Niederdeutschen* (Göttingen 1982).
64. Some idea of the manner by which this was achieved is given in Polenz, *Deutsche Sprachgeschichte. Band I*, pp. 258–69, who makes clear that the elimination of Low German was a precondition for the emergence of a single standard language in the German lands.
65. Compare Ahlzweig, *Muttersprache-Vaterland*, p. 96.
66. Compare Besch, 'Schriftsprache und Landschaftssprachen', pp. 338–40.
67. Mihm, 'Arbeitersprache und gesprochene Sprache', p. 290.
68. Compare Dieter Stellmacher, *Wer spricht Platt? Zur Lage des Niederdeutschen heute* (Leer 1985).
69. See Durrell, 'Pygmalion Deutsch', for a comparison of attitudes towards standard language and dialect in England and Germany.
70. Ulrich Knoop, 'Das Interesse an den Mundarten und die Grundlegung der Dialektologie' in Besch et al., *Dialektologie*, i, pp. 1–23, gives a full account of early dialect study in Germany and its motivation, pointing out and explaining the paradoxical nature of these attitudes.
71. Compare Reichmann, 'Deutsche Nationalsprache', pp. 400–1.
72. Cited in Knoop, 'Zur Begrifflichkeit', p. 338.
73. Cited in Knoop, 'Zur Begrifflichkeit', p. 339–40.
74. Knoop, 'Das Interesse an den Mundarten', p. 5.
75. Grimm, *Deutsche Grammatik*, p. xiii.
76. Cited in Stefan Sonderegger, 'Leistung und Aufgabe der Dialektologie im Rahmen der Sprachgeschichtsschreibung des Deutschen', in W. Besch et al., *Dialektologie*, ii, p. 1530.
77. This view is put forward most clearly in the introduction to Karl Müllenhoff and Wilhelm Scherer, eds, *Denkmäler deutscher Poesie und Prosa*, 2nd edn (Berlin 1863). It is graphically illustrated in Werner König, *dtv-Atlas zur deutschen Sprache*, 10th edn (Munich 1994), p. 92.
78. Cf. Polenz, *Deutsche Sprachgeschichte. Band I*, p. 92. It should be pointed out, though, that the most widely accepted modern view of the development of standard German still involves the selection of variants from

across a wide range of the German regions, compare Besch, 'Standardisierungsprozesse',

79. Alon Confino's chapter in the present volume shows how the notion of *Heimat* was similarly employed at this time to emphasize how regional diversity was interpreted as a crucial aspect of German nationhood.

6
Federalism in the Nazi State

Jeremy Noakes

In 1928 the Länder conference, which had been convened to discuss a reform of the federal structure of the Reich, had concluded its deliberations with the statement that 'the regulation of the relationships between Reich and Länder' was 'unsatisfactory' and required 'a fundamental reform'.[1] The problem had two aspects. On the one hand, there was the lack of geographic and demographic proportion between the sixteen Länder or states that made up the German Reich, which ranged in size from Prussia with three fifths of the area of the Reich and 61 per cent of its population to tiny Schaumburg-Lippe with only 53 195 inhabitants (1941);[2] seven of the Länder had fewer than half a million. On the other hand, there was the issue of the distribution of power and governmental responsibilities between the central Reich institutions and the Länder, which possessed their own governments and parliaments and exercised a wide measure of control over their own internal administration, including the police, judicial and educational systems, and cultural affairs.

Pressure to reform this unwieldy and irrational structure had existed since the proclamation of the Weimar Constitution in 1919.[3] In the negotiations which preceded the drawing up of the Constitution the four south German states – Bavaria, Württemberg, Baden and Hesse – had fought a relatively successful rearguard action against attempts drastically to curtail the rights of the Länder in favour of the Reich.[4] The result was that the Weimar Constitution had left the geography and political structures of pre-1918 German federalism basically intact. Subsequently, all the various proposals for rationalizing the territorial boundaries of the Länder and achieving a broadly accepted balance between the powers of Reich and Länder had been thwarted by the clashes of interest and opinion between the participants. The central

problems were first: what to do about Prussia and, secondly, the determination of the South German Länder, and particularly Bavaria, to
press for maximum sovereignty for the individual Länder. These discussions had culminated in the so-called Länder Conference, which
had a series of meetings between 1928 and 1930.[5] But they had been
brought to an end by the crisis situation of 1930 and the appointment
of the Brüning government.

However, despite the failure of attempts to reform the federal system,
the Weimar years saw a development, which profoundly affected the
relationship between the Reich and the Länder. This was the successful
attempt by the ministerial bureaucracy of the Reich to increase the
powers of the Reich administration at the expense of the Länder. The
crucial development here was the financial reforms enacted by
Matthias Erzberger in 1919, which shifted the balance of financial
power between Reich and Länder markedly in favour of the former.[6]
This process was accelerated by the period of presidential rule between
1930 and 1933.[7] Thus, on 5 December 1931, the Supreme Court stated
that the Reich President could make law in areas which were the
responsibility of the Länder. And in fact the presidential decrees issued
under the emergency article 48 of the Weimar constitution enabled the
Reich to intervene in a wide range of matters hitherto the province of
the Länder and local government. Most ominous was the fact that the
powers of the Länder over their police forces were weakened by a new
formulation of the Law for the Protection of the Republic, dated 24
March 1930, and by the presidential decree to combat political excesses
of 28 March 1931. These measures increasingly had the effect of subordinating the *Länder* Interior ministries to the dictates of the *Reich*
Interior Ministry. At the same time, the Reich bureaucracy seized the
opportunity of the crisis to create new Reich agencies and to appoint
Reich Commissioners such as, for example, the Reich Commissioner
for Labour Service. This process of Reich intervention in Länder affairs
during the Weimar Republic culminated in the appointment by the
Papen government of a Reich Commissioner to take over the government of Prussia on 20 July 1932, a development in which the political
priorities of the nationalist Right conveniently coincided with the
bureaucratic goals of the Reich civil service, and which provided a
model for any future Reich government determined to take control of
the Länder.

This then was the situation at the end of January 1933, when Adolf
Hitler was appointed Reich Chancellor: on the one hand, a movement
to reform the federal structure of the Reich had been frustrated by

irreconcilable differences and by the exigencies of crisis government, on the other hand, an increasing tendency for the Reich ministries to intervene in more and more areas that constitutionally were the responsibility of the Länder or of local government.

As far as popular support for the federal system was concerned, this was located above all in the three southern Länder of Baden, Württemberg and, above all, Bavaria. In Bavaria and Württemberg popular and elite hostility to the unification of Germany under Prussia in 1871 had obliged Bismarck to grant them special privileges, for example, permitting them to retain their own post and telegraph services through exemption from clauses 48–51 of the Reich Constitution.[8] The experience of nearly fifty years and, in particular, of the First World War as part of the German Reich undoubtedly significantly modified this attitude creating a new sense of national identity as Germans.[9] However, the establishment of the Weimar Republic in the aftermath of the Revolution of November 1918 with a Socialist Reich President and, initially a Socialist-dominated government, when combined with the elimination of the special privileges of the south German Länder in the new Weimar Constitution of 1919, and above all the centralizing fiscal reforms introduced by Erzberger in the same year produced strong negative feelings towards the Reich and a determination to defend Länder autonomy as far as possible.[10] Indeed, in the case of Bavaria, during the years 1920–23, the Land frequently acted in defiance of the Reich Government and a separatist mood became quite widespread.[11] This attitude was composed of a mixture of traditional resentment against 'the Prussians' and hostility to 'Red Berlin' and was shared by the Bavarian nobility, the peasantry, and by both the urban and rural petty bourgeoisie. It was strongly encouraged by the Catholic Church, which felt particularly threatened by the new political order and found expression in the dominant political party, the Bavarian People's Party (*Bayerische Volkspartei.*)

Although the political paranoia which had infected Bavaria in the post-war years and which culminated in Hitler's Beer Hall Putsch of 8–9 November 1923, subsided following the end of hyperinflation in 1924 and with a series of moderate conservative Reich governments, nevertheless, many Bavarians continued to retain a suspicion of Reich politics and not only of the Left but also of the *deutschnational* Right. However, within Bavaria itself there were significant variations in the degree of loyalty to the Bavarian identity. In Franconia (most of central and northern Bavaria) for historical reasons the commitment was less strong; indeed, there was some resentment of rule by distant Munich and of what was seen as its domination by the interests of the southern Bavarian provinces. Here in Franconia there was a greater sense of identity with the Reich that was partly also associated with the pre-dominance of the more nationalistic Protestant Church in much of this area. These differences were reflected in differences in voting behaviour. Thus, whereas in southern Bavaria (Oberbayern-Schwaben and Niederbayern) the Nazis won 27 and 21 per cent of the vote in the July 1932 Reichstag election, in Franconia they won 40 per cent (Reich average 37 per cent).[12] These differences were of course bound to complicate any attempt by Bavaria to resist Nazi 'coordination' as a Land.

The Nazis came to power with no clear vision of how Germany's federal structure might be reorganized let alone any concrete planning. The last point (25) of the Nazi Party's programme of February 1920 demanded 'the creation of a strong central state power for the Reich'.[13] However, in his official commentary on the Party programme, Gottfried Feder stated that the

> composition of the German nation from various Länder, each of which was united through their tribal characteristics and history, necessitates the greatest possible independence for the individual federal states as far as their internal affairs are concerned.[14]

However, this appears to have been primarily a statement intended for propaganda purposes. For Hitler had very different views. Indeed, he had embarked on his political career in 1919 with a speech attacking Bavarian separatism and he frequently deplored the anti-Prussian sentiments that were current in Munich in the early 1920s and which he claimed were encouraged by Jews attempting to divide Germans.[15] This was not a stance, which was calculated to win him much popularity. Hitler made clear his contempt for German federalism in chapter 10 of *Mein Kampf*, which had the title 'Federalism as a Mask'.[16] For Hitler the German nation, *das Volk*, was the key political entity and in his view that could only be effectively represented politically by the Reich – the central government, which must, therefore, retain absolute and undivided sovereignty. However, for Hitler the Reich did not mean the central bureaucracy in Berlin but rather the national *political* leadership. Indeed, he strongly disapproved of bureaucratic centralization. He was prepared to delegate authority down to regional and local level but only on the clear understanding that this was *delegated* authority and not the kind of limited sovereignty claimed by the existing Länder or notions of local autonomy or *Selbstverwaltung* asserted by local government. In *Mein Kampf* Hitler insisted 'in these petty federated states we can really see nothing but points of attack for separatist endeavours inside and outside of the German Reich'. 'The importance of the individual states,' he went on, 'will in the future no longer lie in the fields of state power and policy. I see it either in the tribal (*Stamm*) field or the field of cultural policy.'[17] In any case, he argued that modern communications would have a 'levelling effect', which would iron out any 'tribal' distinctions making such Länder superfluous. 'National Socialism', he concluded:

> as a matter of principle must lay claim to the right to force its principles on the whole German nation without consideration of previous federated state boundaries and to educate it in its ideas and conceptions. Just as the Churches do not feel bound and limited by political boundaries no more does the National Socialist idea feel limited by the individual state territories of our fatherland.[18]

On 2 February 1933, three days after his appointment as Reich Chancellor, Hitler reassured the representatives of the Länder in the Reichsrat by promising 'only to regulate and centralize' where it was essential and 'to do everything possible to preserve these historical building blocks of the nation'.[19] However, his dislike of federalism was confirmed by his experiences during March 1933 when his government set about taking over control of the Länder.[20]

Of the sixteen Länder four were already under Nazi control by the end of January 1933, that is before Hitler's appointment – Anhalt (from 21.5.1932), Oldenburg (from 16.6.1932), Mecklenburg-Schwerin (from 13.7.1932), Thuringia (from 26.8.1932). In addition, the Nazi Party had ministers in coalition governments in Brunswick (from 1.10.1930), Mecklenburg-Strelitz (from 6.4.1932) and Lippe (from January 1933).[21] During February, Prussia was rapidly subordinated to the new regime by Göring in his role as acting Prussian Interior Minister. The Nazi leadership postponed moving against the remaining Länder until after the Reichstag election of 5 March. However, during the week following the election, in a series of carefully coordinated actions, beginning with Hamburg on the 5th–6th, they used pressure and intimidation from below through mass demonstrations by SA and SS units to justify the intervention by the Nazi Reich Interior Minister, Wilhelm Frick, to restore law and order. This was done on the basis of Article 2 of the so-called Reichstag Fire decree of 28 February 1933,[22] which legitimated

Reich intervention 'if in any German Land the measures necessary for the restoration of public order are not taken'. Frick appointed Nazi Gauleiters or SA leaders as Reich Commissioners to take over the police and then to orchestrate the takeover of the Länder governments.

Bavaria had posed the greatest problems for its government was determined to resist any attempt by the Reich to repeat the Prussian coup of 20 July 1932.[23] It, therefore, sought and received repeated assurances from Reich President von Hindenburg that there was no intention of sending a Reich Commissioner to Munich. Reassured by this, in the middle of February, Fritz Schäffer, the leader of the Bavarian People's Party which dominated the government, used an election meeting to give a public warning that any Reich Commissioner who set foot across the river Main would be arrested. At the same time, however, both the Bavarian People's Party and the Bavarian SPD gave serious consideration to the appointment of the popular Crown Prince Rupprecht of Bavaria as a State Commissioner as the first step towards a restoration of the Bavarian monarchy. However, the Bavarian Prime Minister, Heinrich Held, was more sceptical and, when it became apparent that Hindenburg would not back the move and that the local Reichswehr units remained loyal to Berlin, it was decided not to proceed with the plan for fear of provoking the very Reich intervention which it had been intended to prevent. The fact that in the Reichstag election of 5 March the Nazis had won 40 and 39 per cent of the vote in the core Bavarian districts of Upper Bavaria-Swabia and Lower Bavaria respectively, which had hitherto proved relatively resistant to the Nazi appeal, suggests that even the most traditional sections of the Land were now proving vulnerable.[24]

Hitler was clearly furious about the Bavarian experience. His first response came in his speech to the Reichstag on 23 March, introducing the so-called Enabling Law, in which he announced that he considered a monarchist restoration 'at this time unacceptable' and he would regard 'any attempt within the individual Länder to solve this problem on their own responsibility as an attack on the Reich and act accordingly'.[25] At the same time, however, in this speech, which was primarily designed to reassure the Conservative elites, he promised that the Government would not use the Enabling Law 'to abolish the separate existence of the Länder'.

However, at a cabinet meeting a week later, on 29 March, he referred to the need for 'a fundamental reform in Reich–Länder relations',[26] and he now proceeded to use the instrument of the Enabling Law of 24 March,[27] which enabled the Reich Government to pass laws independently of the Reichstag and the Reich President, including laws which overrode the Weimar Constitution, systematically to strip the Länder of their democratic bases and their autonomy.

The first move came on 31 March 1933, when a so-called Provisional Law for the Coordination of the Länder with the Reich dissolved the Länder parliaments.[28] After the Communists and subsequently the Socialists had been excluded, Nazi majorities were secured. This law also laid down that, as in the Reich, Länder laws could now override the Länder constitutions.

Then, after his experience with the resistance to the Nazi takeover in Bavaria, Hitler set about devising a constitutional mechanism designed to prevent any future Länder particularism, even if it would now be initiated by local *Nazi* organizations. Thus, at the same cabinet meeting at which he had insisted on the need for a fundamental reform of Reich–Länder relations, Hitler stated that he 'envisaged the future regulation in terms of the Länder receiving Land presidents who would be nominated and appointed by the Reich Government. The Land presidents must in turn receive the power to appoint the Länder ministers. In this way a complete coordination of the policy of the Länder with the Reich can be achieved'.[29]

Just over a week later, on 7 April, Hitler's proposal was implemented in the shape of the Second Law for the Coordination of the Länder with the Reich, which authorized the appointment of so-called Reichsstatthalter or Reich Governors. The substitution of the term Reichsstatthalter for Hitler's original term 'Land President' was evidently designed to stress the importance of maintaining the unity of the Reich. In a speech to the Nuremberg Party rally the following September Hitler once more revealed his anger at the events in Bavaria and announced that 'the Reichsstatthalter law was the initial response of the German nation to these troublemakers undermining the unity and greatness of the German nation'.[30]

The Reichsstatthalter were to be nominated by the Reich President but only on the advice and with the countersignature of the Reich Chancellor. Ten were appointed during the next three months: six for the largest Länder, the other four covered those Länder with a population of less than two million: one for Braunschweig and Anhalt, one for the two Mecklenburgs and Lübeck, one for Lippe and Schaumburg-Lippe, and one for Oldenburg and Bremen.[31] This was an indication of Hitler's willingness, even at this early stage, to ride roughshod over Länder boundaries and sovereign rights. With the exception of Bavaria and Prussia a senior Gauleiter within each Land was appointed.[32] In the case of Bavaria, the appointment of General von Epp, a popular figure who had been responsible for crushing the Communist Republic in spring 1919, and who was a Nazi but not a Gauleiter, was a shrewd move given the deeply divisive nature of the Nazi takeover there.[33] Epp was regarded as the liberator of Munich from the Communist regime of spring 1919. His appointment also avoided the need to make an invidious choice between the four Gauleiters in Bavaria. In the case of Prussia Hitler clearly regarded this as so big and important a Land that he preferred to appoint himself Reichsstatthalter. However, on 25 April 1933 he delegated his powers to Hermann Göring, who had virtually appointed himself Prime Minister of Prussia three weeks previously.[34]

The Reichsstatthalter were not officials and the law said nothing about to whom they were responsible. They had the power to appoint and dismiss Länder ministers, to dissolve Länder parliaments, to order new Länder elections, to draw up and publish Länder laws, and to appoint and dismiss higher Länder officials.[35] However, although they had the right to be kept informed by the government agencies in their area, they did not have the right to give them instructions except in an emergency.

Article 1 of the first Reichsstatthalter law stated that they were to supervise 'the observance of the general policy laid down by the Reich Chancellor'. The use of the words 'Reich Chancellor' was significant. The first draft prepared by the Reich Interior Ministry had referred to 'Reich government'. In a letter to the Reich Defence Minister, dated 19 June 1933, Wilhelm Frick, the Reich Interior Minister, had summed up the position of the Reichsstatthalter as follows: 'In their relationship to the Reich Chancellor the Reichsstatthalter are the Führer's sub-leaders in the Länder ... So the Reichsstatthalter are in every respect dependant on the Reich Chancellor'.[36] Hitler clearly intended them to be his agents in the Länder to prevent the emergence of particularist forces, albeit now in the form of Nazi-controlled Länder governments.[37] For this role only senior Party figures would have the necessary clout. Indeed, arguably, he was trying to turn poachers into gamekeepers. At their induction on 26 May 1933, Reich President von Hindenburg outlined the Reich government's view of their role: 'to be a new bond between the Reich and the Länder ... to facilitate a unified Reich policy and thus strengthen the unity of the Reich'.[38] At the Reichsstatthalter conference held on 28 September 1933 Hitler spoke of their 'supervisory and advising function'.[39] As part of this strategy he initiated an amendment to the Reich Military Law of 1921 dated 20 July 1933, which transferred the right to call on the support of Reichswehr units in the event of a threat to public order from the Länder governments to the Reichsstatthalter.[40]

Hitler clearly intended to give the Reichsstatthalter as elevated a status as possible. With the exception of the Reichsstatthalter of tiny Lippe-Schaumburg-Lippe, they were paid at the same level as Reich Ministers. Moreover, in May 1933 he sought from Hindenburg, who was still Supreme Commander of the Armed Forces, permission for the Reichsstatthalter to be provided with personal adjutants, sentries, and honour guards on important occasions. In fact Hindenburg refused the request, although he agreed to consider the provision of honour guards 'from time to time'.[41]

The first Reichsstatthalter law of 7 April 1933 brought to an end the first phase in the relationship between the Reich and the Länder during the Third Reich, that of Nazi *Gleichschaltung* or 'coordination'. The second phase, which lasted until the Law for the Reconstruction of the Reich of 30 January 1934, a law, which effectively abolished the federal system in Germany, was dominated by two themes. The first was the relationship between the Reichsstatthalter and the new Nazified Länder governments; the second was the planning by the Reich Interior Ministry to carry out a reform of the Reich's federal structure, which would, on the one hand, subject the Länder to its direct control and, on the other, rationalize the Länder in order to achieve a more geographically and demographically balanced arrangement.

On the first point, the relationship of the Reichsstatthalter with the Länder governments, under the law of 7 April 1933 the Reichsstatthalter had not been given the authority to give instructions to the Länder governments except in an emergency. As a result they sought to assert control over the Länder governments by using their powers of appointment and dismissal under this law or endeavouring to do so where, as for example in the case of Hessen, the Land government tried to assert its independence from the Reichsstatthalter.[42] In Lippe, for example, the Reichsstatthalter, Alfred Meyer, dismissed the existing Nazi Prime Minister and replaced him with a Nazi crony from the pre-1933 period.[43] The new Land government then passed a law, on 2 June 1933, which established the Reichsstatthalter's right to give instructions to the Prime Minister and the latter's responsibility to the Reichsstatthalter, thereby effectively subordinating the Land government completely to his control.

However, at the Reichsstatthalter conference on 28 September 1933 Hitler complained that in some Länder ministers had already been dismissed and new ones appointed. He, the Reich Chancellor, should in future be consulted before such decisive steps were taken.[44] Moreover, he went on, the Reichsstatthalter should not interfere with the state administration. This warning reflected a growing concern on Hitler's part that the Nazi revolution was getting out of hand. At their previous conference on 6 July 1933 he had told the Reichsstatthalter that 'revolution is not a permanent state; it must not develop into a lasting state. The full spate of revolution must be guided into the secure bed of evolution.'[45] Hitler also moved to emphasize the importance of the Reich at the expense of the Länder. Thus, at the Nazi Party rally in Nuremberg at the beginning of September 1933, he spoke of the 'liquidation' of the Länder, which he described as 'building blocks of the past' which he no longer recognized as 'pillars' of the present Reich and he declared that he was not prepared to be their 'conserver'.[46]

This new shift in Hitler's policy coincided with efforts on the part of the Reich Interior Ministry to establish its control over a more rationalized administrative structure within the Reich. These were prompted not only by the desire to neutralize the centrifugal forces created by independent-minded Reichsstatthalter in the Länder and the disruptive effects caused by interventions by Nazi Party agencies but also by initiatives being taken by the Prussian government.[47] At the opening of the Prussian State Council on 16 September 1933, Göring had repeatedly spoken of a Prussian 'mission' and the Prussian government now launched a series of legislative initiatives designed to reform its internal administration and local government. These plans, which threatened to pre-empt the Reich Interior Ministry's own projects for reform of the Reich, placed it under pressure to act.

The Reich Interior Minister, Wilhelm Frick, a bureaucrat by profession, and two of his senior officials, Helmut Nicolai and Franz Medicus, wished to create a strong central Reich authority and to replace the Länder with a series of Reich provinces or Gaus more or less equal in size directly subordinate to the Reich Government.[48] They also wanted to create a uniform civil service out of the Reich and Länder civil services and, finally, to integrate the political organization of the Nazi Party into the state as, in effect, a propaganda and indoctrination agency. They envisaged the Reichsstatthalter forming strong intermediate centres or *Mittelinstanzen* between Berlin and the localities, combining the authority of party and state but subordinate to the Reich Interior Ministry. In their role as *Mittelinstanzen* the Reichsstatthalter would exercise a general supervisory authority over all the state agencies at regional level without, however, interfering in their day-to-day operations. At the same time, as simultaneously Reichsstatthalter and Gauleiter, they would be able to coordinate the different roles of Party and State.

This new policy orientation found expression in the Law for the Reconstruction of the Reich of 30 January 1934, the most important single piece of legislation affecting the federal system in the history of the Third Reich.[49] While Article 1, which abolished the Länder parliaments, was of little practical significance since parliamentary democracy had already ceased to exist, the key article was the second which stated baldly: 'the sovereign powers of the Länder are transferred to the Reich. The Länder governments are subordinated to the Reich government.' Article 3 placed the Reichsstatthalter under the administrative supervision of the Reich Interior Ministry. Finally, Article 4 stated that: 'The Reich Government can pass laws concerning the Constitution.'

One of the authors of the law, Dr Nicolai, summed up its significance with the assertion that 'the boundaries of the Länder are no longer Land boundaries but merely administrative boundaries'.[50] Frick proudly proclaimed the 'creation of a powerful national unified state instead of the previous federal state' as marking a 'new page in German history', as 'the beginning of a new historical epoch of the German nation'.[51] Indeed, so far-reaching were the provisions of this law that Frick was correct in describing it as a 'second Enabling Act'.[52] However, the extent to which the law would bring about a major reform of the Reich structure remained to be seen. For the time being, at any rate, the Länder had to remain in existence, since otherwise the Reich government had no means of exercising authority in the field. And so, under the first supplementary decree of 2 February 1934, the sovereign powers claimed by the Reich were delegated back to the Länder. On the surface, therefore, everything appeared to be as it was before.

The first significant measures of Reich reform that followed in the wake of the Law for the Reconstruction of the Reich were: first, the provision contained in its first supplementary decree permitting the transfer of officials between Reich and Länder, the first step towards creating a unified civil service, and secondly, the Decree concerning German Citizenship of 5 February 1934 abolishing Land citizenship and creating a German citizenship.[53]

However, the obvious major area which Reich reform would have to address was relations between the Reich and Prussia.[54] As we have seen, Prussia had already been effectively coordinated by the Reich as early as July 1932 when a Reich Commissioner had been appointed. On 30 January 1933, Franz von Papen had been appointed to that position in the new Hitler government with Hermann Göring as acting Minister of the Interior. At the same time, Alfred Hugenberg was made Minister of Economics and Minster of Agriculture in both the Reich and the Prussian governments. However, Papen stepped down as Reich Commissioner in April 1933 and was replaced by Göring but now as Prime Minister of Prussia. This was to prove highly significant for the future of a reform of the Reich.

On 18 June 1934, Göring announced to the Prussian State Council: 'The Führer has set me the task, within a decade, to merge the Prussian ministries with those of the Reich and to divide up Prussia into Reich Gaus, as he himself shall designate. During this decade, which the Führer has envisaged ... Prussia exists and remains a state concept and will have to be administered.' Moreover, he expressly indicated that, in the meantime, all proposals for reform should be avoided.[55] In fact, while Göring accepted the transfer of the Prussian Interior Ministry to Frick on 1 May 1934, and the merger of all the Prussian ministries, with the exception of the Prussian Ministry of Finance, with their Reich counterparts by the end of the year, he had retained his position as Prussian Prime Minister, and indeed the Prussian cabinet continued to meet during 1936. Moreover, Göring had insisted on keeping control of certain spheres such as the Prussian theatres, which were removed from the new Reich Ministry of Education and Culture, which had been created in May 1934, and forestry, which as a passionate hunter he removed from the Reich Ministry of Agriculture. Thus, Göring's position as Prime Minister of Prussia proved a major obstacle to the abolition of Prussia, since Hitler was extremely loath to antagonize the man whom he proclaimed as his successor.

The most significant of these ministerial amalgamations was that of the Reich and Prussian Interior Ministries, which was finalized on 1 November 1934.[56] For, while the Prussian Interior Ministry had a large bureaucratic apparatus with a huge field administration made up of Oberpräsidenten, Regierungspräsidenten and Landräte, the Reich Interior Ministry was much smaller and lacked a field administration since, under the constitution, internal administration was a matter for the Länder. Not for nothing was the Reich Interior Ministry known as a *Dame ohne Unterleib*. However, in order to make its writ run through the Reich it needed to establish control over the Länder and that now meant over the Reichsstatthalter and the Land governments. As we have seen, the Law for the Reconstruction of the Reich, which abolished federalism and subordinated the Reichsstatthalter to the directives of the Reich Interior Ministry, provided Frick with the legal wherewithal to do this. However, the question was how far would he be able to enforce this law. This would require the creation of a clear-cut chain of command through regional centres (*Mittelinstanzen*) down to the localities.

This, however, raised enormous problems. In the first place in Prussia there were two potential *Mittelinstanzen*. First, there were the *Oberpräsidenten* who were the senior government officials in the provinces and who traditionally had a general supervisory role and only limited direct powers. During February 1933, Göring had appointed Gauleiter to most of the *Oberpräsident* posts.[57] Secondly, there were the *Regierungspräsidenten* who were in charge of the *Regierungsbezirke* and who had direct responsibility for most of the internal administration.

As part of the Reich Interior Ministry's reform initiatives, on 27 November 1934, the Oberpräsidenten were granted increased authority corresponding to the position of the Reichsstatthalter in the Länder.[58] For the aim of the Reich Interior Ministry was to divide up Prussia into its provinces, renamed Reich Gaus, and to turn the Oberpräsidenten-Gauleiter into a strong *Mittelinstanz* coordinating both the various regional branches of the Reich government departments and the agencies of party and state. In practice, however, not only did it find itself frustrated in its attempt to divide up Prussia but it also discovered that several of the Oberpräsidenten-Gauleiters developed alarmingly independent tendencies. The result was that the Reich/Prussian Interior Ministry increasingly found itself relying on its direct line to the *Regierungspräsidenten* with which to by-pass the *Oberpräsidenten* in its attempt to retain control in the Prussian provinces.

Whereas within Prussia the Reich Interior Ministry faced the problem of asserting its authority against independent-minded *Oberpräsidenten-Gauleiter* so outside Prussia there was the problem of recalcitrant Reichsstatthalter. As we have seen, Article 3 of the Law for the Reconstruction of the Reich had established that the Reichsstatthalter were subordinate to directives from the Reich Interior Ministry, apparently transforming their position from being the Führer's sub-leaders in the provinces, and as such powerful regional potentates, to being regional line managers of the Reich government. However, the Reichsstatthalter-Gauleiter, who believed that they had won their authority in their Länder by right of political conquest, were prepared to take their orders only from Hitler not Frick, whom they regarded as little more than a jumped-up bureaucrat. Moreover, in an evident attempt to boost their morale, at a Reichsstatthalter conference on 22 March 1934, Hitler referred to them as 'Viceroys of the Reich' and announced that each of them 'must make of his position what he could'.[59]

This issue came to a head in a confrontation between two Reichsstatthalters, Fritz Sauckel of Thuringia and Wilhelm Loeper of Brunswick-Anhalt, and Reich Interior Minister Frick during 1934.[60] On 9 April, Loeper complained that the position of the Reichsstatthalter was

> unclear at the moment ... One is often in the position of not knowing whether one is allowed to act independently in accordance with the policy of the Führer or whether one is merely an executive organ of the Reich Ministry of the Interior ... I can very well imagine that the professional bureaucracy is happy to make use of the opportunity of reducing the position of the Reichsstatthalter below that intended by the Führer. But I also recall the words of the Führer during a conference of Reichstatthalter: 'You are the first Reichsstatthalters and what you make of this position will deter-mine what it will become.[61]

This is a classic demonstration of Hitler's style of government. It created precisely the kind of uncertainty which the Führer clearly regarded as creative but which in practice caused endless friction and wasted energy on the part of those involved.

On 28 October, Loeper complained again to Lammers that through their subordination to the official supervision of the Reich Interior Minister 'the nimbus of the Reichsstatthalter had been shaken and their real power considerably reduced'.[62] Sauckel had earlier made a similar complaint and Frick had responded to Lammers' query about the situation by claiming that, if the Reich government was to retain its leadership functions, then it was unacceptable to have a Reichsstatthalter appealing to Hitler over the heads of the Reich Ministers. 'On the contrary', Frick continued:

> the decision of the Reich Minister, who represents the Reich Government in his sphere of responsibility, must be accepted by the Reichsstatthalter without allowing him a form of legal redress against the decision of the Reich Minister in the field of legislation.[63]

Lammers then took the matter to Hitler who, while agreeing in principle that he should not be asked to adjudicate on differences of opinion between a Reich departmental minister and a Reichsstatthalter, nevertheless insisted that:

> in the Chancellor's view an exception must be made for those cases which are concerned with questions of special political importance. In the view of the Reich Chancellor such a regulation is consistent with his position of leadership.[64]

Clearly the result of this confrontation was unsatisfactory for both sides. For while on the one hand, Hitler had reaffirmed that for most purposes the Reichsstatthalter were now subject to the direction of the Reich Ministers, on the other hand, he had reserved 'questions of special political importance' for his own decision, but without specifying what such political questions were or who was to decide what matters qualified as such.

However, the Reich Interior Ministry pressed on with its policy of trying to centralize state and party authority in the Länder in the hands of the Reichsstatthalter, and in Prussia in those of the *Oberpräsidenten*. For according to Frick, 'the threads of the whole administration in the Reichsstatthalter's district should come together in the Reichsstatthalter's hands ... in the interests of the unity of the administration in the *Mittelinstanz* of the Reich'.[65] The aim was for the Reichsstatthalter and *Oberpräsidenten* to act as in effect district supervisors or line managers for the Reich government in general and the Reich Interior Ministry in particular, though without having any direct administrative responsibilities.[66]

The next stage in this strategy was represented by the so-called Second Reichsstatthalter Law of 30 January 1935.[67] However, once again Hitler did not allow the Reich Interior Ministry to achieve all it wanted. For it had hoped to bring about the appointment of the Reichsstatthalter as heads of the Länder governments in the interests of strengthening their position as the *Mittelinstanz*. However, Hitler had replaced the word 'will' in the draft law with the word 'may' take over the headship of the Länder governments.[68] In fact Hitler only permitted the Reichsstatthalter of Hessen and Saxony to take over their Land governments (28.2.35) and declined to release the appointment documents of the other Reichsstatthalter which had been drawn up by the Reich Interior Ministry and which he had in fact signed. The Reichsstatthalter of Lippe and Hamburg were, however, subsequently permitted to take over their Land governments on 4 February 1936 and 30 July 1936 respectively.[69]

The situation created by this law and by Hitler's actions produced some extraordinary anomalies. Thus, in Prussia Hitler had delegated his powers as Reichsstatthalter to Göring as Prime Minister and as such Göring was in theory subordinate to Frick as Reich Interior Minister. However, Frick was also Prussian Interior Minister and as such subordinate to Göring as Prussian Prime Minster! Similarly, Sauckel was Reichsstatthalter of Thuringia but also Minister of the Interior and so in theory as such subordinate to the Prime Minister, Willy Marschler.

This issue of whether or not the Reichsstatthalter was simultaneously head of the Land government was very important because, under the 1935 Reichsstatthalter law, the Reichsstatthalter had no authority to issue instructions to the Länder governments. The only way they could do this was if they were simultaneously head of their Land government. At the same time, the 1935 law underlined their subordination to the Reich government. For Article 3 laid down that, in addition to their general subordination to the directives of the Reich Interior Ministry, the Reichsstatthalters were also subject to the directives of the other Reich Ministries in the particular spheres for which they, the Reich Ministers, were responsible. Hitherto, these other Reich Ministries had only been able to issue directives to the Land ministries not to the Reichsstatthalters.[70] This law also transferred the right to appoint and dismiss Land officials from the Reichsstatthalter to the Reich Chancellor, who delegated this to the Reich Ministers. The Reichsstatthalter also lost virtually all the rights to issue pardons in criminal cases and the right to call in the Army, which, as we have seen, they had been granted by the first Reichsstatthalter Law in April 1933.

In a letter to the head of the Reich Chancellery dated 27 January 1938 the Reich Interior Minister, Wilhelm Frick, summed up the development in the office of Reichsstatthalter since 1933 as follows: 'In so far as the Reichsstatthalters have not been assigned the leadership of a Land government, the constitutional development since 1933 has led to their office losing more and more powers and to it becoming primarily a representative position.'[71] This assessment had already been confirmed in a bitter memorandum sent to Hitler in 1936 by the Reichsstatthalter and Gauleiter of Thuringia, Fritz Sauckel, one of the Reichsstatthalter who did not control his Land government. Sauckel complained that:

> The position of Reichsstatthalter has in reality even less substance than that of the Land ministers. The Reichsstatthalter have hardly

any direct legal responsibilities in the day-to-day affairs of state ... It is not true that the activities of a Reichsstatthalter need be restricted to these paltry legal responsibilities. He can act as the official representative of the Reich Government, which he is officially declared to be. He can hurry from rallies to receptions, from public addresses to serious accidents, from dedication ceremonies to meetings – but he can give no orders. He is by no means without influence; he can get somewhere by diplomacy, by persuasion, by threats, or through the Party – but he can give no orders. To make a comparison, he has a similar position in his district to that of the English king in England. He can make quite a lot of his position through his energy and skill but largely outside the legal limits.[72]

Sauckel claimed that the Prussian Oberpräsidenten, most of whom were also Gauleiters, were in a similar position to the Reichsstatthalter.

The issue of territorial reform also remained to be solved. In a speech to Reichswehr officers on 15 November 1934 Frick announced that territorial reform would be decreed on 30 January 1935 to coincide with the publication of the Second Reichsstatthalter Law of that date and as a fitting climax to two years of Nazi rule. [73] Germany was to be divided up into approximately twenty Reichsgaus, each with an average population of four millions, with their respective boundaries to be decided by economic, social and military rather than historic considerations.

This announcement was the culmination of a whole series of plans and discussions concerning the territorial aspect of *Reichsreform*, which had occurred over the previous two years.[74] For the state the lead role was taken by the Reich Interior Ministry and for the Party by the Gauleiter of Munich-Upper Bavaria, Adolf Wagner, appointed by Rudolf Hess to head a department for 'The Reconstruction of the Reich' within the Staff of the Führer's Deputy. However, as a result of the continuing differences between Party and state, apart from a few boundary adjustments such as that between Hamburg and Prussia, virtually nothing happened in relation to this aspect of Reich reform throughout the entire Third Reich. The only Länder to suffer a fundamental change of status were the two Mecklenburgs, Schwerin and Strelitz, which were merged from 1 January 1934 on the initiative of their Reichsstatthalter, and the city state of Lübeck, which was merged into Prussia in January 1937.[75] The problem was that no Reichsstatthalter wished to give up any part of his Land territory and, while Göring was prepared to discuss the break-up of Prussia as a long-term project, as the current Prime Minister of Prussia he had no desire to hurry the project on.

Hitler himself was extremely cautious about moving on the issue at a time when he had other priorities, notably restoring the economy and mobilizing the nation's resources for war.[76] He was aware of the administrative upheaval it would cause and also how much concern and dissension it would be liable to provoke both among the Nazi leaders who lost out in the reform and among the populations of the Länder or provinces affected. There was also opposition from the Wehrmacht to any major territorial changes, since it already had its own system of military districts. Above all, perhaps, Hitler was unwilling to have his future options limited by a reform which would concentrate power in the hands of a bureaucratically minded Reich Interior Ministry. As a result, in November 1933 public discussion of the territorial reform of the Reich was banned, a ban that was subsequently reiterated, for example on 14 March 1935.[77]

These bans did not, however, prevent the Reich Interior Ministry from continuing to press for a territorial reform of the Reich. During 1937, Frick approached the Reich War Minister in an attempt to persuade him to agree to a reorganization of the defence districts to correspond with a reorganization of the Reich into 17 Reich Gaus and two city Gaus.[78] However, at the meeting with Hitler on 1 December 1937, at which the issue was discussed, Hitler vetoed it on the grounds that he did not want 'the reform of the Reich to be pre-empted by administrative changes'.[79]

The issue arose again the following year with the attempt to merge Schaumburg-Lippe into the Prussian province of Hanover and Lippe-Detmold into the Prussian province of Westphalia.[80] This initiative was sparked off by Göring's decision to replace Freiherr von Lüninck, the Conservative Oberpräsident of Westphalia, with Dr Alfred Meyer, the Reichsstatthalter of Lippe and Gauleiter of Westphalia-North. Frick decided to seize this opportunity to bring about the two mergers in the hope that Meyer's appointment as Oberpräsident of Westphalia would provide sufficient compensation for his loss of the Reichstatthaltership of Lippe. Significantly, the Reich Interior Ministry had the support of both Göring as PM of Prussia and of the Party leadership in the shape of the Staff of the Führer's Deputy. The Interior Ministry wrote to Meyer pointing this out and appealing to him to agree to the changes. However, Meyer knew that without Hitler's support the other leaders were powerless, and so he replied pointing out that Hitler had forbidden further moves on *Reichsreform* and arguing that it would be unfair to Lippe and Schaumburg-Lippe if they were the only small Länder to be abolished. Hitler indicated that he was unwilling to consent to the reform for the time being and so Meyer was able to add the post of Oberpräsident in Westphalia to his Reichsstatthaltership in Lippe. Finally, the attempts of Göring and Viktor Lutze (Oberpräsident in Hanover) to incorporate Bremen into Prussia were frustrated by a similar combination between the resistance of the local Reichsstatthalter, Carl Röver, and Hitler's unwillingness to act.[81]

To sum up the situation so far, then: during the period 1933–5 the Länder had been effectively subordinated to the Reich government. The turning point here was the law for the Reconstruction of the Reich of 30 January 1934, which, by removing the sovereignty of the Länder, had effectively abolished federalism. However, the Länder themselves had not been abolished. Indeed, §2 of the first decree implementing the Reconstruction Law had transferred the Reich's new powers back to the Länder but now as powers derived from the Reich; they were now '*mittelbar*' or indirect. At the same time, the powers of the Reichsstatthalter, which under the First Reichsstatthalter Law of April 1933 had made them powerful regional potentates, 'viceroys' in Hitler's phrase, had been steadily whittled away, particularly in the case of those Reichsstatthalter who were not simultaneously heads of their Länder governments, and transferred back to the Reich Government in general and the Reich Chancellor in particular. Finally, apart from the merger of the two Mecklenburgs on 15 December 1933 and the absorption of Lübeck into Prussia as part of the so-called Greater Hamburg Law of 26 January 1937, further major territorial reform of the Reich had been blocked by Hitler for the reasons already given.

Despite his unwillingness to proceed with a reform of the federal system at this point, Hitler clearly considered it desirable once the coming war had been won. And when victory appeared to be on the horizon he returned to the matter. Thus, during a conversation with the Reich Propaganda Minister, Dr Joseph Goebbels, on 4 February 1941, he expressed the view that a reform of the Reich was 'urgently necessary':

Prussia must be broken up. Only the Führer can do that; he has the authority for it and also the moral right, for he has broken up his Austrian homeland. But the cultural centres in the Länder must remain intact and be supported by the Reich, viz. Vienna and then later Munich, Dresden etc. The Wehrmacht, money matters, finance – the Gaus will get the necessary money from the Reich – the tools of leadership such as radio, film, press etc. will remain with the Reich. It must remain inviolable ... As in the Party so in the state the central authority must be made as strong as possible. But it should not administer but lead. It has the money, the power and the right to launch major initiatives.[82]

Just over a year later, on 22 June, when the situation still looked reasonably hopeful, Hitler returned to the matter.[83] According to Goebbels, he expressed strong opposition to 'a schematic approach' and responded to the plans of the Reich Interior Ministry 'with a healthy mistrust'. By this was presumably meant the plan to divide Germany into Reich Gaus of more or less equal size. Instead, Hitler advocated a hierarchy in which only the senior Gauleiters were *Reichsstatthalter*. Thus, he wanted to appoint 'the most prominent representatives of the Party to an office in the state as was the case with the old prince electors'. The *Reichsstatthalter* had to have the opportunity of rising and

> although they must all have the same rights within their Gaus, the Gaus themselves did not need to be of equal rank. He considered it a very good idea to construct a sort of hierarchy in this way so that young Gauleiters could gradually climb up the ladder and increase their status through their achievements. Hitler was opposed to the office of Gauleiter and *Reichsstatthalter* always being combined. On the contrary, becoming a *Reichstatthalter* must be a desirable goal for a Gauleiter.

Two days later, at dinner, Hitler commented that he intended to apply the lessons he had learnt organizing the Nazi party before 1933 to the organization of the Reich:

> If at the time I made the Gauleiters into Kings of their Gau, who received from above only the broadest possible instructions, I now intend to give to our Reichstatthalter the same wide freedom, even if this should sometimes bring me into conflict with the Ministry of the Interior. It is only by giving the Gauleiter and the Reichsstatthalter a free hand that one finds out where real capability lies. Otherwise, there will eventually spring up a stolid, stupid bureaucracy ...

However, he pointed out that

> while giving my Gauleiter and Reichstatthalter the greatest possible liberty of action, I have at the same time demanded of them the

strictest possible discipline in obedience to orders from above, it being understood of course, that the central government is not concerned with matters of detail, which vary greatly in different parts of the country.

Nevertheless, he concluded by saying that 'there is nothing more harmful than over-centralization and limitation of local power. The lawyers among us hanker constantly for such limitation' and referred to the French *Départements* as a warning example.[84]

A year later, on 11 May 1943, Hitler returned to the subject, criticizing the Reich Interior Ministry for creating 'an enormous bureaucratic apparatus, which lies on public life like a sponge absorbing all initiative'.[85] He argued that 'to centralize the leadership tasks of the Reich and to decentralize the tasks of implementation was a high art, an art that the Interior Ministry was unable to comprehend'. However, although this criticism was aimed at Frick, whom Hitler had come to regard as a typical bureaucrat, according to Goebbels, following his appointment as Reich Interior Minister, Heinrich Himmler had demanded 'a strengthening of the central powers of the Reich' and declared that 'in his role as Reich Interior Minister he would ruthlessly support that'.[86]

Meanwhile, Hitler had issued instructions blocking any attempt at reforming the Reich, including 'the abolition of Länder governments which no longer had any point to them'.[87] Goebbels, who was anxious to rationalize the administration as much as possible in order to release resources for the war effort, concluded regretfully that 'in this situation it won't be possible to carry out what we intended: a modest reform of the Reich through total war measures without bothering about legal niceties'.

One can see from these various statements that Hitler's future plans envisaged subordinating the need to reform the administrative structure on the basis of bureaucratic rationality to his notions of the importance of competition in generating performance. Of course, the problem with this was whether these modern 'prince electors' and 'Gau Kings' would be prepared to see their role reduced to that of 'administrators', while the Reich ministries 'led', or even whether Hitler himself would have actually approved of this, since he continued to regard the *Reichsstatthalter* and Gauleiters as his direct personal representatives in the provinces. He was clearly torn between, on the one hand, the desire to give the Reichsstatthalters and Gauleiters as free a hand as possible and, on the other, a recognition of the need for central control. However, the point was that he was not prepared to yield that central control to a Reich bureaucracy that he regarded as infected by a legalism which prevented them from following political priorities.

Although Hitler was unable to put his plans into effect, his views had an indirect influence through his support for the party vis-à-vis the state apparatus. In fact, the development of the German federal system during the following decade, 1935–45, was marked by two fundamental developments. The first was the growing tendency for Reich agencies to establish their own field administrations within the Länder and increasingly to usurp the functions of Land and local government. The second development was the growth in power of the Nazi Party, particularly during the war years and a corresponding development of Gau particularism.

On the first point, the expansion of Reich influence in the Länder: this was of course inevitable given the abolition of Länder sovereignty by the Law for the Reconstruction of the Reich of 30 January 1934. It was most striking in the case of Prussia. By the end of June 1934, with the exception of the Minister of Finance and the Prime Minister, all the Reich and Prussian Ministries had been nominally merged with their Reich counterparts. In May 1934 a Reich Ministry of Education and Culture was established to which the Prussian Minister of Education and Nazi Gauleiter of Hanover-South-Brunswick, Bernhard Rust, was appointed.[88] In the same month Frick was appointed Prussian Minister of the Interior and in November 1934, the Reich and Prussian Interior Ministries were completely merged into one ministry, though it continued to be called the Reich and Prussian Interior Ministry. In June 1934 the Reich Minister of Justice, Franz Gürtner, was appointed Prussian Minister of Justice and, on 5 December 1934, all control over judicial matters passed to the Reich, and in April 1935 all Land justice authorities became Reich authorities and all Land judicial officials became Reich officials.[89] In January 1935, a Reich Local Government Law introduced a uniform constitution for all local government in place of the variety of constitutions, which had hitherto existed between and, in the case of Prussia, within the Länder.[90] In perhaps the most significant development of all, on 17 June 1936, the Reichsführer SS, Heinrich Himmler, who had already taken control of all the political police forces of the Länder during 1933–4, was appointed to the new post of Chief of the German Police, bringing all the Länder police forces under his control.[91] As such he remained nominally but not actually subordinate to the Reich Interior Ministry.

However, more ominous for Land autonomy than this process of nationalizing existing Länder government departments was the emergence of new Reich agencies, such as for example Goebbels' Propaganda Ministry and the Todt organization. For they now developed their own field administrations removing responsibilities from the existing Land government departments, albeit in their nationalized form. Moreover, this process was fatal for the Reich Interior Ministry's dream of a strong Reich *Mittelinstanz* and a well-coordinated administration.

The end of parliamentary democracy and the rapid demise of cabinet government after 1933 had led to the fragmentation of the Reich government into its component departments, each of which pursued its own agenda.[92] Since the federal reform legislation had allocated power and responsibility over the Länder to the individual Reich ministers rather than to the government as a corporate body, the Reich ministries were in effect encouraged to act as autonomous agencies within the Länder. These Reich departments and agencies were further prompted to establish their own field administrations by the intense rivalry over spheres of competence which existed between government departments and in particular with local Party agencies, a situation encouraged by Hitler. Reich government departments and agencies, therefore, resisted attempts by the Reich Interior Ministry to use the offices of Reichstatthalter and Oberpräsident to coordinate the activities of the various Reich field offices in the *Mittelinstanz*, since they merely regarded this as an attempt by a rival to encroach on their spheres of competence. Gauleiter Sauckel of Thuringia summed up this situation very well in his memorandum to Hitler of 1936, already referred to in connection with the powers of the Reichsstatthalter:

The Reich government departments clearly desire – and all of them are more or less forced by one another's actions to follow suit – to establish for themselves their own self-contained field organizations with a separate identity, imposing sharper and sharper lines of demarcation from the other administrative bodies and seeking to achieve independence of them. These huge administrative bodies are, therefore, bound in the long run to diverge more and more from one another; each one creates a state within the State. Instead of seventeen Länder (Saar) there will be in the end fourteen departmental bodies which at their middle and lower levels are cutting themselves off more and more from one another. It only requires the shock of a crisis to bring about public chaos.

Instead of Länder particularism we are getting departmental particularism.[93]

This memorandum was written in 1936 before this process had gone very far. However, fragmentation of the Reich administration at the lower levels was further compounded by the proliferation of new Reich agencies created by Hitler, above all during the war years.[94] By 1942, for example, there were 28 different Reich departments operating in Hamburg independently of the Land authorities and taking their orders from Berlin.[95]

Meanwhile, the Länder were not only confronted with Reich departmental particularism but with Gau particularism. The boundaries of the Gaue basically followed the lines of the Reichstag electoral districts. Sometimes, they happened to correspond to Länder or historic borders, as was the case, for example, with Baden and Württemberg or East Prussia and Pomerania. But in many other cases there was no such relationship. The Prussian province of Hanover was, for example, divided into three Gaue – Hanover-South Brunswick, Hanover-East and Weser-Ems, and the latter Gau contained the Länder of Oldenburg and Bremen as well as Prussian territory in East Friesland.

The Gauleiters had come to power through political organization and propaganda.[96] They identified their own personal political fortunes with the status and importance of their Gau and so were determined to increase them if possible by acquiring new territory, economic resources or administrative functions or at any rate strongly to resist any reduction in them. Thus the Gauleiter of Westphalia-North strongly resisted the merger of the Protestant Church of Lippe with that of Hanover even though he had no direct responsibility for the matter and was not a Christian.[97] After 1933, the Gauleiters continued to see their main role as being directly responsible to Hitler for the mobilization of the population of their Gau through propaganda and indoctrination for the goals of the regime and, above all, for the maintenance of its morale. And this is undoubtedly how Hitler saw their role.

As far as the Gauleiters were concerned this involved the creation of a personality cult in which they adopted a persona which embodied elements of a traditional *Landesvater* with those of a modern *Volksführer*.[98] They established political surgeries to which people could come and bring their concerns and were effectively encouraged to complain about the administrative decisions of the Land and city authorities, bypassing the official channels. In Hamburg, for example, between January and March 1937 alone 15 000 complaints were made, some of which the

Reichsstatthalter-Gauleiter, Karl Kaufmann, dealt with personally.[99] They sponsored arts festivals and produced plans for massive building projects to glorify the Gau, the Party and themselves. They were the star turn in a constant round of district and Gau Party rallies and benefited from the reflected glory of visits to the Gau by national leaders. All these events were extensively reported in the local press in what one historian has described as 'ritualized reporting on ritualized events'.[100]

The Gauleiters often adopted a kind of populist socialism. The most striking example of this was the 'People's Socialist Self-help' *(Volkssozialistische Selbsthilfe)* organization, which Gauleiter Bürckel initiated in the Palatinate in 1933.[101] This was basically a programme by which the Party put pressure on state and local government officials and local businesses to contribute to a fund that would 'enable the Palatinate to stand on its own feet and be no longer dependent on any help from the Reich or the state'.[102] Bürckel, who was on the 'left' wing of the NSDAP, also introduced a number of other fairly radical measures designed to solve the unemployment problem, which was particularly acute in his Gau. However, his ultimate aim, which was to establish the basis for an independent social policy in the Palatinate, was thwarted when the VS was forcibly absorbed in the Reich welfare scheme, the *Winterhilfswerk*. Other Gauleiters also adopted forms of populist socialism. Much of this was rhetorical but could also involve gestures, such as the Gauleiter of Hamburg projecting himself as the protector of the dock workers by defending their high wage levels.[103] Gauleiters tried to project an image as benevolent patriarchal rulers by presenting Christmas gifts to needy children and visiting bombed out families. During the war, the Agriculture Ministry allocated special allowances of coffee, cigarettes and chocolate for distribution to cities in the immediate aftermath of serious air raids, popularly known as Zitterkaffee, and significantly these were distributed by the Gauleiters.

How then did this affect German federalism? After the war the Reich Finance Minister, Schwerin von Krosigk, recalled that some of the Gauleiter 'proved to be more hard-bitten federalists than their Länder Prime Minister predecessors'.[104] Gauleiter Kaufmann of Hamburg is a particularly striking example of a Gauleiter who developed a role as the advocate of his Land's interests.[105] Thus, through the Greater Hamburg Law of 1937 he secured the acquisition of Prussian territory in the shape of Altona and Harburg-Wilhelmsburg. He also pressed the interests of the Hamburg economy at a time when it was finding it difficult to recover from the depression. At the end of 1934, Kaufmann initiated a meeting between Hamburg's political and business leaders and the

Reich ministers attended by Hitler himself, at which Hamburg was given official status as a distressed area. He continued his lobbying on behalf of Hamburg business interests into the war years, securing the placement of Hamburg political and business leaders in key posts in the various German occupation administrations.

Finally, on a semi-comic note, the Reichsstatthalter and Gauleiter of Saxony, Martin Mutschmann, complained repeatedly to the propaganda minister, Joseph Goebbels, about the prevalence of jokes about the Saxons on the radio. According to Goebbels, Mutschmann 'watches out like a gun dog to see whether anything is going to be done to the Saxons. In general, the result is that he makes the Saxons even more ridiculous than they are already'.[106] This suggests that Mutschmann, who came from Saxony, had a certain loyalty to his Land and its people and was prepared to act on it, although his corrupt lifestyle and crude and brutal behaviour made him unpopular within the state.[107]

The key Nazi concepts of 'national community' (*Volksgemeinschaft*) and compatriot or national comrade (*Volksgenosse*) dominated official discourse about the political identity of the individual with the clear aim of submerging or at least subordinating other identities and loyalties including those of Land, region or locality. However, in the cultural sphere attempts were made to sustain some traditions that could be incorporated into the official Nazi narrative by giving them a particular gloss. Thus, for example, in those cases where their Gau boundaries coincided with historic or Länder borders the Gauleiter could and did encourage and exploit regional traditions as a means of legitimizing their rule vis-à-vis both the population of their Gau and the Reich leadership. This was the case, for example, in the Palatinate, where the Gauleiter, Josef Bürckel, tried hard to achieve independence from Bavaria, though he also sought a merger with the newly acquired Saar, thereby indicating that his main goal was an expansion of his own power.[108] Where the Gau did not coincide with such boundaries the Gauleiter often still tried to encourage and instrumentalize the various regional traditions within their Gau to legitimate their rule. For example, Alfred Meyer, Gauleiter of Westphalia-North and Reichsstatthalter of Lippe-Detmold developed a cult of Hermann the Cherusker, the German tribal chief who defeated the Roman army in an epic battle in the Teutoburg Forest and whose exploits had already been commemorated by the erection in the late nineteenth century of an enormous statue near Detmold.[109] Meyer also organized an annual Grabbe festival to celebrate the nineteenth-century playwright, Dietrich Grabbe. Grabbe was viewed as an appropriate subject for Nazi celebration because he sought to develop an original German dramatic style and his plays dealt with heroic historical figures. The attempt to develop a Nazi literary icon for the Catholic Münsterland by projecting Annette von Droste-Hülshoff as a precursor of Nazi 'blubo' values proved less effective.

Finally, in order to integrate the industrialized western part of the Gau into the symbolic world of the Nazi 'national community' the Party adopted the figure of the coal miner as a Nazi icon. In the words of an article in a Gelsenkirchen paper: 'From the dark pit to the bright light of day the miner daily wends his hopeful way ... And so for us the miner's lamp becomes a symbol of Germany's rise, a sign of the honesty of hard work, a symbol of our comradeship and national community from which nobody is excluded.'[110] Moreover, they popularized this image by associating the Party with the immensely popular and successful football club, Schalke 04, which was based in the Westphalian coal fields.[111]

However, significantly, where the interests of the Gau clashed with those of a historic province or Land the Gauleiter invariably gave priority to the interests of his Gau. Thus, when, during the 1930s the route of the new east–west autobahn was being planned through north-west Germany, Alfred Meyer refused to intervene on behalf of the Land Lippe of which he was Reichsstatthalter for fear of antagonizing the population of the other part of his Gau Westphalia-North who also had an interest in the autobahn.[112] Similarly, during the war, two successive Gauleiters of Westphalia-South sought to split the province of Westphalia in two, so that they could become Oberpräsident of a new province instead of being subjected to Gauleiter Meyer of Westphalia-North as Oberpräsident. Significantly, however, Hitler blocked their move.[113]

The threat of Gau particularism became increasingly acute from 1938 onwards as a result of two separate developments. The first occurred when Germany began annexing new territory in Austria, Czechoslovakia, and Poland. For here the German authorities could afford to act as if they were dealing with a tabula rasa and impose their own system of administration without the same fear of arousing vested interests that existed in the so-called *Altreich*. The model that was employed was the one that had been developed in the Reich Interior Ministry during the early years of the regime but which, with the exception of the Greater Hamburg Law of 1937, they had not been able to introduce because of Hitler's veto – the *Reichsgau*.[114] Thus, the Sudetenland was established as a so-called Reich Gau in October 1938 and, on 14 April 1939, Austria was divided into seven Reich Gaus. This involved a powerful *Reichsmittelinstanz* in the shape of a Reichsstatthalter who was simultaneously Gauleiter but who had greater powers than his equivalent in the *Altreich*.

The intention was clearly for the new *Reichsgaue* to be in turn the model for the future administrative structure of the whole of the Greater German Reich to be introduced in the *Altreich* as soon as circumstances would permit. However, in fact there was a lack of conviction within the Reich Interior Ministry about whether the Austrian and Sudetenland Reich Gaus, which in any case differed from one another, would actually provide an appropriate model. In particular, there was a sharp difference of views about the role of the Reichsstatthalter in the Reich Gaus between the Reich Interior Ministry on the one hand and the Party leadership on the other. Thus, while the Interior Ministry continued to envisage the Reichsstatthalter being subordinate to itself, the Party leadership in the shape of the Staff of the Führer's Deputy/Party Chancellery regarded the Reichsstatthalter as primarily Party officials who would set the political guidelines independently of the Interior Ministry and would treat the state officials in the Reich Gaus as their executive agents implementing an agenda set by the Party.[115] However, the Reichsstatthalter of the new Reich Gaus saw themselves as subordinate neither to the Reich Interior Ministry nor to the Party Chancellery but rather as directly answerable to Hitler, a view that he officially endorsed.

The second development, which encouraged the growth of Gau particularism, was Hitler's decision on the outbreak of war to appoint in each of the 12 military districts a Gauleiter to the new post of Reich Defence Commissioner, who was responsible for coordinating defence matters on the home front.[116] Initially, their functions were limited, basically because at that stage very little defence was needed since Germany was on the offensive. However, from 1942 onwards, as the pressures of war on the German home front increased, with the Allied air raids and the increasing need to mobilize all available resources for the war effort, so the role of the Reich Defence Commissioners increased and in 1942 Hitler abandoned the division according to military districts, and replaced it with one based on the boundaries of the Party Gaus, so that now every Gauleiter (there were 41) was a Reich Defence Commissioner. This change reflected Hitler's belief that only the Party had the determination and the ideological commitment to see the war through to a successful conclusion. There was also the fact that, with the growing difficulties of administration, increasingly only senior Party officials had the political clout to cut through red tape and take emergency action.

The other state and military agencies then began to adapt their administrative boundaries to this new Gau arrangement. For example, on 20 April 1942, Gau Economic Chambers were established,[117] and, on 1 August 1943, Gau Labour Offices were created in place of the existing Land labour offices, reflecting the fact that the General Plenipotentiary for Labour Mobilization, Fritz Sauckel, had nominated the Gauleiters as his representatives in the regions.[118] Finally, as the crisis on the home front deepened after 1942 so, in a desperate attempt to fulfil their main function of maintaining the morale of their Gaus, and not least in an attempt to sustain their own personal reputations, the Gauleiters began to assert the interests of their Gaus at the expense of the broader Reich interests as articulated by the Reich ministries. Hence they fought to prevent local businesses and plants being closed down and even resorted to confiscating the contents of food and fuel transports passing through their Gaus.[119]

Thus, by 1945 German federalism had long since ceased to exist. The German Länder had effectively become hollow shells, their powers drained away by, on the one hand, a centralistic but fragmented Reich administration, which was increasingly paralysed by the jungle of competencies created by Reich departmental particularism and, on the other, by a Gau particularism, in which the Nazi party challenged the authority of state and local government at every level and was trying to impose its own administrative boundaries, the *Gaue*, in place of those of the traditional Länder.

Notes

1. F. A. Medicus, *Reichsreform und Länderkonferenz* (Berlin 1930), pp. 65ff.
2. T. Kirk, ed., *The Longman Companion to Nazi Germany* (London 1995), p. 75.
3. See especially G. Schulz, *Zwischen Demokratie und Diktatur*, i, *Die Periode der Konsolidierung und der Revision des Bismarckschen Reichsaufbaus 1919–1930* (Berlin 1987).
4. See Wolfgang Benz, *Süddeutschland in der Weimarer Republik. Ein Beitrag zur deutschen Innenpolitik 1918–1923* (Berlin 1970).
5. See Schulz, op. cit., pp. 564ff.
6. On Erzberger and his reforms see Klaus Epstein, *Matthias Erzberger and the Dilemma of German Democracy* (Princeton 1959), pp. 381ff., and Gerald D. Feldman, *The German Disorder. Politics, Economics, and Society in the German Inflation* (Oxford and New York 1997), pp. 161ff. According to Feldman, Erzberger's tax reform, which basically transferred the administration of

taxation and income tax from the Länder to the Reich, 'next to the actual creation of the Republic itself ... probably was the most revolutionary act in the history of the Weimar Republic' (ibid, p. 161).

7. For the following see K. D. Bracher, *Die Auflösung der Weimarer Republik,* 3rd edn (Villingen 1966), pp. 571ff.
8. For the Reich Constitution of 1871 see Hans Boldt, ed., *Reich und Länder. Texte zur deutschen Verfassunsgeschichte im 19. Und 20. Jahrhundert* (Munich 1987), pp. 456 ff, for these clauses pp. 469–71.
9. For the crucial role of school teachers in this process in Bavaria see Werner K. Blessing, *Staat und Kirche in der Gesellschaft: Institutionelle Autorität und mentaler Wandel in Bayern während des 19. Jahrhunderts* (Göttingen 1982).
10. For the relevant clauses of the Weimar Constitution (§§1–19) see Boldt, *Reich und Länder*, pp. 490–4. On South Germany during this period, see Wolfgang Benz, op. cit.
11. On Bavaria during these years see K. Schwend, *Bayern zwischen Monarchie und Diktatur. Beiträge zur bayerischen Frage in der Zeit 1918 bis 1933* (Munich 1954).
12. Reichstag election statistics in J. Noakes and G. Pridham, eds, *Nazism 1919–1945,* i, *The Rise to Power* (Exeter 1983), p. 83.
13. *Das Programm der NSDAP und seine weltanschaulichen Grundgedanken von Dipl. Ing. Gottfried Feder* (Munich 1927), p. 22.
14. Ibid, p. 38.
15. *Mein Kampf* (London 1969), pp. 199. For an example of a Hitler speech along these lines see Eberhard Jaeckel, ed., *Hitler. Sämtliche Aufzeichnungen* (Stuttgart 1980), p. 106.
16. *Mein Kampf*, pp. 505–26.
17. Ibid, pp. 524–5.
18. Ibid, p. 526.
19. W. Baum, 'Die "Reichsreform" im Dritten Reich' in *Vierteljahrshefte für Zeitgeschichte* 3.1.1955, p. 37.
20. For the following see K. D. Bracher, W. Sauer, G. Schulz, *Die nationalsozialistische Machtergreifung. Studien zur Errichtung des totalitären Herrschaftsystems in Deutschland 1933/34* (Opladen 1961), pp. 136ff.
21. See Albrecht Tyrell, *Führer befiehl ... Selbstzeugnisse aus der "Kampfzeit" der NSDAP. Dokumentation und Analyse* (Düsseldorf 1969), pp. 384–5.
22. *Reichsgestzblatt (RGBl.,)* I, 1933, p. 83.
23. See Bracher, Sauer, Schulz, op. cit., pp. 137ff.; K. Schwend, *Bayern zwischen Monarchie und Diktatur*, pp. 506ff.
24. See Noakes and Pridham, *Nazism*, p. 83.
25. Max Domarus, *Hitler Reden 1932 bis 1945,* i, *Triumph* (Wiesbaden 1973), pp. 231–2.
26. K. Repgen, ed., *Akten der Reichskanzlei. Die Regierung Hitler 1933–1938*, Teil I, 1933–4, Bd 1 (Boppard 1995), Doc. Nr. 78, p. 273.
27. *RGBl.* I, 1933, Nr 25, p. 141.
28. *RGBl. I*, 1933, p. 153f.
29. See note 26 above.
30. *Völkischer Beobachter,* 2.9.1933.
31. Diehl-Thiele, *Partei und Staat im Dritten Reich* (Munich 1969), pp. 43–4.
32. On Gauleiter as Reichsstatthalter see P. Hüttenberger, *Die Gauleiter. Studie zum Wandel des Machtgefüges in der NSDAP* (Stuttgart 1969), pp. 75ff. On

Gauleiter, see also Walter Ziegler, 'Gaue und Gauleiter im Dritten Reich' in H. Möller, A. Wirsching and W. Ziegler, eds, *Nationalsozialismus in der Region. Beiträge zur regionalen und lokalen Forschung und zum internationalen Vergleich* (Munich 1996), pp. 139–60.

33. On the position in Bavaria see Jochen Klenner, *Verhältnis von Partei und Staat 1933–1945 dargestellt am Beispiel Bayerns* (Munich 1974), pp. 44ff.
34. I. Kershaw, *Hitler 1889–1936: Hubris* (London 1998), p. 470.
35. *RGBl. I*, 1933, p. 225. For the genesis and operation of the first Reichsstatthalter law see Bracher, Sauer, Schulz, op. cit., 464ff., Peter Diehl-Thiele, *Partei und Staat im Dritten Reich* (Munich 1969), pp. 37ff, and Hans-Jürgen Sengotta, *Der Reichsstatthalter in Lippe 1933 bis 1939. Reichsrechtliche Bestimmungen und politische Praxis* (Detmold 1976), pp. 9ff.
36. Sengotta, op. cit., p. 23.
37. See Hüttenberger, op. cit., pp. 82ff.
38. Baum, op. cit., p. 39.
39. K. Repgen, ed., *Akten der Reichskanzlei. Die Regierung Hitler 1933–1938*, Teil I 1933–34, Bd 2 (Boppard 1995), pp. 185ff.
40. Sengotta, op. cit., pp. 138ff.
41. Ibid.
42. Diehl-Thiele, op. cit., pp. 50ff.
43. Sengotta, op. cit., pp. 120ff.
44. See note 29 above.
45. K. Repgen, op. cit., vol. 1, no. 120.
46. See note 20 above.
47. For the following see Bracher, Sauer, Schulz, op. cit., p. 589 and Baum, op. cit., p. 40.
48. For the following see Baum, op. cit., p. 41, Bracher, Sauer, Schulz, op. cit., pp. 586ff., Diehl-Thiele, op. cit., pp. 81ff, M. Broszat, *Der Staat Hitlers* (Munich 1969), pp. 151ff., Günter Neliba, *Der Legalist des Unrechtstaates. Wilhelm Frick. Eine politische Biographie* (Paderborn 1992), pp. 99ff.
49. *RGBl. I*, 1934, p. 75.
50. A. Lepawsky, 'The Nazis reform the Reich', *American Political Science Review,* 30 (1936), p. 327.
51. Baum, op. cit., p. 42.
52. Bracher, Sauer, Schulz, op. cit., p. 598.
53. RGBl. I 1934, p. 85.
54. For the following see Bracher, Sauer, Schulz, op. cit., p. 600, and Baum, op. cit., pp. 40ff.
55. Baum, op. cit., p. 49 and R. G. Wells, 'The Liquidation of the German Länder', *American Political Science Review* 30 (1936), p. 360.
56. Bracher, Sauer, Schulz, op. cit., p. 602; Broszat, op. cit., p. 156.
57. For the following see Diehl-Thiele, op. cit., pp. 113ff, and Hüttenberger, op. cit., pp. 75ff.
58. *RGBl. I,* 1934, p. 1190.
59. Broszat, op. cit., p. 150.
60. Diehl-Thiele, op. cit., pp. 68, Broszat, op. cit., p. 152; Sengotta, op. cit., pp. 33ff.
61. Bundesarchiv Berlin (BAB), R 43 II/1376.
62. Broszat, op. cit., p. 152.

63. Diehl-Thiele, op. cit., pp. 68–9; Broszat, op. cit., p. 153.
64. Ibid.
65. Sengotta, op. cit., p. 41.
66. Hüttenberger, op. cit., p. 89, footnote 43.
67. *RGBl. I*, 1935, p. 65.
68. Diehl-Thiele, op. cit., p. 72; Broszat, op. cit., p. 157; Sengotta, op. cit., p. 41.
69. Diehl-Thiele, op. cit., pp. 46ff. After the Greater Hamburg Law of 26 January 1937, which created a 'city Gau', Kaufmann also took over control of local government reducing the Bürgermeister Karl Krogmann to a subordinate role.
70. This subordination was underlined by a letter from the Reich Interior Minister to the Reichstatthalter of 30 January 1935, which warned them that they only had the power to issue *provisional* instructions to the Länder governments *(Reichsmittelbehörden)* without consulting the relevant Reich ministry in an emergency. 'The Reichstatthalters do *not* have *a general right to give instructions.'* Italics in the original. See *Akten der Reichskanzlei. Die Regierung Hitler Band II 1934/1935. Teilband 1* (Boppard 1996), p. 343.
71. Sengotta, op. cit., p. 58.
72. Bundesarchiv Berlin (BAB), R 43 II/494.
73. Wells, op. cit., p. 360.
74. For the following see Bracher, Sauer, Schulz, op. cit., pp. 607ff, and Broszat, op. cit., p. 158.
75. Wells, op. cit., p. 359.
76. For the following see Broszat, op. cit., pp. 158ff, and Baum, op. cit., pp. 46f., 50.
77. Baum, op. cit., pp. 42, 28.
78. Ibid, p. 50.
79. Ibid, p. 51.
80. For the following see Sengotta, op. cit., pp. 388ff.
81. Baum, op. cit., p. 51.
82. Elke Fröhlich, ed., *Die Tagebücher von Joseph Goebbels*, Teil I, *Aufzeichnungen 1923–1941*, Band 9, Dezember 1940–Juli 1941, (Munich 1998), p. 127.
83. Elke Fröhlich, ed., *Die Tagebücher von Joseph Goebbels*, Teil II, *Diktate 1941–1945*, Band 4, April–Juni 1942 (Munich 1995), p. 585.
84. *Hitler's Table Talk. Hitler's conversations recorded by Martin Bormann*, ed. Hugh R. Trevor-Roper (Oxford 1988), pp. 533–4.
85. Elke Fröhlich, ed., *Die Tagebücher von Joseph Goebbels* Teil II, *Diktate 1941–1945*, Band 8, April–Juni 1943 (Munich 1993), p. 271.
86. Elke Fröhlich, ed., *Die Tagebücher von Joseph Goebbels* Teil II, *Diktate 1941–1945*, Band 10, Oktober–Dezember 1943 (Munich 1994), p. 72.
87. Wells, op. cit. p. 332.
88. *RGBl. I*, 1934, p. 375.
89. *RGBl. I*, 1934, p. 1214.
90. *RGBl. I*, 1935, pp. 49ff.
91. *RGBl. I*, 1936, p. 487.
92. Broszat, op. cit., pp. 162ff.
93. See note 59 above.
94. See D. Rebentisch, *Führerstaat und Verwaltung im Zweiten Weltkrieg* (Stuttgart 1989), pp. 283 ff.
95. F. Bajohr, 'Gauleiter in Hamburg. Zur Person und Tätigkeit Karl Kaufmanns', *VjZG*, 43 (1995), p. 282.

96. On the Gauleiters in general, see Hüttenberger, op. cit.
97. Sengotta, op. cit., pp. 157ff.
98. For the following see especially Bajohr, op. cit., H-J. Heinz, *NSDAP und Verwaltung in der Pfalz. Allgemeine innere Verwaltung und kommunale Selbstverwaltung im Spannungsfeld nationalsozialistischer Herrschaftspraxis 1933–1939. Ein Beitrag zur zeitgeschichtlichen Landeskunde* (Mainz 1994), pp. 105ff and passim, and H. J. Priamus, 'Alfred Meyer-Selbstinszenierung eines Gauleiters', in H. J. Priamus and S. Goch, eds, *Macht der Propaganda oder Propaganda der Macht. Inszenierung nationalsozialistischer Politik im 'Dritten Reich' am Beispiel der Stadt Gelsenkirchen* (Essen 1992), pp. 48–67.
99. Bajohr, op. cit., p. 284.
100. Priamus, op. cit., p. 66.
101. For the following see Heinz, op. cit., pp. 246–305.
102. Ibid., p. 249.
103. Kaufmann also lobbied against a proposed wage-cut for building workers in Hamburg in spring 1935, while Gauleiter Mutschmann of Saxony lobbied against the abolition of Sunday and Public Holiday bonuses on the outbreak of war. See Timothy W. Mason, *Arbeiterklasse und Volksgemeinschaft. Dokumente und Materialien zur deutschen Arbeiterpolitik* (Opladen 1975), pp. 1132–4.
104. Broszat, op. cit., p. 154.
105. Bajohr, op. cit., passim.
106. Diary entry for 2.2.1942 in Elke Fröhlich, *Die Tagebücher von Joseph Goebbels*, Teil II, *Diktate 1941–1945*, Band 3, Januar–März 1942 (Munich 1994),p. 357.
107. On Mutschmann see Hermann Weiss, ed., *Biographisches Lexikon zum Dritten Reich* (Frankfurt am Main 1998), p. 330.
108. Heinz, op. cit., pp. 105–241.
109. H. J. Priamus, 'Regionale Aspekte in der Politik des nordwestfälischen Gauleiters Alfred Meyer' in H. Möller, A. Wirsching and W. Ziegler, eds, op. cit., pp. 182ff.
110. Ibid, p. 189.
111. Ibid, p. 190 and S. Goch, 'FC Schalke 04 – Instumentalisierung des Zuschauersports', in H. J. Priamus and S. Goch, eds, op. cit., pp. 81–92.
112. Sengotta, op. cit., pp. 282ff.
113. K. Teppe, *Provinz, Partei, Staat. Zur provinziellen Selbstverwaltung im Dritten Reich am Beispiel Westfalens* (Münster 1977), pp. 127ff.
114. For the following see D. Rebentisch, op. cit., pp. 163–282, Baum op. cit., pp. 51f, Broszat, op. cit., pp. 162ff., Hüttenberger, op. cit., pp. 138ff., Heinz, op. cit., pp. 198 and passim, A. V. Boerner, 'Towards Reichsreform – The Reichsgaue', *American Political Science Review*, 33 (1939), pp. 853ff.
115. See Teppe, op. cit., pp. 225ff., Rebentisch, op. cit., pp. 273ff.
116. *RGBl., I*, 1939, p. 1565 and Rebentisch, op. cit., pp. 132ff.
117. *RGBl., I*, 1942, p. 189.
118. A. Kranig, *Lockung und Zwang. Zur Arbeitsverfassung im Dritten Reich* (Stuttgart 1983), p. 158.
119. A. Speer, *Inside the Third Reich* (London 1970), pp. 219, 311ff, 412; Hüttenberger, op. cit., pp. 183ff.

7
Democratic Centralism and Regionalism in the GDR

Mary Fulbrook

Germany is renowned for its federal traditions. The Federal Republic of Germany, with its own experience of relatively successful regional devolution, was at the heart of moves towards closer European integration in the latter half of the twentieth century. And, at the turn of the millennium, in a situation of increasing globalization with the proliferation of international and multinational organizations and global cultural trends, when the nation-state seems no longer to be the location at which all decision-making and identity formation is automatically concentrated, there has been a new interest in and re-evaluation of a degree of devolution of sovereignty and identity downwards as well as upwards. Suddenly, traditions of federalism and regionalism have become the focus of more positive interest.

One might add: it was not ever thus. At least among Anglo-Saxons, the nation-state has long been a taken-for-granted unit of analysis, the automatic focus of sovereignty and identity formation. For a long time, decentralization, or 'failure' to do The Decent Thing (along the lines of England and France) and develop a centralized nation-state, was seen as a fatal flaw in Germany's long-term trajectory on the road to 'belated' nationhood and a root cause of the Nazi catastrophe. However, the teleological narrative of Germany's alleged 'failure' to centralize can very easily be inverted, given Germany's specific twentieth-century experience of more wilfully centralized states. After Hitler, decentralization in the new guise of federalism has suddenly been seen one of the more positive lessons of German history for a post-Holocaust world. Perhaps, however, the lesson of these ruminations should be more abstract. Centralization and federalism should not automatically be equated with the question of dictatorial control or democratic input at whatever level.

We need however to make a more important distinction. While federalism refers to a rather specific form of political structure (varying degrees of institutionalized regional devolution within a larger political whole), regionalism is an altogether vaguer concept. It may refer to informal as well as formal structures and bases of power; to regional differences in dialect or accent; distinctive regional socioeconomic profiles; or to the pronounced development and maintenance of distinctive regional cultural identities. While presupposing some sort of 'whole' within which distinctive regions can be identified on one or more of a set of criteria agreed to be relevant, this 'whole' need not be nearly so clearly or institutionally defined as in discussions of federalism.

Let us then focus specifically on the German Democratic Republic. This nicely demolishes any notion of teleology or assumptions about federalism being a key element in some alleged German national identity, coexisting as it did with the western Federal Republic of Germany, yet rapidly demolishing traditions of federalism (if not entirely of regionalism).

The five Länder from which the GDR was constituted were abolished by the ruling communist SED (Socialist Unity Party) within less than three years of the state's foundation. The new system of 'democratic centralism' was, at least by most western interpretations of the terms, more centralist than democratic. The GDR thus presents an interesting test case with respect to the supposedly centuries-old German traditions of federalism and regionalism. Any central power which is so apparently successful in overcoming such allegedly deep-rooted traditions of regional diversity must be able to provide lessons on the conditions under which regional identities both develop and vanish. Moreover, there may be a little more to be said about the nature of the relations between the centre and the regions, or the centre and the grass roots (if not any actual federalism) in the GDR, to try to understand in a little more detail the complexities of the system which did develop in place of a formal system of political federalism.

There are thus two general sets of questions which I shall address in this chapter. I shall look first at the ways in which a new political system developed and explore what the official concept of democratic centralism meant in theory and practice, with respect to the relations between state and society, or 'ordinary people' at the grass roots. Second, I shall switch to the altogether more amorphous question of regionalism, or the maintenance and transformation of distinctive regional identities. I shall focus particularly on two examples: the implications for SED rule of regionally based religious subcultures; and the case of the linguistically and culturally distinct Sorbian population of the Lausitz region.

I shall present two main sets of theses. First, I shall argue that we do, indeed, need a model of power in the GDR which emphasizes centralism rather than democracy (at least as understood in the western sense of the term); but that this could only work through a system embedded in the regions, and diffused through the relative willingness of large numbers of people to abide by the rules of the system and cooperate with its mode of functioning over long stretches of time, under particular historical circumstances. Not all means were repressive, and not all motives were malign. Elsewhere, I develop the notion of a 'participatory dictatorship' to encapsulate this peculiar mode of involvement of the people.[1]

Second, I shall argue that while a sense of regionalism is to some extent an inherited cultural idiom, as outlined by Maiken Umbach in the Introduction to this volume, it is also in large measure a product of political and socioeconomic experience, and as such is historically malleable and open to change. Institutional regionalism of the one remaining autonomous social institution, the Christian churches, did pose a major problem for the SED's policies of co-option and control. The institutional devolution and regional diversity of the churches proved problematic for the state's attempts to control dissent under the umbrella of the churches in the 1980s. But even here, the state ironically produced a form of 'GDR-Christianity' which subsided with the collapse of the GDR itself. A more diffuse regionalism in a cultural sense was sustained in the GDR only when and where it was in the SED's interests to do so, for purposes such as fostering tourism, international respectability with respect to furtherance of minority cultures, and co-option of particular subcultural groups. Regionalism in the wider cultural sense was overridden by other social, economic and political developments in the GDR, such that regional identities became ever less salient. In their place grew a sense of 'GDR identity', further confirmed by distinctive differences between East and West Germans (*Ossis* and *Wessis*) after the fall of the Wall and formal political unification. Thus the main legacy of the SED to the history of German regionalism to date is to have created a new 'ex-GDR' wide regional identity, arguably overriding, or coexisting with, previously existing conceptions of regionalism in this geographical area: that of the *Ossis*.

The general moral of all this is that regionalism is not some intrinsic historical and geopolitical given in the German-speaking area of central Europe, but is a constantly changing phenomenon, susceptible to relatively rapid historical reshaping and transformation. Federalism, or regionally relatively autonomous institutions of one sort or another can clearly play an important role in serving to maintain or indeed even create and foster regional diversity.

'Democratic centralism' and inputs from below

The undoubted fact of communist control in a centralized state has led many scholars to adopt the concept of totalitarianism to summarize the political structure – and indeed in some cases the entire history – of the GDR. This cold war concept – combining as it does castigation with a claim to description and explanation – has witnessed a remarkable resurrection with respect to analyses of the GDR, adopted even by the parliamentary committee of inquiry, the *Enquetekommission*.[2] However, a closer look suggests that we need a more complex model than is offered by analyses presupposing a simple pyramid of power, even where these assume that the attempts at total control will never be totally successful, totally without opposition or resistance.[3] Scholars in the traditions of social history and the history of everyday life have been playing with the idea of a *'durchherrschte Gesellschaft'*, a 'society drenched through with political authority'. First coined by Alf Lüdtke, and taken up in an influential article by Jürgen Kocka, this concept appeared to offer a better purchase on the everyday experience of power in the GDR.[4] However, there remain problems. On the one hand, critics such as Klaus Schroeder consider that use of a notion of 'authority' rather than 'power' fails adequately to distinguish between the GDR and western societies where the state also intimately affects all manner of aspects of society.[5] On the other hand, even those sympathetic in principle with a social history approach have pointed out that there is something of a mirror image involved here, with a shift of focus to resistance from below rather than oppression from above, but still essentially presupposing some form of pyramid of power. In the context of these wider debates over interpretation, an analysis of both the formal structures and the character of the exercise of power – particularly the links between centre and grass roots – is of some importance.

On its foundation in 1949, the GDR was formally a federal state, consisting of five reconstituted Länder (as well as Berlin), with both a lower house and an upper house of parliament. Formally, its federal constitution was quite compatible with that of the western Federal Republic of Germany, although of course in practice communist manipulation of the political process rendered it less than democratic in the western sense of the term. It was not long before the constitutional landscape was brought into line with the new political realities. As sizeable political units with considerable strength and importance in terms of regional government, the five Länder were abolished in 1952 and replaced by 14 much smaller *Bezirke* (15 if one includes East Berlin), which in turn were subdivided into 191 rural *Kreise* and 28 urban *Kreise* (the larger of which were again subdivided into *Stadtbezirke*). In 1958 the upper house of parliament, which supposedly represented the Länder, was formally abolished too. The new constitution of 1968 finally confirmed these changes formally.

These changes in political organization took place as part of the dramatic reorganization of life in the GDR in the summer of 1952, under Ulbricht's slogan, proclaimed at the Second Party Conference in July 1952, of the 'Building of Socialism' (*Aufbau des Sozialismus*). Following Stalin's abortive initiative in March 1952 to propose a united neutral Germany (the so-called 'Stalin Notes'), in a failed attempt to prevent the integration of Adenauer's West Germany into western military alliances, a new hard line was adopted in the Soviet bloc. A 'People's Army' was to be formally established in the GDR ('Create a people's army without uproar – pacifist period is over', as Pieck noted after a discussion with Stalin in April)[6] with increased expenditure on militarization accompanied by a visibly more aggressive tone in the propaganda of class warfare. In May, there was a dramatic tightening up of the border with the creation of the closed area or *Sperrgebiet*, which involved the forcible expulsions of around 12 000 people who were categorized as 'politically unreliable elements' from the five-kilometre strip along the inner-German border. At the July Party Conference, new socioeconomic measures were announced, including the enforced collectivization of agriculture into LPGs (*Landwirtschaftliche Produktionsgenossenschaften*) and PGHs (*Produktionsgenossenschaften des Handwerks*). Once any possibility of reunification with West Germany had faded from the perceived political agenda (though not yet from popular aspirations or general discourse), the construction of a very different state and society within fortified borders was to be pushed ahead as fast as possible in East Germany. The replacement of the Länder with smaller *Bezirke* was part of this massive set of wider shifts in emphasis and direction.

General accounts of this territorial reorganization tend to emphasise enhanced central control (the 'centralism' part of 'democratic centralism'). Ulrich Maehlert, for example, summarizes it as follows:

The transformation of the Länder into fifteen administrative districts (*Verwaltungsbezirke*) permitted a further centralization of the political system as well as a reorganization of the state and party apparatus, which was accompanied by a renewed 'cleansing' of personnel and thus corresponded to the security interests that had already been formulated, months earlier, by the Soviets.[7]

Klaus Schroeder tells us that the result was the creation of 'a socialist centralized non-pluralist state (*Einheitsstaat*) on the Soviet model'.[8]

Even GDR Prime Minister Otto Grotewohl's justification to the Volkskammer comments remarkably frankly on the obstacles which the democratic process of parliaments and governments in the Länder had put in the way of achieving SED goals:

> The state apparatus in the Länder, with their parliaments and governments, has proved to be a constraint on our [great political] task, a source of bureaucratic obstacles and falsifications, in the realization of our progressive goals.[9]

There was then a clear political impetus behind the abolition of the Länder: the enhancement of SED control and the more efficient implementation of policies which had been decided at the centre, without undue hindrance from strong regional governments and local bureaucracies getting in the way.

Having removed the intervening layer of the Länder, the new system was designed to achieve an integrated system from the highest to the lowest levels – from the central organs of party and state down through the parallel state and party bodies in the *Bezirke* and *Kreise* through to the level of the basic organizations in the factories, combines and residential areas.

While the 'centralism' aspect is thus clear enough, there are several questions to be addressed with respect to the 'democratic' part of the concept of 'democratic centralism'. Needless to say, the self-representation of the meaning of 'democratic centralism' by the SED was a little different from interpretations current in the west. The official definition of course emphasized the ultimate power of the central party apparatus, and the crucial importance of collective responsibility and party discipline. It also, however, at least formally gave a much larger role to input and control from below than is usually noted. For example, the definition in the *Kleines Politisches Wörterbuch* includes the following phrase, which is more interesting in reality than might at first blush appear (particularly when embedded in the less than enthralling dense text of this encyclopedia):

> unconditional binding nature of the decisions of the higher organs for the lower organs and the membership, whose manifold experiences flow into the decisions of the higher organs.[10]

A two-way process is specifically envisaged here. Moreover, there is to be a quite specific and explicit division of labour between the decisions of principle to be taken at the top and the manner of realization of these decisions at the grass roots:

> In the process, central state leadership and planning of social processes is to be increasingly concentrated on informed decisions on fundamental questions, and personal responsibility and initiative for the realization of state goals is to be fostered on the part of local state organs, *Kombinate*, factories, cooperatives, and institutions.[11]

It is therefore crucial to explore the extent to which real input from below was or was not possible.

It is important to emphasize at the outset that the general parameters of the GDR's existence were not open for discussion. What we are looking at here is the extent to which those operating within those parameters had any real input into discussions of policies on a more domestic scale: that is, the extent to which they could discuss and affect the ways in which the system, which could not itself be put into question, operated in practice. And the striking and almost self-contradictory summary of such an investigation must be that, for all the general existential problems of the GDR – the need effectively to imprison a population attracted by the affluence and democracy of the West, the spiralling cycle of economic decline – the attempt of a centralized state to extend very deep and very local roots among the population was remarkably successful. Within the general framework set by the all-encompassing state net, there were more real, if circumscribed, opportunities for widespread popular participation and political dialogue than is commonly recognized.

Certainly the system of smaller *Bezirke* and *Kreise*, in place of the old federal states, assisted the SED's aims of exerting increasing communist control. The various organizations of party, state and mass organizations, as well as the notorious state security police, the *Stasi*, formed a comprehensive network which went right down to the lowest levels of workplace, school and housing estate. Youth organizations, work brigades, leisure activities, all came in some way within the comprehensive web of GDR party-state organizations. Virtually no activity (with the notable exception of religious practice, to which we shall come in a moment) could be carried out in an institution or organization which was not part of a centralized state network for reaching deep into the localities.

The system took a long time to develop and become routinized. The main initial problem was that of unreliability of local functionaries, at least through the 1950s and the greater part of the 1960s. A key issue here appears to have been the ways in which local functionaries were embedded in local networks of family, friendship, and subcultural ties.[12] The 'cadre system' was of great importance here: at every level of every organization, those who were particularly promising in one way or another were selected, trained, their careers in the party hierarchy fostered. Alongside this was the system of party discipline and demotion of those who proved unreliable. What is remarkable is the way this was in large measure successful by the 1970s and 1980s. There was a clear generational shift between those who had memories of life before the GDR, and those born into the East German state who tended to take the organizational and institutional landscape more for granted, however critical, distanced or disaffected they might be. Conformity was the norm for the vast majority until the changed international landscape of 1989 dramatically altered the parameters of their existence.

By the 1980s, one in five of the adult population was a member of the SED. There was widespread and relatively willing participation in mass organizations. Virtually the entire adult working population were members of the state trade union organization, the FDGB. Although not an independent union in the western sense (since it tended to represent the state to the workers rather than the workers to the employers), the FDGB offered its members a variety of real benefits, ranging from services as primary organizer of excursions and holidays, to functions in dealing with conflicts at work, inadequate management, or poor working conditions. It was, in short, not simply or only a stooge of the state and propaganda organ of the party. And much of the evidence suggests a degree of involvement in other aspects of working life and organization, such as the socialist work brigades which were locations of gossip and camaraderie if not actual commitment to 'socialist overproduction'. Similar examples could be taken from other areas of

GDR social life in mass organizations, many of which offered real benefits and opportunities to their members, ranging from small animal breeding and cacti collection at one end of the spectrum, to the camping holidays and excursions of the state youth organization, the FDJ, or the superior sporting facilities offered by the paramilitary youth organization, the euphemistically named *Gesellschaft für Sport und Technik* (GST), at the other.

It is hard to ascertain how many – or perhaps better, how few – people were not involved at all in any of these organizations and activities once they were of school age. And in view of the question of relations between central control and grassroots input, it is important to note the way in which these organizations were not only means of exerting state control and influence over the population. Some of the organizations undoubtedly facilitated certain popular activities; all of them fulfilled functions not only of seeking to influence, but also trying to tap, and to respond to, popular opinion on a wide range of matters.

Even individual citizens could be drawn directly into the political process. An interesting example is provided by the purposes and practice of *Eingaben* (roughly, citizens' petitions), which might be in the nature of complaints, comments, requests, or responses to questions. Citizens' petitions or *Eingaben* were a constitutional right, first introduced in Article 3 of the 1949 constitution, periodically refined or amended (as in the *Erlass* of 27.2.1961) and reaffirmed in Article 103 of the 1974 (and 1968) constitution. They were intended to allow citizens to take an active part at all levels and in all institutions of the state, and to voice their grievances where there appeared to be problems. Citizens were entitled to an appropriate response within clearly specified and relatively short time periods (depending on the level of the body to which the complaints were addressed). These could be interpreted as a very direct form of grassroots input at the level most immediately relevant to a particular question, although it should be noted that citizens could only act as individuals, on the basis of individual grievances, and not as organized groupings with common platforms or programmes.

The records of state responses to *Eingaben* in the period from the mid-1960s to the late 1980s suggest on the whole that petitions were indeed taken seriously by the authorities. Complaints do appear in the main to have been thoroughly investigated and sources of dissatisfaction dealt with as well as possible under the circumstances in each case.[13] There appears to have been no predetermined pattern concerning whose side was taken on any particular type of issue: for example, investigations into disputes in factories where there were difficulties with the introduction of new technologies or new methods would come up with some surprising culprits: one could not assume in advance that it would be either the workers, or the managers, with whom fault would automatically be found. Even where there was no realistic possibility of delivering satisfaction (as with the frequent complaints about housing, where the GDR faced a well-nigh insurmountable problem) the SED functionaries who had to deal with the questions appear to have treated them with a high degree of earnestness and genuine concern to try to make at least some improvements, however limited.

Of course it is possible to criticize these *Eingaben*, from a number of perspectives. They were more or less automatically restricted to matters of everyday life: fundamental topics to do with the very existence and character of the SED state could not be addressed. And there were certain rituals and unspoken rules which had to be observed when citizens put their petitions forward.[14] Nevertheless, it would be quite mistaken either to dismiss them entirely as sham democratic, or to try to insert them into a theoretical framework which emphasizes solely control from above, resistance from below. They do indicate at least some minimal level of grassroots input into the system, with not always entirely unfounded hopes of satisfactory response or redress, on the part of a significant minority of people.

The SED intended the *Eingaben* system, as so much else, to be an asymmetrical two-way street, in which the leading party would never lose the upper hand, but in which active and willing grassroots participation and input would be genuinely fostered, and real grassroots enthusiasm encouraged. Of course these and other SED methods of encouraging a dialogue between state and society, such as the well-orchestrated discussions about issues such as the 1968 constitution, or the abortion law of 1972, were also intended to persuade and change, rather than just reflect, popular opinion; as such they were not comparable to any western form of democratic process. But at the same time the SED was very keen to tap into and where possible respond to popular opinion, and there is some evidence to suggest that certain viewpoints were to a degree respected or taken into account when formulating policy.

There was clearly no space for legitimate debate or 'democratic input' over those areas of policy which were in a sense existential: crucial to the character, essence, and continued existence of the GDR. Thus, one could not debate, for example, such fundamental topics as the leading role of the SED, the general onward march of history on the road to communism, or the legitimacy of specific measures which the SED deemed to be necessary means to achieve the ultimate goals, however disagreeable such means might appear to be (such as the Wall).

However, reading through the records of this undoubtedly central-ized state, it is quite striking to note the extent to which there was also, at the grass roots, the possibility of often remarkably frank and open input into discussions of matters which fell *inside* the general parame-ters thus defined. And to some extent this input took place at levels which appeared to operate according to the renowned principle of sub-sidiarity: taking decisions at the lowest possible level, closest to the issues at hand. The means were clearly not those with which western democrats are familiar. We are certainly not talking here about free, open elections in which there is a degree of choice between parties with alternative programmes and policies. Nevertheless, a greater degree of popular input was possible than one would think if one emphasized only the centralism aspect (as do the totalitarian theorists).

In other words there was a genuine interaction between 'above' and 'below' rather than a purely dictatorial relationship predicated solely on the threat or use of force, however cynical one is justified in being when using the word 'democratic' with respect to the GDR. Insofar as there was such interaction, it tended to take place at the level most immediate to the locality: a form not exactly of extreme devolution, but certainly of very local experience of (restricted) debate and input into central decision-making processes. The fact that this took a differ-ent form from those of western democracies (whether organized on federal principles or otherwise) should not lead us automatically to assume that it was purely a matter of central dictates from on high with absolutely no reference to those below. Politics in the GDR was not solely a matter of force, coercion and repression, but also of con-trolled and channelled incorporation of popular opinion in ways which, over a period of many years, came to seem increasingly 'normal' to the majority of those involved.

Regionalism in a centralized state

What then of historic patterns of regional identity under these chang-ing political conditions? In looking at regionalism in the GDR, it rapidly becomes apparent that strong institutional bases and specific socioeconomic and cultural profiles were vital for the preservation of any particular regional identity or subculture. But the only subculture that had sufficiently powerful institutional bases and international support not only to survive but even to challenge the SED's power was that of the Christian churches. Let us look first at the question of regional diversity in rather general terms, and then take a closer look at the specific examples of the Sorbs as an ethnic-linguistic, regionally based minority, and the regionally based Protestant churches as a cultural minority.

Regional diversity

The GDR was a relatively small state, with nevertheless quite distinctive regions. Geographically, the flat, sparsely populated, primarily agricultural north, with its extensive lakes and waterways, bordering on the sand dunes of the Baltic Sea, contrasted with the hillier south with its larger urban areas and higher concentrations of industry. Culturally, there were contrasts between the vast majority of primarily Protestant regions, and the small pockets of Catholicism (particularly in the Eichsfeld, a region of Thuringia straddling the border between East and West). Linguistically and culturally, the small Sorbian population in lower and upper Lusatia was an indigenous minority group with its own language, traditions, customs, culture; immigrant minorities tended to be dispersed across the GDR, though usually housed in segregated hostels rather than integrated into GDR society.[15] East Berlin – or, to use its official name, Berlin, Capital City of the GDR (*Berlin, Hauptstadt der DDR*) – tended to occupy a dominant position over all else. And a most unwelcome pocket was of course that little outpost of the West, a small capitalist island in the sea of communism, West Berlin.

Regional diversity in a socioeconomic or geographical sense was to some extent actively fostered in the GDR, not least because of the economic importance of specialization of function (agriculture versus industry, fruit-growing versus cattle or grains, tourism versus heavy chemical production, and so on). It was also was heavily emphasized in tourist literature, which played up 'historic traditions' – Meissen china, the Wartburg castle at Eisenach and the Luther trail, Goethe and Weimar, folk traditions in picturesque villages and waterways, the national heritage of ancient castles and medieval churches, former royal residences such as Schloss Sanssouci in Potsdam, now open for the enjoyment of the common people. Tourist literature also exploited geographical and climatic diversity, with brochures sporting idyllic images of winter sports in the Thuringian mountains, sandy summers at the

Baltic sea coast. This is regionalism appropriated by a centralized state, with a centralized tourist industry – Berolina – exploiting regional diversity to attract customers, particularly those from the West paying for pre-booked tours and overpriced Interhotels with hard western currency (the majority of East Germans had less choice in the matter of holiday destination). Although the point should not be over-stated (since the SED had far more obvious and arguably more important strategies for seeking to transform loyalty and gain popular support for the socialist project) the maintenance and fostering of apolitical regional traditions also appears to have played some role in SED attempts to root loyalty to a constructed, essentially artificial state in a more genuine sense of belonging to one's locality or immediate homeland – *Heimat* – in the classic pattern of a new state seeking to centralize loyalty by forging links between local, regional and national identities.[16] Thus regional traditions, names and related emotional investments were fostered through festivals, clubs or associations, and periodicals, under the supervisory umbrella of the mass organization for culture, the *Kulturbund*.[17] In this respect, older cultural idioms were preserved (if at the same time transformed through their communist reappropriations) and hence were readily available as part of the taken-for-granted cultural repertoire for rapid resurrection with the fall of the Wall.

However, undoubted geographical differences and state fostering of regional diversity for tourist purposes or the construction of loyalty to the new state do not necessarily amount to any persisting sense of regional identity based in active popular notions of self and otherness. We know that, historically, the areas which formed the GDR had very strong stereotypes of regional difference (urban/rural, Prussians versus Saxons, for example), but, apart from some reverberations in literary texts such as Günter de Bruyn's *Märkische Forschungen* or Brigitte Reimann's *Franziska Linkerhand*, these seem to have become of decreasing importance over time. There is some very limited evidence of East German versions of 'country bumpkin' images, or tensions between rural and urban areas, and there were of course jokes about regional dialects or accents, such as those centred on Walter Ulbricht's speech patterns (*'sächseln'*) or on the distinctive linguistic patterns of Berlinese. But on the whole historically rooted regional identities appear to have become less salient with the emergence of new GDR-created regional commonalities and differences, to do with distinctive patterns of privilege and deprivation.

A new politicized form of regional identity was to some extent created by the perceived privileges and consumer priority status for some areas rather than others: the showcases of East Berlin, always, and Leipzig at the times of international trade fairs, were the occasion of widespread criticism and regional envy. But at the same time, regional identities were less salient in everyday life than the conditions and constraints of living within the new communist state.

In very general terms, it can be argued that collective identities are a product of: common current experiences in everyday life; the construction of salient histories about a common past; and a strong sense of a common fate or common destiny rooted in the perceived demands and threats of the present.[18] Once one even begins to look at any one of these aspects in the GDR, it rapidly begins to become clear why a GDR identity began to emerge which overrode previous regional identities.

The GDR was not a state one could ignore. From the moment of entry into a state-run crèche or nursery onwards, GDR citizens were exposed to a distinctive mixture of ideology and collective experience (from collectivized potty training through the collective activities of the state youth organizations, to the work brigades and mass organizations of adult life). Increasing central control of all aspects of life, most notably the educational institutions and the workplace, served to reduce any inherited experience of regional difference and diversity (which had in any event been dramatically disrupted by the experiences of the war and its aftermath, with associated massive population upheavals). Stories about a common past had a supraregional flavour too. Whether these stories were the tales told in the home – about experiences on the eastern front, or in prisoner of war camps, or in flight from the Red Army, or rape at the hands of Soviet soldiers – or whether they were the bland tales of anti-fascist heroes presented in schools, museums, exhibitions, war memorials and concentration camps, the overwhelming weight of the German past and the GDR-specific presentation of that past overrode local legends and regional myths. And once one comes to look at the issue of a sense of common fate or common destiny, the importance of living within the GDR as a whole, rather than any specific region of it, becomes even more apparent. Boundaries are crucial to the construction of any collective identity (identifying who is 'in the same boat'; who is 'one of us' and who is 'other'); and there could be no more compelling boundary than the Wall. By the time of unification, it was the Wall, rather than Hitler, which appeared to be the most important fact in recent German history to the largest number of East Germans.

What we see therefore over forty years of the existence of the GDR is the growth of experiences and constraints which were of far greater

importance than historic regional differences. Among younger generations (the '*Hineingeborene*', those born into the GDR) factors such as the
Wall, division, the grumbles and shortages of everyday life, the uncertainties and vicissitudes of unpredictable politics, and so on, took
precedence over 'historic' regional differences between Mecklenburgers
and Thuringians, Saxons and Berliners.

Furthermore – at least until the fall of the Wall and the discovery or
construction of differences – a sustained sense of all-German identity
remained of major importance. East Germans remained vitally interested in the West, and retained a strong sense of mutual belonging,
sustained at least by the official lip-service paid by the West German
governments to a notion of common citizenship and brotherhood.
That socioeconomic and to some considerable extent also cultural differences are more important in the construction of collective identity
than a common language or citizenship rights only became apparent
after the fall of the Wall.

Under what conditions, then, could distinctive regional subcultures
survive in the GDR? Let us take a closer look at two contrasting examples, one small regional subculture – that of the Sorbs – and one large
international culture, that of Christianity, with a regional institutional
structure within the GDR. I shall spend rather longer on the case of the
Sorbs, who seem to me to present the most important candidate for
the role of genuine regional subculture in the GDR, than on the case of
Christianity, which serves here largely as an example to emphasize the
importance of a supranational as well as regionally devolved organizational base.

Preserved and undermined: the Sorbs as a regional subculture

Since the Sorbs constituted the one distinctive minority population in
the GDR, it is worth taking a slightly closer look at the rather contradictory features of their experience.

The Sorbs (or Wends) are perhaps best defined as a regionally based
and linguistically distinctive subculture rather than an ethnic minority.
They were concentrated in areas of the south-east of the GDR, around
Bautzen and Hoyerswerda and in the Spreewald; they lived primarily in
the *Kreise* of Bautzen, Kamenz, Niesky, Hoyerswerda, Cottbus-Stadt and
Cottbus-Land, Weißwasser, Guben, Forst, Calau, Lübben and
Spremberg. Estimates of population numbers vary from
32 061 in the census of 1956 to a figure of around 100 000 in a Lexikon
of 1964; most likely, those designating themselves as Sorbs fluctuated

in the region of 45–50 000.[19] In other words, what we are talking about is a population of somewhat less than the average British parliamentary constituency, or between one and two per cent of the population of Wales, thinly spread out over a number of mainly rural areas.

The Sorbs were not internally homogeneous, but divided between Upper and Lower Sorbs, speaking different dialects of Wendish. They were distinctive not only for their language, but also by virtue of particular traditional costumes (*Trachten*) and customs, such as riding festivals, distinctive houses, boats and river traffic in the Spreewald area, and the production of highly decorated hand-painted Easter eggs. Most (at least among the older generations in rural areas) were Catholics. The existence of a Catholic regional subculture with distinctive clothing, festivals and customs was not in itself anything unusual in midtwentieth-century Germany; anyone familiar with, say the Alpine borders of Upper Bavaria in the 1950s could equally have witnessed regionally distinctive processions with men and women in traditional dress (*Dirndls* and *Lederhosen* in this case), highly decorated carts and horses (even cows) on the occasion of particular high days and holy days. What was additionally distinctive about the Sorbs was their language, which was not a dialect of German. They were, in essence, a long-lost survival of those days in the high and later Middle Ages when the Germanic tribes had moved eastwards, colonizing areas of central Europe inhabited by Slavic populations. They were an ancient population pocket who had remained, and, given their location within the borders of the 'Altreich', survived even the extraordinary population upheavals unleashed by Nazi resettlement and 'Germanization' policies in central Europe.

In contrast to the Nazis, the SED sought to protect and preserve the linguistic and cultural heritage of the Sorbs, whose status as a distinctive linguistic and cultural group was constitutionally guaranteed. Article 40 of the constitution (in its 1974 version) stated that: 'Citizens of the German Democratic Republic have the right to protection and care [*Pflege*] of their mother tongue and culture. The exercise of this right will be fostered by the state.'[20] But the SED's proudly proclaimed 'nationalities policy' had strings attached.

The strings had as usual to do with the SED's characteristic strategy of co-option of a subgroup for the achievement of communist aims. The Sorbs possessed their own representative institution, the Domowina (meaning *Heimat*), which was founded in 1912 as part of a *Heimatbewegung* ('homeland movement'), attacked and in 1937 closed down by the Nazis, then refounded in 1945 and reorganized in the GDR as a mass organization. As such, it served the characteristic purposes of all GDR mass organizations: controlled coordination of and influence over grassroots opinions and interests by an apparently representative body ultimately subservient to, and populated by loyalists towards, the SED. It would be too simple to portray this as a body simply for the control from above of a distinctive subgroup below (as in the totalitarian model of power), or as a body of genuine representation of interests (as it might be with a western representative body). Rather, it was something of a mixture, with an asymmetrical relationship. Undoubtedly the balance of power lay with the state, but there were some genuine benefits in return – particularly in cultural matters – for the subcultural group.

As far as the SED was concerned, the compliant members of the Domowina were party to a pact in which, in return for assistance in the preservation of Sorb culture, they put across SED policies with respect to socioeconomic and political change. They facilitated, for example, the formation of collective farms or LPGs in rural areas; they supported socialism in principle; they fostered support for the GDR as the fatherland and the SED as the leading force. A flavour of the SED expectations are given in the *Grußadresse* of the Central Committee of the SED to the Domowina on the occasion of its 'high point', the *VII. Bundeskongreß* on the occasion of the twentieth anniversary of the GDR, held under the revealing banner slogan 'The love, faith and strength of the Sorbs [are given to] our socialist fatherland, the German Democratic Republic!':

> We highly value the work of your organization, the Domowina, in the process of winning over Sorbian people to the creation of the developed social system of socialism. In this work, it has been proven that the Domowina has always proceeded from the unity of the political, economic and cultural tasks, and has shaped its political endeavours such that Sorbian working people have developed into carriers and fellow shapers of our socialist social order.

The speech goes on:

> The socialist national culture of the German Democratic Republic, of which the socialist Sorbian culture is a firm constituent part, is developing on the basis of our economic successes and the all-round security and stabilization [*Festigung*] of our socialist state. We accord

great significance to the renewed flowering of socialist Sorbian culture, because this helps to stamp its mark on the socialist face of the Sorb.[21]

Clearly the Sorbs were to have little choice in the matter of what sort of state and society they were to live in and contribute to; only 'socialist' Sorbian culture seemed worthy of repeated mention in approbatory tones. The pay-off, however, was supposed to be the preservation of the Sorbs' language and at least some of their customs, if not all aspects of their traditional culture.

In furtherance of such cultural preservation, the regime supported a variety of institutions. These included a German-Sorbian Volk Theatre in Bautzen, a Museum for Sorbian folk customs, a daily and a weekly newspaper, respectively entitled the *Nowa Doba* (New Epoch) and *Nowy Casnik* (New Times), and the Domowina's own Sorbian language publishing house. In addition there were around sixty schools of two types (A and B) according to whether Sorbian was the main language of instruction, or was taught alongside other subjects. Cultural events, traditional customs and festivals were encouraged and promoted. The status of Sorbian as an official minority language was underlined by the use of dual-language public signs, even in major urban centres such as Bautzen.

Like many other areas of policy in the GDR, however, apparently laudable aims in one area were simultaneously in conflict with or undermined by conflicting priorities in another area. As nearly always, the shortcomings and the priorities of the economy proved to be the undoing of high-minded ideals in this area. The main problem for the Sorbs, as a distinctive regionally based group, was that they were being dispersed by two irreversible wider processes: long-term trends towards industrialization and urbanization, and specific SED energy policies with respect to brown coal mining. The first set of trends meant that younger Sorbs, who wanted to leave their villages and get jobs in the surrounding towns and cities, felt little incentive to learn Wendish at school since it would hardly help in any career, and once they had left their villages rapidly became Germanized in language and culture, as well as being subject to the general processes of secularization. Increasingly embarrassed by their heritage in urban society, they often became critical of and distanced from the older generation at home. The latter set of policies meant that whole villages were removed at one swoop, as and when it suited the SED to clear them for purposes of the extensive and shallow lignite mining. As many as 88 per cent of village demolitions in the GDR were of Sorbian villages (70 per cent of which took place after the oil crisis of 1973 and the switch to searching for a homegrown energy supply). Once uprooted and physically moved into the anonymous concrete housing estates or *'Plattenbauten'* of the new towns, Sorbish communities disintegrated even more rapidly. The customs and traditions became ever more artificial, preserved for a wilting tourist trade of fellow travellers or already converted admirers of the SED's 'nationalities policy' (as well as the occasional anthropologically inclined westerner).

In this sense, then, one can perhaps say that the SED's policy with respect to a specific regional identity was, if self-contradictory, at least in some respects successful. Those who sought to sustain a distinctive Sorbian cultural identity and literary presence appear to have made the compromises necessary with respect to co-option by the SED. Those who did not were quietly submerged into the anonymous masses of the Workers' and Peasants' State. Those remaining, who stood out by their difference, could provide visible evidence of how different the GDR was from its predecessor, the Nazi regime.

Institutional decentralization: the Christian Churches

A rather different story about the importance of institutional devolution and international significance can be told with respect to the Christian Churches in the GDR. The Christian Churches proved to be the one major social institution which the SED was, for a variety of reasons, incapable of either abolishing or successfully co-opting and bringing under a degree of central control. What concerns us in this context is the relationship between the democratic centralist notions of the SED and the regional devolution of the Churches' political structure. The institutional decentralization of the Protestant Churches, in particular, proved to be crucial for the growth of domestic dissent in the 1980s.

The majority of East German Christians were Protestants, with declining numbers (from fifteen million formally having membership in the eight different regional Lutheran and Reformed Churches in the early 1950s to an estimate of four or five million active Protestants in the rather different circumstances of the 1980s), out of a total population of seventeen million. There were around one million Catholics in the GDR, with concentrated minority pockets in particular areas, such as the Eichsfeld.

Christianity could not be successfully attacked by the SED head on, for a variety of reasons, including the record of some individual

Christians alongside communists in the fight against Hitler, as well as the cross-border character of the churches and the strength of international support in a still very uncertain world political situation. After some stormy attempts at confrontation in the 1950s (such as the controversies over the *Junge Gemeinde* and the *Jugendweihe*), a more subtle politics of infiltration and subordination was adopted by the SED. The internal regional (as well as, more importantly, political) diversity of the Protestant Churches could be exploited to the SED's advantage, as it sought from the mid-1950s onwards to infiltrate and influence regional churches. The Thuringian church, led by the compliant Bishop Mitzenheim, proved the first and easiest to infiltrate; developments there could then be used to influence developments elsewhere in the East German Protestant church government.

The long history of power and influence of the Churches played a role in sustaining regional cultural diversity in certain pockets, particularly, for example, among older generations in Catholic rural areas. Nevertheless, general trends towards secularization were evident in the GDR as in the West in the 1960s and 1970s, with increasing numbers of people living in urban areas where the church no longer acted as a traditional social centre (and sometimes, in new urban areas, where there was no church at all). The political discrimination against young people who were committed Christians deterred many of those who even thought about the issue; but for the vast majority of young GDR citizens, religion was increasingly a matter of next to no interest in any event. The churches started to fight a spirited battle against this politically assisted process of secularization, with attempts to attract young people through popular music, 'blues masses' and the like, as well as outreach work among alcoholics, drug addicts and other 'a-socials'. Yet, had it not been for an unexpected turn in the political significance of the Churches in the changed domestic and international circumstances of the 1980s, Christianity as a subculture might well have continued to be on the wane in the GDR.

It was paradoxically only when the SED's insidious attack on the Churches appeared most nearly successful that the regional devolution of the Churches' institutional structure proved to be a major obstacle for the SED. Following the 'summit meeting' (*Spitzengespräch*) of 6 March 1978, in which Honecker and compliant church representatives reached a form of mutual accommodation which ultimately proved to be a most ambiguous pact, the SED thought it had finally succeeded in bringing the Churches under state control: co-opting them much like any other mass organization in the GDR. However, some

Christians thought otherwise. The Churches suddenly became a space in which free discussion appeared possible, even officially sanctioned.

In the changed environment of the 1980s, not all church representatives or local pastors felt bound by the hidden compromises of the pact reached at the top. What was agreed by one church representative, or put into effect in one church region, was not necessarily adhered to by another, or in another area; the pact was exploited for the loopholes and spaces it opened up, while being ignored with respect to the more Faustian elements. A Manfred Stolpe might plead with unruly spirits not to put the Church's protected status in jeopardy, while at the same time a Rainer Eppelmann would be organizing unorthodox concerts of dissident young people or mounting symbolic protests with piles of rotting rubbish in the churchyard. Institutional devolution and cultural diversity in the Churches played a role too in the kind of regionally based and distinctive civil courage evidenced in the Leipzig Monday demonstrations which proved so important in igniting the sparks of the 'gentle revolution' of 1989.

What does this (essentially counter-) example show? Even in this case, it was only because of the political salience of the institutional role of the Churches in the 1980s that the religious subculture suddenly appeared more widely relevant. And it became such, not as a set of regional subcultures within the GDR, but in respect of the GDR as a whole. The 'Protestant Revolution' was a GDR phenomenon, rooted in and made possible by a regionally diverse institutional structure, but not in any respect a product of cultural regionalism within the GDR. Rather, the SED's policies unintentionally served to produce a supraregional, distinctive GDR-Christianity. It is also interesting to note that there has been a dramatic decline in religious practice in the GDR since the collapse of the regime in which it took on such significance.

Conclusions: regional diversity and centralization in the GDR

As far as the question of federalism, or rather the lack of it, is concerned, we need a far more differentiated understanding of the character of the East German dictatorship than has been prevalent in the largely black-and-white literature of the decade or so since unification. A more detailed analysis of the practice and experience of 'democratic centralism' in the provinces can help us to understand precisely how the GDR was able to survive with such apparent stability over such a long period of time. It indicates the deep local roots of an apparently extraordinarily centralized system. Insofar as there was a democratic element to this centralism (and serious reservations of course have to be entered on this point) it was one which operated about as close to the ground as it is possible to get – certainly as close to the everyday gripes of the people as is found in virtually any federal system operating under the rules of representative democracy.

Second, as far as regionalism or regional identities in the wider sense is concerned, the system appears to have stamped its mark very clearly. The comparison between the strong regional structure of the Christian Churches on the one hand, and the limited local cultural bases of the Sorbs on the other, proves very revealing. The somewhat self-contradictory policies of the SED with respect to the Sorbs were of more benefit to the GDR's image (and tourist trade) than to any real preservation of regional Sorbian traditions, language and culture, rooted as these were in rural communities which were progressively undercut (often literally!) by a combination of SED energy policies and the imperatives of industrialization. By contrast, in part because of their very strong regional institutional bases which were at the same time rooted in a much wider international framework, the continued regionalism of the Christian Churches proved to be part of the SED's ultimate undoing. Unlike the Prussian absolutist rulers of the eighteenth century, the atheist SED was not able successfully to coopt the Christian Churches, even under a heterodox variant, to totally subservient and state-sustaining vessels. But even in its own unmaking, the SED produced a supraregional form of Christian-GDR identity.

Regionalism became ever less important in the construction of collective identities in the GDR. Given the overriding importance of politics and centrally determined (if not always provincially effective) policies in the GDR, a much broader general GDR identity developed which overrode pre-existing regional diversity. In the changed circumstances of 'united' Germany, this east German regional identity continues to play a major role in the enlarged Federal Republic of today.

Yet the SED's fostering of regional identities for the purposes of attracting tourism, and in the attempt to link the new claims to legitimacy of the GDR with a longer-standing, more deep-rooted emotional identification with a local or regional *Heimat,* served to keep notions of regional culture alive. Nor were regional variations in speech patterns or food preferences much affected in a state which, despite the growing availability of western television channels in the 1970s and 1980s, did not participate extensively in the general trends of the later twentieth century towards globalization and takeover by multinationals (the advance of the American hamburger was stopped by the Wall; McDonalds outlets only began to sprout after unification). Moreover, regional identities were to a large degree apolitical. Hence, they were available, relatively uncontaminated, for speedy resurrection when pragmatic considerations brought this onto the agenda of the day.

In 1990, with the rapid collapse of the East German economy as thousands of East Germans continued to haemorrhage to the West, political unification came to be seen as the only possible solution far more quickly than anyone – even West German Chancellor Helmut Kohl – would have thought possible in the closing weeks of 1989.[22] Under the constitutional provisions of the *Grundgesetz* or Basic Law of the Federal Republic of Germany, there were two possible routes through which (re)unification could take place. Under Article 146, the two German states could come together to devise a new constitution for a new united German state. This would be a slow and politically arduous process. It would have had much to recommend it in terms of representing a genuinely new start, rather than what later came to be seen by many disillusioned East Germans as colonization or takeover by the West. But the dramatic and sudden collapse of the East German economy (particularly following the currency union in July 1990, devised on economically disastrous terms which had been politically advantageous to the CDU in the March elections) did not allow the luxury of pursuing this route; and Helmut Kohl as well as the CDU-led East German coalition government opted instead to deploy Article 23 of the Basic Law. This entailed a reconstitution of the Länder, which would then allow their application to be incorporated into an expanded Federal Republic. Hence their rapid resurrection and the return of eastern Germany to political federalism.

It was then all too easy to throw over the traces of the discredited GDR by resuscitating cultural notions of old federal traditions and recreating the Länder, disregarding the historical malleability of such regional political entities. And (re)constructed regional identities could be deployed as camouflage in disputes rooted in exceedingly strong contemporary political and economic interests, as in the resistance of Brandenburg to merger with Berlin.[23] Those who would wish to argue that strong regional identities had persisted in some subterranean manner, and were simply allowed to re-emerge relatively intact, as it were, from below the ice, should note that few ex-Prussians appear to have mourned for Prussia, or sought to reconstitute this state which had been so significant for German history for two centuries or more, and had been dismantled so recently following the defeat of Hitler.

The distinctive legacy of the SED to the story of regionalism in German history is to have forged a new region: that of the ex-GDR, in the euphemistic phrase the 'five new Länder', in perhaps more colloquial terms the land of the *Ossis*. Distinctive political, cultural and socioeconomic experiences over the forty years of division, and the unprecedented place of these newly recreated Länder in the new Germany after 1990, proved far more important than any regional diversity among them. This is not to say, of course, that such regional identifications cannot be reconstructed (witness the slogans which sprouted so rapidly in the wake of the GDR's collapse, such as 'Thuringia, the green heart of Germany', and so on). But it is to argue that regionalism is a phenomenon rooted not so much in the soil (a form of geopolitical determinism) as in political and cultural experience; as such it is open to perpetual, and often very rapid, shaping and reshaping in changing historical circumstances.

Jokes are often a good indicator of what is salient and what is sensitive in everyday life. The vast repertoire on variants of the 'Englishman and Irishman' or 'Englishman, Welshman, Scotsman' jokes in England/Britain since at least the time of Shakespeare tells us something about identity construction in what became the (not always terribly) United Kingdom; Jewish jokes function both in the obvious denigratory anti-Semitic sense, and often also as part of a humorous in-group self-definition. Jokes are always on the threshold of what it is not quite acceptable to talk about openly; they may sublimate other tensions which cannot be negotiated overtly. Jokes during the GDR appear to have been overwhelmingly about the regime and the way the state operated, not about members of a particular region told by those from another. The rapid proliferation of *Ossi/Wessi* jokes after the *Wende* illustrates only too clearly the processes of construction, negotiation, and transformation of new regionally based identities, as differences between East and West Germans drowned out the proclamation of being 'one people' (*ein Volk*) prevalent in the demonstrations of autumn 1989. Given that there is a widespread view that the Germans are a dreadfully serious people (and even that 'a German joke is no laughing matter'), this may ultimately prove to be the most positive legacy of democratic centralism to the history of German federalism.

Notes

1. A concept I develop in a book entitled *Perfectly Ordinary Lives? A Social History of the GDR* (Yale, forthcoming).

2. See particularly Klaus Schroeder, *Der SED-Staat* (Munich 1998); for a critique of this, see M. Fulbrook, 'Jenseits der Totalitarismustheorie? Vorläufige Bemerkungen aus sozialgeschichtlicher Perspektive' in P. Barker, ed., *The GDR and its History: Rückblick und Revision. Die DDR im Spiegel der Enquete-Kommissionen* (Amsterdam 2000).
3. See particularly Klaus-Dietmar Henke, ed., *Totalitarismus. Sechs Vorträge über Gehalt und Reichweite eines klassischen Konzepts der Diktaturforschung* (Dresden, Hannah-Arendt-Institut für Totalitarismusforschung e.V. an der T. U. Dresden, Berichte und Studien Nr. 18, 1999).
4. See particularly the essays by Lüdtke and Kocka in Hartmut Kaelble, Jürgen Kocka and Hartmut Zwahr (eds), *Sozialgeschichte der DDR* (Stuttgart 1994).
5. Schroeder, op. cit., pp. 632–3.
6. Quoted in Ulrich Maehlert, *Kleine Geschichte der DDR* (Munich 1998), p. 61.
7. Maehlert, op. cit., p. 63.
8. Klaus Schroeder, op. cit., p. 104.
9. Otto Grotewohl, quoted in Schroeder, op. cit., p. 104.
10. *Kleines Politisches Wörterbuch*, 3rd edn (Berlin 1978), p. 158.
11. Ibid, p. 159.
12. Cf. M. Fulbrook, *Anatomy of a Dictatorship* (Oxford 1995), and *Perfectly Ordinary Lives?* (forthcoming), for further details of this argument. See also Daphne Berdahl, *Where the World Ended* (Berkeley 1997), for the curious case of the Christian mayor of Kella.
13. These points are explored further in *Perfectly Ordinary Lives? A Social History of the GDR*.
14. See for example the jokes in Ernst Röhl, ed., *Wenn's mal wieder **anders** kommt* (Berlin 1996), p. 26.
15. The position of foreigners in the GDR has not yet as yet been the subject of adequate scholarly research, despite the relevance of this in post-*Wende* debates about the roots of racism and neo-nazism in eastern Germany; very interesting work on this topic is being undertaken by Damian mac con Uladh at University College London.
16. See the discussion in Chapter 4 of this volume.
17. See the forthcoming work on *Heimat* in the GDR by Jan Palmowski of King's College London.
18. See M. Fulbrook, *German National Identity after the Holocaust* (Cambridge 1999).
19. See for these figures and more general discussion of the constitutional position of the Sorbs in the GDR, Siegfried Mampel, ed., *Die Sozialistische Verfassung der Deutschen Demokratischen Republik* (Frankfurt am Main 1982), pp. 821–4.
20. Mampel, op. cit., p. 821.
21. *Die Sorben. Wissenschaftswertes aus Vergangenheit und Gegenwart der sorbischen nationalen Minderheit*, 3rd edn (Bautzen 1970), pp. 89–90.
22. It should be remembered that Chancellor Kohl's 'Ten Point Plan' of 28 November 1989 only envisaged an evolutionary process of ever closer confederation, possibly moving towards unification over a period of a decade – a notion to which the then British Prime Minister, Margaret Thatcher, reacted with horror.
23. The case of Land Brandenburg is particularly interesting because of the position as Premier of Manfred Stolpe, formerly occupant of a senior position in

the East German Protestant Church and long-time informant to the Stasi, hence embodying in his own person some of the ambiguous problematics of life in the GDR. Stolpe uniquely stood out and survived the general post-*Wende* witch-hunt of former Stasi-IMs in high places, as well as being a rare example of an East German, rather than a western colonizer, holding high political office.

8

German Federalism from Cooperation to Competition

Charlie Jeffery

Introduction: the decline and fall of cooperative federalism?

This contribution is about the demise of what has become known as cooperative federalism in Germany. This term is a convenient and apt shorthand for the distinctive features which characterized West German federalism by the mid-1970s:

- a functional division of competence between federal legislation and Länder administration;
- the entrenched role of the Bundesrat in the federal legislative process;
- a commitment to securing consensus among the Länder and between Länder and federation on policy formulation and implementation, which was facilitated by a multitude of coordinating committees;
- the consequent bureaucratic 'entanglement' (*Politikverflechtung*) of the two levels of government;
- and the relative marginality of the few remaining exclusive competences still exercised by the Länder and their Landtage;

The term 'cooperative federalism' can increasingly be seen *also* as evocative of an era which seems to be drawing to a close. This era might be defined as that in which the institutions of the federal system were seen and used as instruments with which federation and Länder purposefully sought in cooperation to maintain a 'uniformity of living conditions' across the Federal Republic.

In contrast to most federal systems, German federalism was not conceived as an instrument and guarantor for territorial diversity, but rather dedicated to the delivery, through institutional cooperation, of common standards of public policy and services across the federal territory. While this commitment to maintain common standards formally remains in the late 1990s, in practice it has been undermined by the post-unification realities facing the German federal system. In particular, the integration of the five eastern Länder after 1990 has placed a large question mark over the feasibility of *achieving*, let alone 'maintaining' uniform living conditions across the post-unification federation. The scale of the problems of economic adaptation in the east and the relatively slow pace of the economic catching-up process hitherto mean that the prospects for ensuring uniformity have faded at the very least into a long-term goal.

The pursuit of common standards has also become a highly contested goal. The implications of even trying to work collectively towards uniformity are increasingly unwelcome for many of the Länder. Unification has brought with it a much wider differentiation of Länder interests. The notion of collective action through cooperative structures to secure common goals now implies for any one Land a much greater degree of compromise of its political interests than it did in the West German past. As a result a growing sense of having to make unjust sacrifices for the benefit of others has emerged and has led to the questioning of both the mission of uniformity and the mechanisms and spirit of cooperation which were developed in the pre-unification federal system to secure it.

There is, in other words, intensifying pressure for change in the way the federal system works. And that is what this contribution is about: how cooperative federalism has become increasingly contested and subject to change in the direction of what has come to be known as 'competitive federalism'. It starts with an account of *how* cooperative federalism has become unsustainable by looking at how the preconditions which had supported its evolution have largely fallen away, mainly since unification, but in some respects beforehand as well. And then it looks at how change in the direction of a more 'competitive' federalism has been manifested. And on this point the evaluation differs from the many commentaries on the German federal system which have looked with pessimism and trepidation at the failure of one reform initiative after another through the 1990s to reshape the federal system to fit the new post-unification realities. Among the more prominent of these failures have been the 'non-reform' (or at least highly marginal reform) of the federal system proposed by the Joint Constitutional Commission of Bundestag and Bundesrat in the early 1990s, the inability of negotiations surrounding the 1993 Solidarity

Pact to update the principles underlying the system of financial equalization in the federal system,[1] and the rejection of the Berlin-Brandenburg merger in 1996.[2]

Focusing on just these failed initiatives seems an unnecessarily formalistic perspective on 'change', no doubt reflecting the strong role in research on the federal system played by the German constitutional law tradition. Though it may not square easily with the (over-)formalism of this tradition, change does not have to be effected through constitutional engineering or other formal institutional mechanisms. It can just happen. New forms of political practice and new ways of thinking about politics can emerge as part of the process of coming to terms with changed social or economic realities. Changes which emerge in this way may stand in tenuous relationship with the constitution's formalities, but may nevertheless still generate some new and workable political modus operandi. One day, the constitution might even 'catch up' with the new reality and formalize the new modus operandi.

The history of post-war German federalism itself provides examples of this process of change in practice and ideas subsequently being 'caught up' by an amended constitutional framework. For example, the constitutional reforms undertaken in 1969 which provided a formal capstone for the cooperative federal system – joint tasks, joint federal–Länder investment financing and a revised and more 'entangled' financial constitution – effectively only formalized *what was already happening* and placed it on a more systematic basis. In other words, German federalism had *long before* become pervaded by mixed financing of policy initiatives, financial interdependence and a wider fabric of cooperative federal–Länder working relationships. The political practice of German federalism has therefore before demonstrated a capacity for flexibility and adaptation; and although the constitutional framework may be 'sticky', it does seem eventually to 'catch up'. The question driving this contribution is whether German federalism is currently located in an era in which constitutional stickiness lags behind changing practice. As the pursuit of uniform living conditions recedes to a distant and contested goal, are the structures and spirit of the *cooperative* federalism which were dedicated to their maintenance evolving anew to create a 'new model federalism' in Germany?

These are questions which will be addressed in the second and third sections, which look in turn at how, in the late 1990s, (a) *changed practices* have emerged the federal system, and (b) how these have become pervaded and, to an extent, legitimized, by *new ideas* on how the federal system should work. First, though, the changes in wider political context which have made cooperative federalism increasingly unsustainable are discussed.

The preconditions for a cooperative federalism

The system of cooperative federalism which had emerged by the mid-1970s rested on a number of foundations. A first, resulting in particular from the SPD's entry to federal government after 1966, was a confidence in the capacity of government economic intervention to secure economic and social goals. Given the functional division of labour which had merged between federal legislation and Länder implementation, interventionism had the effect of extending federal–Länder cooperation in policy-making by the end of the 1970s across such major policy fields as taxation policy, infrastructural investment, educational and health policy.

The scope of this interventionism put public policy flesh on the constitutional bones of the commitment to secure uniform living conditions, in the process cementing a second precondition for a cooperative federalism: West Germany's relatively high degree of social and economic homogeneity. With the partial exception of Bavaria, West Germany had always been a state without significant, territorially embedded socio-cultural divides; the era of interventionism ensured a diminution of territorial economic disparities. As Roland Sturm put it: 'regional diversity seemed to be something obsolete, which had to be overcome.'[3]

Third, patterns of voting behaviour had stabilized by the 1970s to underpin a process of party concentration in a 'two-and-a-half' party system which operated congruently at the federal and Länder levels, facilitating both 'vertical' intra-party coordination between, for example, the federal SPD and the SPD in the Länder, but also allowing for regularized and predictable patterns of interaction within and across parties throughout the federal system.[4] This in turn underpinned a fourth precondition: the consensual spirit of decision-making which operated at the meeting point of territorial and party politics in the Bundesrat and reached from there into the Bundestag. It was striking that two classics of postwar German political science, each highlighting one aspect of the consensualism of the federal system, were both published in 1976: Fritz Scharpf's pioneering work on the institutional 'entanglement' of federation and Länder in delivering public policy;[5] and Gerhard Lehmbruch's more historically rooted work on 'party competition in the federal state'[6] which set out how a de facto grand coalition, stretching across Bundestag and Bundesrat, had emerged to qualify the nominal governing majority held by the social-liberal coalition.

However, this complex of preconditions of federal-Länder and cross-party cooperation focused on intervening to maintain social and economic homogeneity, which inspired Scharpf and Lehmbruch 25 years ago, manifestly no longer exists today. Though Germany did not board the bandwagon of neo-liberal reform as enthusiastically or far-reachingly as the UK or the US, Kohl's *Wende* after 1982 signalled a trimming of the commitment to interventionism which has been gradually extended since, if at times rather fitfully. Schröder's adoption of a Blairite 'Third Way' is arguably little more than an updated version designed to meet the greater rigours of turn-of-the-century globalization.

Rolling back the state naturally means rolling back the scope of the areas in which federation and Länder cooperate in defining common national standards. It also, inevitably, led to a widening of economic and social disparities between the Länder. Unification then of course overlaid its own stark east–west dimension on the existing West German pattern of economic and social disparity while simultaneously exhausting the resources which might otherwise have been focused on maintaining earlier levels of homogeneity. The post-unity era has also injected a new volatility into patterns of voting behaviour which have exploded the former neat congruence between party formations at the federal level and in the Länder and rendered much more complex and in part unmanageable intraparty coordination between the federal and Länder levels.

The net outcome has been a new prominence of territorial interests. The Länder, in part disengaged from structures of cooperation by the turn away from interventionism, differentiated by greater economic disparities, especially since 1990, and released from former disciplines of intraparty coordination, have shed some of the consensualism which governed their relations among themselves and with the federation in favour of a new, more hard-nosed politics of self-interest. The question is whether a federal system structured in many ways rather rigidly to concert and coordinate interests and policy across a much less diverse society can adapt to this new situation. The pessimistic answer from many commentators is no, not really, because a system constructed to concert inevitably contains numerous veto points which will tend inherently to block change. To quote Heidrun

Abromeit in an article resignedly subtitled 'the alternative-lessness of cooperative federalism':

> Let me put forward a heretical thesis: German federalism is unreformable. It is capable only of minor adaptation. This is problematic given that in the 1990s the objective need for reform has grown starkly – i.e. the cleft between need for reform and ability to reform has opened up massively.[7]

Others are scarcely more optimistic. Rainer Olaf Schulze warns of possible dysfunctionalities and systemic instabilities arising from the post-unity situation,[8] Uwe Leonardy presents a pessimistic alternative of *re*form now or risk the *de*formation of the structures and function of German federalism,[9] Christian Stolorz issues a scholarly sigh and says the 'outlook' is 'depressing'.[10]

The prognosis here is, by contrast, rather more optimistic about the capacity of the federal system to adapt to a new situation. The next section seeks to justify this optimism in a discussion of how, and with what effect, the Länder have begun to *do* politics differently during the 1990s, reflecting the diversities which increasingly differentiate them.

New practices of federalism in Germany: interest divergence among the Länder

Cooperative federalism has rested on a capacity and will for coordination and compromise. One of the striking characteristics of Länder politics in the 1990s has been the erosion of that capacity and will. The following traces this process of erosion under four headings: financial equalization, policy differentiation, competence issues, and EU politics.

Money talks: financial equalization

The financial equalization process which regulates the allocation of resources between federation and Länder and among the Länder is, by common consent, deeply flawed. It is, first and foremost, extraordinarily complex and intransparent, running, apparently, across 100 separate calculations[11] which divide up and then variously reallocate tax revenues in a way which leaves no real opportunity for citizens to identify who has raised what tax for which purpose. Equally unsatisfactorily, the equalization system allows the federal level to legislate on issues for which the Länder have to pick up the tab, *Sozialhilfe* being the most obvious and controversial.

But more than anything else, if one is to take the term 'equalization' at face value, the system has been a profound failure. Though in operation in more or less its present form since 1969, only one Land – Bavaria – has shifted in that period from being in the position of recipient of equalization transfers to that of provider of transfers. Others have either fallen down the ladder, or simply stayed near its bottom rung, notably the Saarland. Although of course other factors are at play here, such as structural decline in key, regionally concentrated sectors, a central problem is that the structure of the financial equalization process lacks appropriate incentives.[12] Whatever the starting point, all the Länder are ultimately brought up to a position where each has at least 99.5 per cent of the average tax revenue per head of the Länder as a whole. There is therefore little incentive for revenue-weak Länder to improve their performance. At the same time, revenue-strong Länder see themselves losing most of the fruits of what they understand as their superior economic management in order to haul others up to the 99.5 per cent level.

Nothing in this is new. These same problems have existed since 1969 (and, indeed, led in the 1980s to a number of constitutional complaints). What is new is that the sums of money flowing through the equalization system have multiplied since unification. The current sum is roughly DM 33 billion yearly, or as Brandenburg's Minister of Finance put it: 'For the same sum, someone playing the lottery would have to win DM one million every weekend for 630 years.'[13] Inevitably, resentments have grown, especially among the net contributor Länder, leading three of them – Baden-Württemberg, Bavaria and Hessen – to construct new complaints to the Constitutional Court designed to limit their financial support for their less affluent counterparts, an enterprise generally felt to have met with some success in the Court's ruling of November 1999.[14]

Debate on the unfairnesses and tensions of resource allocation has also spilled over into other areas. Predictably these include schemes of territorial reform to rid Germany of Länder condemned by size and economic structure to remain perpetual supplicants. Less predictable and rather more controversial was the idea raised by Bavaria to regionalize the social insurance funds on the basis that large parts of the unemployment insurance contributions Bavarian citizens make leak out support to some other Land's unemployed. Again, such ideas have a wider resonance in the affluent south; apparently some

30–50 per cent of Baden-Württemberg's unemployment insurance contributions have been used to support the unemployed outside Baden-Württemberg.[15]

Going it alone: growing policy differentiation

One might respond to such concerns by suggesting that such transfers, and cross-Länder subsidization more generally, have wider benefits in terms of social cohesion. There appears, though, to be a narrowing of perspective among at least some of the Länder which filters out wider concerns and focuses primarily on territorial self-interest. This can be observed in a more general sense in a move away from past practices of seeking coordinated, inter-Länder solutions to policy problems to introducing new, territory-specific measures. These have been most evident in the management of the regional economies of the Länder, presenting the key message of a body of work by Arthur Benz, Jens Hesse, Klaus Goetz and others often dubbed as 'dynamic federalism'.[16] Work on 'dynamic federalism' took issue with the research tradition inspired by Fritz Scharpf's *Politikverflechtung* which had identified and criticized a deep immobilism and inadaptability in the policy repertoires of cooperative federalism.

Benz and colleagues found instead, and in particular in regional economic policy, where older cooperative structures – notably the Joint Task for regional economic development – have become less important than new emphases on 'endogenous' economic conditions and potentials within the various Länder. Significantly, Benz has also emphasized that these considerable changes in policy practice have taken place despite an unchanged constitutional framework stipulating detailed procedures for cooperative policy-making. In other words, constitutional 'stickiness' in this field has certainly not impeded significant policy change on the ground.

Increasingly, similar patterns of differentiation can be seen in other policy fields. What is more, they have become more politically salient – i.e. one Land defines and legitimizes its own form of policy in distinction to that of another Land. For every attempt by Bavaria to retain a solid Christian base in its education system, North Rhine-Westphalia might, for example, argue that its system is more efficient, or Brandenburg that liberalized religious instruction is better.

The *level* of differentiated policy-making is generally less widespread in the east – not least because of the lack of financial resources for ambitious autonomous policy initiatives – but there one can still observe a different version of the move away from policy coordination: the collective eastern Länder pursuit of federal financial support in high expenditure policy fields such as health, higher education and regional economic development, which has been won partly at the expense of formerly federation-wide federal–Länder programmes. East–west differences have had as their result a recalibration of relationships between federation, western Länder and eastern Länder, with the latter entering a new and asymmetrical relationship with the federation, and the western Länder increasingly inclined – or left with no choice but – to go it alone.

We (or some of us at least) want our competences back!

Some of the Länder, especially the wealthier ones in the west, have given the prospect of 'going it alone' an enthusiastic thumbs-up, not least because it might be employed as an instrument for a further loosening of the bindings – *'Entflechtung'* – of cooperative solidarity. The focal point of their concerns has been Article 72 of the Basic Law, which determines whether federation or Länder have the right to legislate in the fields of concurrent and framework powers. This was one of the few clauses where the constitutional reforms recommended by the Joint Constitutional Commission of Bundestag and Bundesrat of 1992–3 had a significant impact on the federal system. Two changes were implemented. On the one hand the hurdles which the federation has to overcome to claim the right of legislation were raised and explicitly made subject to constitutional adjudication. And on the other the possibility was established, via federal legislation, of restoring to the Länder legislative rights hitherto claimed by the federation.

The latter point was a particular concern pursued by Hessen in the constitutional reform debates in the early 1990s. In fact Hessen had wanted to go rather further by establishing a process for reclaiming legislative rights which could be triggered by autonomous Länder initiative rather than requiring federal legislation. This however foundered on the resistance of those Länder, especially in the east, which were 'groaning too much under the weight of existing Länder competences to regret their diminution in favour of the federation',[17] and did not share Hessen's enthusiasm for taking on further legislative competences. The Hessian baton was then taken up by Bavaria, which proposed in 1995 that the Bundesrat draw up a federal bill designed to make use the possibility of restoring legislative rights to the Länder under the new provisions of Article 72. Bavaria was accordingly given the task of drafting the bill, and came back with a radical proposal to 'repatriate' some twenty fields of legislation to the Länder, mainly on the grounds that earlier arguments setting out a need to maintain uniformity of living conditions via common federal legislation could no longer be justified.[18]

The Bavarian proposal, which was supposed by the end of 1997 to have produced a consensual bill for introduction into the federal legislative process, was, however, effectively shelved. It was too ambitious, too overtly autonomy-driven to gain the approval of a Länder majority. Nevertheless, the Bavarian initiative still gives an impression of the growing pressures in some parts of the federation to abandon both the spirit and the structures of cooperation in favour of more cross-Länder differentiation. As Edmund Stoiber, expressed it in November 1996, 'we need made-to-measure suits, not a unitary corset'.

Interests and autonomy in the European policy arena

All of the above indications of differentiation in Länder politics – the pursuit of financial self-interest, differentiation of policy interests, arguments for greater policy autonomy – can also be seen in the European policy arena. This has a certain irony. In the years following the Single European Act, the Länder in the west before unification and in both east and west after unification had maintained a closed and united front in pressing the federation to acquiesce to their demands for fully constitutionalized rights of access to European decision-making. And the rights they eventually won in the 1992 'European amendments' to the Basic Law were an unexpectedly complete success, amounting to an extension of the domestic policy structures of cooperative federalism to European policy-making.

Winning rights is only part of the story, though; much depends on how they are used. And while the Länder are able on most European policy issues to work through these structures to generate common positions, there are indications – just as in the domestic arena – that in some fields effective cooperation is either hard to sustain, or simply irrelevant to a group of increasingly disparate territorial units which have differentiated policy priorities.

For the eastern Länder in particular, money again talks in the form of Objective One Structural Funding status (awarded to support structural adjustment in 'regions whose development is lagging behind').

For them the continued award of Objective One status into the current funding round which extends through to 2007 has been an overriding objective which has concentrated their energies on one field – regional economic policy and structural funding – in which the other Länder have expressed at best a far lesser interest.

Other Länder equally have pursued policy interests relevant to their particular structural characteristics, for example: Hessen in air transport policy (given the importance of Frankfurt Airport in the Hessian economy); Brandenburg in relations across its (and the EU's) border to the east; and Bavaria in agricultural policy (given the size of its agricultural sector). The pattern is broadly similar to that in the domestic arena: 'going it alone' in EU politics is a straightforward corollary of the loosening of the intensity of cross-Länder policy coordination at home.

The corollary extends further: some Länder have sought to increase their opportunities to 'go it alone' by arguing for reductions in the scope of European regulation and its concomitant: additional scope for autonomous regional policy-making. Anti-regulationist arguments have been especially prominent in the field of competition policy, and in particular the European Commission's policing of the EU's subsidy controls. This was a concern high on the agenda for Baden-Württemberg in the 1980s which resented the limits the Commission imposed on the activist regional economic policy of the then Minister-President, Lothar Späth. The same concern re-emerged amid considerable controversy in 1996 when Volkswagen was ordered by the Commission to repay a locational subsidy paid to it by the Land government in Saxony, leading the Saxon government to mount a highly vocal, but ultimately unsuccessful strategy of defiance.[19] In both cases, the view from the Länder was that they should have the right to manage the regional economy as they see fit and in accordance with priorities determined in the Land and not in Brussels.

The same viewpoint, but on a much wider front, has been expressed with some vehemence by Bavaria during the Minister-Presidency of Edmund Stoiber. Bavaria has in recent years protested against the extension of European competence in the field of media regulation, and issued highly detailed policy prescriptions for the slashing of bureaucratic and financial intervention in the fields of the Common Agricultural Policy and the Structural Funds (the latter also linked with a loosening of subsidy controls). The thrust of Bavaria's concern is captured in three characteristic Stoiber quotes: 'our own regional policy, with our own resources'; 'we know better ourselves in Bavaria how the work of our farmers for the preservation of our cultural landscape should be rewarded'; and (in respect of the Saxon subsidy controversy) 'the right to save jobs through subsidies'.[20]

In other words, taking together all the above examples from financial equalization to Euro-regulation, Länder across Germany have begun to prioritize new forms of political practice focused on territorial self-interest alongside, and in some cases instead of, the more orthodox practices of cooperative federalism. A new dynamic is developing, even within the structural parameters set by cooperative federalism. This is something which might be described as an emerging 'Sinatra doctrine' of German federalism, with each Land increasingly tending and tempted to do it 'My Way'!

Change in German federalism is, in other words, just happening, with this new 'my way' rationale increasingly underpinning Länder politics. The changes set out in this chapter have been, though, essentially ad hoc and unconnected, with some Länder responding to the perceived inadequacies of the federal system's structures, and all increasingly prioritizing internal, Land-specific issues and goals. There is, though, another dimension of change which may be in the process of legitimizing, systematizing and, perhaps, extending the kinds of political practice I have discussed – and that is change in ideas about German federalism.

Changing ideas of German federalism

More precisely, there is quite clearly a conflict of ideas about German federalism under way. Cooperative federalism is not just a set of institutions and procedures, but also a set of ideas focused on solidarity, consensus and the desirability of common standards across the federation. That set of ideas in increasingly under challenge from a rival set focused on self-responsibility, autonomy, and differentiation, or what has become known as competitive federalism.

The process of diffusion of these rival ideas is an interesting one, and one in which Bavaria has played a particular role. It is no coincidence that in all the areas of interest and policy differentiation noted earlier, Bavaria has been especially prominent, with its advocacy of an autonomous politics of 'made-to-measure suits'. This advocacy is worth dwelling on for a moment. More openly than any other Land Bavaria has profiled the problems the old cooperative federal structures are facing in meeting the new demands of a much more differentiated, post-unification Länder community. Bavaria thinks this differentiation is a good thing which ought to be encouraged in the context of a changed 1990s political environment. To quote Ursula Männle, former Minister of State for Federal Affairs in the Bavarian Land government:

> The unification of Germany, the opening of our borders, further-reaching European integration and economic globalization pose new demands for our principles of [federal] political organization. The distinguishing feature of these challenges is competition. In order to be successful, we need a principle of political organization in which competition, self-responsibility and differentiation have their place alongside cooperation and consensus: we therefore need a competitive federalism.[21]

This commitment to competitive federalism has a solid ideological foundation. Bavaria has a far stronger sense of distinctive identity than any of the other Länder, based in its historic traditions of statehood, peculiarities of social structure (notably its persistent small farming tradition), its political Catholicism, and so on. It can plausibly claim, with due reference to Catholic social thought on subsidiarity, that it should be able to reflect this distinctiveness in autonomous policies capable both of reflecting the Bavarian sense of difference and of mobilizing it to secure economic advantage.

Bavaria's competitive federalism also has, though, a more pragmatic impetus. Bavaria's economic success in recent years has turned it unambiguously into one of the biggest contributors to (or 'losers' of) the financial equalization process. Despite having 'won' from financial equalization in the past, it has decided to pursue a political interest of limiting its obligations to the rest of the Länder community by arguing – as per Männle – for the injection of an element of 'self-responsibility and differentiation' alongside 'cooperation and consensus', so that it can devote its financial and identitive resources to a definition of Bavarian priorities unencumbered by the need to seek accommodation and maintain solidarity with the rest of the Länder community. One can just imagine Stoiber saying in connection with this shift away from earlier understandings of solidarity: 'Regrets? I've had a few – but then again too few to mention.'

This combination of ideology and pragmatic self-interest has been pursued on broad front: Bavaria has taken the most vigorous line on reforming financial equalization, territorial reorganization, the reclaiming of competences and opposing Euro-regulation. The manner of that pursuit is interesting. To a large extent it has bypassed, initially at least, inter-Länder coordination structures. Policy papers are presented either unilaterally, or with one or two selected partners with similar interests (most often Baden-Württemberg). Their purpose is to set the agenda, not seek consensus. Most often they are voted down, partly because their content is not (nor meant to be) capable of generating consensus, partly because the style of presentation – the fait accompli – does not easily make friends.

Nevertheless, the agenda-setting function is important, raising awareness of the Bavarian conception of more autonomous Länder politics and competitive federalism. This conception has attractions for other of the Länder, some of which have begun to pursue issues consistent with the agenda Bavaria has set out, adding further momentum to the drive for 'made-to-measure suits' and investing a growing legitimacy into arguments for a loosening of cooperative federalism. The results of this widening advocacy have been quite substantial. There was a carefully synchronized joint campaign of Baden-Württemberg and Bavaria in 1996–7 focused on the theme of territorial diversity as a basis for innovation and economic success. This in turn fed into the 1998 joint constitutional complaint of Bavaria and Baden-Württemberg on financial equalization. This was based on a controversial paper by the Mannheim lawyer Hans-Wolfgang Arndt which, while much criticized as a legal argument, was extremely powerful in terms of political presentation.[22] Its core argument was based on the effects of financial equalization on tax revenues per capita across the Länder. This suggested that while Bavaria was number 3 before equalization, it fell to 15th out of 16 afterwards, with Baden-Württemberg, North Rhine-Westphalia, Hamburg and Hessen suffering similar drops. Bremen and the Saarland, the perpetual supplicants, of course ended up in the top two places.[23]

This is just one example of a powerful presentational capacity which is good for diffusing ideas. It was striking that Hans Eichel, then Minister-President of Hessen, set out his own agenda of 'competitive federalism' in his inaugural speech as Bundesrat President in November 1998. Though he preferred the more neutral term of 'plural diversity', he raised most of the same themes as one can find in the average Stoiber speech on the state of German federalism. The impetus continued in a programmatic joint paper by Stoiber, Erwin Teufel and Roland Koch (Eichel's successor) in July 1999 on the theme 'Modernizing Federalism – Strengthening the Self-Responsibility of the Länder'.

Striking too has been the evident closeness of views of Stoiber and Wolfgang Clement, Minister-President of North Rhine-Westphalia.[24]

But perhaps most striking has been the reception and reproduction of ideas of a competitive federalism outside the ranks of the federal system insiders. Former Federal President Roman Herzog spoke in May 1998 of the benefits of the Länder acquiring more room for manoeuvre for bold experiments and for new ideas.[25] And Wolfgang Schäuble and Karl Lamers incongruously devoted four paragraphs to the theme in their paper 'Considerations on the Development of the European Integration Process' of May 1999, arguing forcefully that:

> Financial equalization between the Länder has taken on such extremes that it kills off any incentives for improved performance. The practice of German federalism is the opposite of competitive federalism. Federalism and a certain amount of competition are, however, synonymous. Whoever wants diversity must promote competition; and the precondition for competition is diversity, so that the best solutions can be identified and rewarded'.[26]

The competition theme has also been reproduced much more widely: the FDP and the Friedrich-Naumann-Stiftung, the head of the BDI, the *Sachverständigenrat*, the Friedrich-Ebert-Stiftung and even the OECD have all done so. The Bertelsmann Foundation added its considerable weight in a major initiative on 'Disentanglement 2005' launched in May 2000.[27] The ways in which these various bodies have understood federal competition have of course differed, with the Friedrich-Ebert-Stiftung[28] being more circumspect and some of the private sector views[29] frankly off-the-wall in their attempted translation of neo-liberal economics into a principle of political organization.

Nonetheless, these various examples are indicative of a growing weight of opinion which accepts not just the need for change, but also a way of conceiving of it: a move away from the cooperation imperative of the past and an acceptance that greater diversity and autonomy are normatively good things against which the various dissatisfactions and examples of ad hoc differentiation of practice discussed in the earlier sections of this chapter can be rationalized and made sense of.

And it is this positive loading of the notion of competition in the federal system which is tremendously important. If a vision of change is seen positively, then this has implications for those arguing for the defence or at best incremental adaptation of the status quo. And in any case those overtly arguing for the status quo are becoming a smaller group. While only Bavaria and Baden-Württemberg were pressing the competition agenda back in 1996, Hessen, Hamburg, North Rhine-Westphalia, Saxony and Thuringia are now on board, certainly to the extent that they did not back a paper rejecting the notion of competitive federalism published by the other nine Länder in September 1999.

This shifting balance suggests a growing transformative potential, as the changing practices of post-unification federalism mesh with the process of reconceptualizing German federalism pushed forward by Bavaria. It is entirely conceivable that this potential will develop the power in the coming years to overcome the obstacles to reform some German commentators worry and sigh about so much – the constitutional 'stickiness' mentioned earlier – and have the Basic Law 'catch up' with the changes that have already happened to capture the new quality of competitive federalism in Germany.

Notes

1. For a discussion of these two instances of 'non-reform', see Charlie Jeffery, 'Plus ca Change ... The Non-Reform of the German Federal System after Unification', *Leicester University Discussion Papers in Federal Studies*, No. FS93/2 (1993).
2. Cf. Christian Stolorz, 'Bedrückende Perspektiven des Föderalismus im vereinigten Deutschland', *Zeitschrift für Parlamentsfragen*, 28 (1997).
3. Roland Sturm, 'Der Föderalismus im Wandel. Kontinuitätslinien und Reformbedarf', in Eckhard Jesse, Konrad Löw, eds, *50 Jahre Bundesrepublik Deutschland* (Berlin 1999), p. 85.
4. A more detailed account of these interactions between party politics and territorial politics is presented in Charlie Jeffery, 'Party Politics and Territorial Representation in the Federal Republic of Germany', *West European Politics*, 22 (1999).
5. F. Scharpf et al., *Politikverflechtung. Theorie und Empirie des kooperativen Föderalismus in Deutschland* (Kronberg 1976).
6. G. Lehmbruch, *Parteienwettbewerb im Bundesstaat* (Stuttgart 1976).
7. Heidrun Abromeit, 'Zwischen Reformbedarf und Reformunfähigkeit – Die Alternativlosigkeit des kooperativen Föderalismus', in *Leistungen und Grenzen föderaler Ordnungsmodelle. Ettersburger Gespräche*, Weimar: Thüringer Ministerin für Bundesangelegenheiten in der Staatskanzlei (1996), p. 36.
8. Rainer Olaf Schulze, 'Föderalismusreform in Deutschland: Widersprüche – Ansätze – Hoffnungen', *Zeitschrift für Politik*, 46 (1999), p. 179.
9. Uwe Leonardy, 'German Federalism towards 2000: To be Reformed or Deformed?', in Charlie Jeffery, ed., *Recasting German Federalism: The Legacies of Unification* (London 1999).
10. Stolorz (1997), op. cit.
11. 'Wie die Länder dem Bund ein Stück Macht entwenden möchten. Zur Modernisierung des Föderalismus II', *Frankfurter Rundschau*, 26 July 1999.

12. Cf. Stefan Homburg, 'Anreizwirkungen des deutschen Finanzausgleichs', *Finanzarchiv*, 51 (1994).
13. Quoted in Martin Grobe Hüttmann, 'Die föderale Staatsform in der Krise', *Der Bürger im Staat*, 49 (1999), p. 107.
14. Bundesverfassungsgericht, BvF 2/98 vom 11.11.1999, downloaded at www.berfge.de.
15. *Frankfurter Allgemeine Zeitung*, 14.9.1998.
16. For example Arthur Benz, *Föderalismus als dynamisches System. Zentralisierung und Dezentralisierung im föderativen Staat* (Opladen 1995).
17. So Gottfried Müller, then President of the Thuringian Landtag, in 1992. Quoted in Jeffery, op. cit. (1993), p. 225.
18. See Ursula Männle, 'Grundlagen und Gestaltungsmöglichkeiten des Föderalismus in Deutschland', *Aus Politik und Zeitgeschichte*, no. B24/97 (1997), pp. 8–10.
19. Rudolf Hrbek, 'Eine politische Bewertung der VW-Beihilfen-Kontroverse', *Wirtschaftsdienst*, 10 (1996).
20. Quoted respectively in *Focus*, 12.8.1996, 37; *Münchner Merkur*, 21.9.1996; and *Münchner Merkur*, 17.8.1996.
21. Männle, op. cit. (1997), pp. 10–11.
22. Hans-Wolfgang Arndt, *Finanzausgleich und Verfassungsrecht*, manuscript (1997).
23. Cf. ibid, Übersicht 4.
24. Cf. *Focus*, 20 (1999).
25. Quoted in *Frankfurter Rundschau*, 24.7.1999.
26. Quoted in *Frankfurter Allgemeine Zeitung*, 4.5.1998.
27. *Disentanglement 2005*, report of the Bertelsmann Foundation Commission on Constitutional Politics and Government Capacity, manuscript (2000).
28. See Wolfgang Renzsch, 'Modernisierung der Finanzverfassung: Möglichkeiten und Grenzen', *FES-Analyse* (April 1999).
29. Compare the discussion of a 'cannibalism of the Länder' in *Frankfurter Allgemeine Zeitung*, 14.9.1998.

9
Challenges and Perspectives for German Federalism

Wolfgang Renzsch

Reforming German federalism is not a new idea. The debate started soon after the implementation of the 1969 *Finanzreform* – the reform of intergovernmental fiscal relations. Two pioneering books, both published in 1976, pointed out the 'traps' of the German type of cooperative federalism. With the theory of interlocking federalism, Fritz Scharpf and his collaborators[1] drew attention to political immobility arising out of joint decision-making both in Germany as well as in the European Union.[2] Gerhard Lehmbruch focused on the different modes of decision-making within the two chambers of the German federal legislature: decision-making by negotiation and by competition.[3] The 'incongruence' of both modes will eventually produce political gridlock. It should be pointed out however that both works depicted dangers, not necessities. Therefore, the question remained open: When do the traps click shut? Another question would be: What is the price Germany has to pay for avoiding the traps? In this respect it would be quite enlightening to compare the processes of decision-making in the failed tax reform in 1998 and in the successful one in 2000.

After the path-breaking studies by Scharpf and Lehmbruch, an extensive debate about the shortcomings and virtues of German federalism started. It is not the purpose of this paper to offer yet another learned contribution to this debate. But it would not be unfair to say that among academic observers there is a broad agreement that more flexibility, more competition, more responsibility and less entanglement are needed in order to improve the policy output of the German polity. Media, Land parliamentarians and even a former Federal President have participated in this debate. However, those in real positions of power have remained comparatively silent. The federal as well as the Länder governments – except a few – got only reluctantly involved in the debate. 'Practitioners' in the federal as well as the Länder administrations often talk about the advantage of cooperative intergovernmental relations. Officials from various departments – finance, economic development, research, housing, transportation – report that in spite of competing interests, they tend to achieve better results through practical administrative cooperation than they would if federal or Länder decision-making were autonomous.[4] Regrettably the opinions of those who operate the system are rarely reflected in academic discussions.

Although most practitioners of German politics have shown little enthusiasm for an overhaul of the system, the federal government and Länder governments have agreed to start a project called the 'modernization of the Federal State'. Under this heading, however, the government's policy on the issue remains unclear and hesitant. Among the 16 Länder governments, ten are rather reluctant, if not opposed, to reform. Only four openly support change. Under these circumstances, the prospect of fundamental change is remote. The modernization of the federal constitution will therefore not be decided by which academic drafts the best blueprint; it is rather a question of political feasibility.

In practical terms, too, there is considerable pressure to develop the federal system further. Two challenges in particular will require a rethink of German federalism. These challenges are the *budgetary crisis* and *European integration*. To date, the Federal Republic has responded to neither of them in a satisfactory way. This chapter will examine each in turn, starting with the budgetary crisis.

The German budgetary crisis is essentially home-made. Its origins can be traced back to the second half of the 1960s and the first half of the 1970s. Then, Keynesian models of economic steering which were supposed to create continuous economic growth were fashionable, and – at least originally – quite successful. This was a time when West Germany modernized her infrastructure. However, it soon became obvious that only one part of Keynes's theory worked well: deficit spending. The other part did not. According to the theory, governments are supposed to repay debts during boom periods. That part of the model was never carried out, for political reasons. It has never been all that difficult to convince a parliament to accept expenditure cuts during a time of economic recession. However, when money is readily available, it seems to be near impossible to get cuts accepted to free the funds for debt repayment. The late Franz-Josef Strauß, former federal minister of finance, is said to have once remarked that it was more difficult to keep a parliament from spending surpluses than training a bulldog to watch beef. Furthermore, expectations of growth are hardly ever fulfilled. As West Germany reached maturity, each slump of the business cycle became more costly to fight; each time the results of the recovery were less convincing. The revenues of growth never paid for the money spent on promoting growth. Unable to resolve this dilemma, two federal ministers of finance, Alex Möller and Karl Schiller, resigned in the 1970s.

At the beginning of the 1980s, it was well understood that something had to be done to avoid the trap opened by rising indebtedness and interest payments. Governments were increasingly in danger of losing their ability to act because of financial restrictions. The perception that Chancellor Helmut Schmidt was not in the position to achieve a U-turn in public finance was one of the reasons why the Liberals changed coalition in 1982. Yet their hopes for an improvement in financial policies were frustrated again. Beyond some cosmetic changes, Chancellor Helmut Kohl never managed to reduce public deficit spending. Unexpected German reunification increased the calamities of public finance. Expecting a fast and self-financing process of East Germany catching up with the West, the price of unity was initially financed by loans. As a result, in 1992, German interest rates reached a peak, which in turn caused a crisis of the European Monetary System. Great Britain saw herself forced to leave the system in order to avoid suffocating her economic recovery, which had only recently got under way. Later, the German federal government changed its strategy and raised taxes and levies to finance the unification process.[5]

It would, however, be short-sighted to regard German unification as a principal reason for the total public debt, currently amounting to more than DM 2300 billion. According to federal government figures, the transfer payments to the East constituted roughly 4.5 to 5 per cent of annual GNP in the mid 1990s. At the same time, the tax burden was raised by roughly 3.5 per cent. The final net deficit of 1 to 1.5 per cent of the GNP is undoubtedly significant, but it is an insufficient excuse for the dimensions of the public deficit increase of those years.

The size of the debt and the resulting interest payments are the main reason for the budgetary crisis which the Federal Republic has run into. From 1974 until 1997, interest payments on the public debt rose from 2.8 per cent to 7 per cent of total public expenditure. A further reason for the financial calamity is rising expenditure for welfare, social security and old age pensions. In the same time span, from 1974 to 1997, public expenditure on these items increased from 47.2 per cent to 51.2 per cent. Jointly, both categories rose from 50 per cent to 58 per cent of the total of public expenditure.[6]

At the same time, public investment in the future – education, science, research, etc. – remained comparatively small. From 1975 to 1997, its proportion of the total public expenditure dropped from 11.3 per cent to 9.9 per cent. The real decrease was even more significant: in interpreting these figures, we have to take into account that a large part, probably the largest part, of the expenditure on these items goes on paying the salaries of those working in education and research. In the period under consideration, the average age of employees in these fields has risen considerably, resulting in increasing expenditure on salaries. The German pay schemes for the civil service pay a 60-year-old person about twice as much as a 30-year-old of the same qualification. The decrease of about 10 per cent thus veils much larger cuts in these areas.[7] In an international comparison, the Federal Republic of Germany today pays more than most other nations to honour past spending commitments. These include interest payments, old age pensions and at least part of social security system. Investments in the future are small by comparison. It would not be unfair to say that an entire grandparents' generation has lived and will live to a large extent at the expense of their grandchildren. These grandchildren will have to pay for the debts their grandparents will leave behind, at least as far the public sector is concerned. The foreseeable dynamics of expenditure tend to suffocate the German polity. The trap opened by rising payments for past commitments is closing. In the private sector, however, the picture is quite different. Tremendous wealth will be inherited during the next years and decades.

What is less well known is the extent to which the asymmetry between public expenditure on these past commitments and future investments can be attributed to the mode of federal decision-making. The federal government is able unilaterally to reduce expenditure caused by programmes which are administered by federal agencies. Cuts in federal spending often lead to increased expenditure of the Land governments. For example, when the federal government cut the length of time during which people could receive unemployment benefit, this caused increased welfare burdens for the Länder, who are responsible for social security payments. The Land governments had to find the money to pay for these increased costs. To do so, they can pursue budget reductions, but only in those policy areas which are their sole jurisdiction. Of these, the most significant are precisely those that are commonly regarded as vital investments for the future: education, research and culture.

What is to be done? The easy ways out of the dilemma are blocked. Raising taxes would make Germany unattractive for private investment, diminishing the competitiveness of German industry. The obvious alternative, increasing loans, offers no solution. Increasing the public debt might help for the moment, but it would aggravate the budgetary dilemma in the long run. In addition, Europe does not permit increased deficit spending. As a member of the European Monetary Union, Germany has to respect the Maastricht criteria which forbid a public deficit of more than 3 per cent of the GNP. Furthermore, the goal of the EMU is to reduce public deficits further. The federal government wants to reduce its deficit to zero by 2006, as Federal Minister of Finance Hans Eichel repeatedly declared. It is difficult to see how the crisis can be resolved in such a way as not to strain the financial relationship between the federal government and the Länder yet further. This could have profound repercussions for the future of the federal constitution.

The second important challenge for the federal system is the process of European integration. Until about twenty years ago, most of the Länder lived quite comfortably under the German federal umbrella. German federalism guaranteed both: a coherent national policy framework that was based on the consent of the Länder governments, and decentralized policy delivery. The relative loss of the Länder's autonomy was compensated for by their increased influence on federal policy. Within a densely populated, fairly homogeneous country, this was deemed an appropriate compromise. The weaker Länder were quite content that the federation took over tasks which might have overburdened them. Most of the Länder governments did not miss legislative powers of their own; the contrary was (and partly remains) true: many Länder are not unhappy that the federation has taken over this job. They were relieved of the responsibility of drafting laws, thus avoiding the blame for unpopular legislation. At the same time, as far as domestic politics was concerned, the federation could hardly legislate without the consent of the Länder. In practice, the stronger Länder were often able to block federal policies which violated their interests, or at least to redefine those policies considerably. This deal seemed to be of advantage for all: the federal government, especially the federal branch of the governing parties, could extend its scope of action, the weaker Länder were relieved from tasks which might have overburdened them, and the stronger Länder could use their role as caucus leader within their party grouping to exercise an above-average influence.[8]

Since the 1980s, the process of European integration, notably the Single European Act, has changed the terms of trade. Responding to this changing context, the governments of the stronger Länder have begun to request more regulative autonomy for themselves. They demand that powers currently exercised by the federal government be handed back to the Länder. Why this change of approach?

As a result of European integration, the German Länder experienced a threefold loss of influence. First, they lost regulative powers which were transferred to Brussels. Since the Länder had already handed over many responsibilities to the German federal government, any further diminuition of their jurisdiction was considered unacceptable. Delegating further responsibilities to Brussels was all the more painful because, unlike in their power-sharing arrangement with the German federal government, at the European level, the consent of the Länder was no longer required, and not compensated for by extended co-determination. Second, the Länder governments also lost indirect influence on what had traditionally been federal policies, when these were transferred to the European Union. In these areas, the powers of Länder in the Bundesrat became inconsequential. Third, via Brussels, the federal government gained influence in policy areas which used to be under the sole jurisdiction of the Länder but were now under European jurisdiction. This development was heavily criticized by the Länder governments, especially by Bavaria and North Rhine-Westphalia. After all, in terms of their population and their economic strength, each one of these Länder is comparable to a medium-sized member nation of the EU. Both of these Länder thus envisaged themselves playing an active and more prominent role in European affairs. In order to do so, they created the necessary administrative manpower within their civil services. The smaller Länder are barely in the position to compete with them for this kind of role.

The increasing strength and involvement of this sub-national level of government is one side of the coin of European integration. The other is the weakening of national governments as a result of the asymmetry between globalized markets and national polities. The four liberties of the European single market – freedom of movement for commodities, people, capital and services – have transcended national boundaries. These boundaries still represent restrictions in terms of national economic regulation; however, they do not hinder anybody from crossing them, thus leaving the area of a specific national jurisdiction. Markets without borders limit the political options of national governments considerably. The 'big' issues, such as currency, interest rates, trade policies, etc., are controlled on Community level. These general regulations are the same within the whole single market. The 'small' issues, by contrast, such as local infrastructure, access, labour force, etc., are dependent on regional or local decision-making. Therefore, competition for investment is no longer a competition between nations; it has largely become competition among regions.

The single market in Europe has thus also offered new opportunities to the German Länder. They have started to develop networks with other European regions. It is not surprising that those Länder which are economically strong and play an important role in international markets, and which do also employ a comparatively large bureaucracy are the ones to request more scope for their own decision-making. Expanded Länder autonomy is high on the agenda of Bavaria and North Rhine-Westphalia in particular.

Undoubtedly, the challenges of the budgetary crisis and European integration cannot be ignored for much longer. Mechanisms of resource allocation which were allowed to continue without modernization will run dry eventually. Constitutional inefficiencies can no longer be compensated for by the revenues of economic growth. Germany has already become a country of slow economic growth; the boom expected in East Germany after unification did not take place. However, it is very difficult to predict when the consequences of stalled reforms will become sufficiently painful to overcome the politically motivated reluctance to overhaul the federal system.

After many years of political standstill on this front, the issue of modernization of the federal state has been placed on the political agenda in two important moves. First, in December 1998, Chancellor Gerhard Schröder agreed with the minister presidents of the Länder to establish a joint working group in order to develop measures for a reform of the federal system. Second, on 11 November 1999, the Federal Constitutional Court ruled on the constitutional status of the current system of financial equalization.[9] Prior to that decision, the procedures of the Karlsruhe court provided an obstacle to the debate over reforming the federal system because some Länder insisted on awaiting the court's decision first, expecting that the ruling might support their interests. Not only has this waiting period now come to an end. The Court also obliged the legislature of Germany to re-examine the whole financial equalization system. The Court did not prescribe a precise new mechanism itself, and ruled only on the procedures to be adopted for the reform process. Within the next two years, general criteria have to be developed which should serve as a yardstick for financial equalization. By the end of 2004, a new law concerning the actual equalization must be passed. Looking at the progress the negotiations among the Länder governments and between the Länder governments and the federal government have reached early in the year 2001, observers are disappointed. It has become quite obvious that the status quo, not change, seems to be the guideline of the majority of those who are involved in the process of decision-making. However, the Bundestag, the German parliament, has just started its deliberations. The ruling of the Federal Constitutional Court which intended reform, has produced the contrary: because the political process now concentrates on finance, the issue of federal reform was actually postponed. Because there will be no federal reform, the debate on finance will most probably end up at the status quo.

Nevertheless, the necessity of reform is thus established beyond dispute. It is now time to turn to the obstacles that continue to stand in the way of change. First, it is important to focus on what might be termed the structural logic of German 'functional' federalism. Federal regulation of the national markets, adopted with the consent of Länder governments which implement federal regulation under their own responsibility, and a federally determined tax system combined with a highly equalizing system of tax distribution provide for a coherent system. It is difficult to see how its basic structure can be changed without destroying the functional relations that depend on these structures. Therefore, proposals which suggest reforming or removing crucial parts of the system such as the role of the Bundesrat or the financial equalization mechanism, based, as they are, primarily on current requirements, might not improve but destroy the system.

It appears that there is no scope for a radical change in the direction of a system of 'jurisdictional' or 'dual' federalism. After all, the German model of functional federalism has solved the problem of coordination between the two levels of government better than most other types of federalism. Article 37 of the *Grundgesetz* – federal enforcement – has never been used against any Land government. The financial whip or 'golden rein' which in many other federations serves to force the member states or provinces to adopt the policies of the federal government has never played an important role in German intergovernmental relations. In a geographically small and densely populated country with no truly fundamental linguistic, cultural or religious subdivisions, functional federalism has succeeded in delivering a remarkable degree of equalization between living conditions in the member states. Whatever radical fringe politicians suggest, on election day the

German electorate has never supported regional parties which have been hostile towards the customary degree of uniformity among the German Länder. Trying to tell a German motorist to cope with five different Land-based traffic regulations during a single car journey from Berlin to Munich would be an undertaking doomed from the start. German parties and governments have learned to take such expectations into account. Recently, the federal Conference of Ministers of the Interior discussed a ban on bull terriers. Despite having their own jurisdiction in place, the Länder governments realized that nothing short of unitary regulation on the national level could provide a convincing solution to the problem.[10] Any other regulation would open up loopholes and ultimately subvert the policy in question, which in turn would be considered politically irresponsible by public opinion.

The race between decentralizing and centralizing forces often resembles the fairy-tale race between the hare and the tortoise: the tortoise of centralization sat on the finishing line while the hare of decentralization was still running energetically. We need to remember, however, that the tendency towards unitary federalism corresponds to another feature of the German political system, namely the existence of integrated national parties. German political parties have always tried to act more or less consistently on all levels of government, usually paying little respect to the demarcation lines between different tiers of Land and federal decision making in this. Characteristically, the recent Land election which took place in North Rhine-Westphalia was labelled a 'small general election' by the media.

Unitary or 'cooperative' federalism and political competition between nationally integrated parties are mutually stabilizing: party competition pushes for consistent national solutions. In comparison to North America, for example, German parties tend to act with much more closed ranks across the different levels of government. The federal chancellor and the federal opposition leader both campaigned during the last Land elections in North Rhine-Westphalia. In such campaigns, political parties hardly distinguish between different jurisdictions: federal policy issues dominate campaigns at Land level, Land policy issues are discussed at the federal level. Additionally, the proportional electoral system fuels the tendency towards unitary policies. Even for parties with clear regional strongholds it is vital to win a share of the vote elsewhere, too, by offering a policy approach that transcends the boundaries of the region in question.[11] And that is indeed what the electorate expect: many instances in Germany's recent past have shown that disunity will be punished on election day.

All these circumstances have militated against regionally differentiated solutions. However, the German political parties have changed during the last two decades or so. If there is a general trend, it is surely that they have become more 'federalized', in the sense that regional leaders have gained considerable influence. Consequently, party ideologies have become less important, controversial issues no longer follow the simple paradigms of 'left' and 'right', and regional diversity has increased. Therefore, the parties' grip on policy formulation has been loosened. As a result, we can expect the unifying effect of party competition on the federal system to decrease – to an extent. However, on issues likely to gain a high public profile, contradictory positions adopted by two Land branches of the same party, or by the federal and a Land branch of one party, will surely continue to be used by the other parties as proof of the disunity of the party concerned, and used as evidence that it has lost the ability to act cohesively required by a party of government.[12] Despite a certain shift of emphasis, it is clear that the agencies of political legitimation, the institutional setting and the modes of political competition continue to restrict the potential for dramatic change considerably. It would be misleading to expect that German federalism will diverge from the historical path of functional federalism and turn towards a model of competitive federalism.

Having said that, change within the framework of functional federalism is not only possible, but it is becoming probable. First, there is a change in the historical circumstances to take into account. When the fundamental decisions about the German federal structure, in particular about federal finance, were first taken, the political imperative was unity. When the *Grundgesetz* was drafted in 1948–9, the re-emerging German polity had to address the challenges of the immediate post-war period. Under condition of immediate and dramatic scarcity, basic provisions had to be provided for all. There was hardly any room for differentiation or competing solutions. Even in 1968–9, when the *Finanzreform* was adopted, the goal was to provide equal standards and opportunities for those regions which suffered from disadvantages. And in 1992–3, when the Eastern Länder were financially integrated into the federal system, East Germans demanded to be accepted on an equal footing with West Germans. An added consideration throughout this period was that the Cold War put West Germany in a kind of ideological competition with communist East Germany. This East–West confrontation must form a cornerstone of any explanation for West Germany having developed such a highly elaborate unitary welfare system.

Although the process of development and regeneration in East Germany will take another decade or more, the historical circumstances which pushed Germany in the direction of unitary federalism have disappeared. Instead, there are forces pushing in the opposite direction. These forces are emerging out of the budgetary crisis, and the dual processes of European integration and economic globalization. With regard to the budgetary crisis, some Länder have come to the conclusion that federally set standards of their policy delivery can be unnecessarily costly. For example, North Rhine-Westphalia plans to offer civil servants special retirement schedules at the age of 55 when their jobs become effectively redundant. Since legislation concerning civil servants at all levels of government is officially under the control of the federal government, the government of North Rhine-Westphalia can only act after a change in the federal law. However, the procedure to amend federal laws is not only time-consuming; it is also uncertain whether the necessary political majorities can be gathered. Other Land governments disagreeing with the policy pursued by North Rhine-Westphalia have already made their resistance public. They are afraid that their civil servants will demand the same privileges. This example illustrates one of the more prominent difficulties. Party governments do not necessarily put their common concern with increased Land autonomy first: they also take party interests into account, at least as long as they do not contradict government interests. It seems increasingly likely that regulation concerning civil servants might be one of the powers which eventually will be handed back to the Land legislatures.

Federal regulation is not only costly for the Länder. It also provides hurdles to economic progress. In the member states of the European Union, the general rules are predominantly set at European level. At the same time, decisions about investment often depend on local (or regional) conditions. National regulation has lost importance, it can even can become an obstacle for the competing regions. One example is that despite European deregulation, German regulations on manual trades (the so-called *Handwerke*) still place obstacles in the way of setting up new businesses and training apprentices. German national regulations require higher qualifications and longer training periods for these professions than European regulations. It is extremely difficult to change such federal regulations. By comparison, it would probably be much easier to change such regulations at Land level. Currently, a decision of the European courts on whether or not German law is incompatible with European law is pending. The general trend is for regions – in the German case, the Länder – to push for the right to regulate the conditions for investment in their home territory themselves. This applies especially to the stronger regions. A change of attitude of the Länder can thus be expected, as the deregulation entailed by coordinated European legislation opens up new scope for expanding the competence of Europe's regions.

First indicators of this change can be observed already. In 1998, European guidelines on the protection of fauna, flora and habitat had to be made into national law. In this instance, the combination of European decision-making and budget constraints resulted in a decentralized solution. The German federal government tried to introduce uniform compensation payments for ecologically motivated restrictions on agricultural production. Of course, the compensation was to be paid for by the Land governments. The majority of Länder opposed the proposal, and demanded that the issue be settled according to Land legislation. Under mounting pressure – the deadline for translating European guidelines into German law had already passed – the federal government finally agreed. This saved the Länder a lot of money, as Land legislation proved to be less costly than the federal legislation would have been.[13]

These days, even the German federal government appears increasingly inclined to accept a more decentralized mode of decision making. It has even used the prospect of decentralization as a bargaining chip. In 1999, some Länder governments requested a reintroduction of property tax through federal law. Other Land governments and the federal government itself opposed this policy. To reach a compromise with the protesting Länder, the federal government offered to open up this part of tax legislation to the Länder. However, none of the Land governments pushing for the reintroduction of property tax was interested in doing so via Land legislation, as they were not ready to take the blame for imposing new taxes on their citizens. The federal government's plan, to transfer competence to the Länder level in the expectation that they would be reluctant to introduce this tax individually, paid off.[14]

Can we conclude, then, that the forces pushing German federalism in a unitary direction are decreasing while those force pushing in the opposite direction are increasing? And if so, what are the effects? As we have seen, after decades of purely academic debate, a reform of the German federal system has been put on the political agenda. However, for reasons mentioned above scepticism rather than optimism is advised when we look at the probable results.

The majority of the 'fiscally conservatives' on the Länder side wish to avoid any substantial change to the equalization system. In the Länder camp, there is currently a 'group of ten' defending the existing system and opposing the 'gang of four' demanding a move towards greater autonomy for the Länder. Two further Länder are as yet undecided. North Rhine-Westphalia, one of the gang of four, tries to mediate between the two opposing camps. Sources from inside the political system have suggested that the federal minister of finance is in favour of maintaining the status quo among the Länder, but advocates some limited structural change.[15]

Starting federal reform with finance is doomed to fail. The majority of the weak Länder – ten out of sixteen – will block any change which would be at their expense. As long as there are no incentives for them they will defend the status quo. Therefore, the proper path of reform would be, first, to give the Länder more scope for discretion and, second, to change the nature of inter-Länder relations. The frequently and correctly criticized development towards increased financial equalization follows a traditional tendency towards more and more material unitarization. To break the vicious circle of increasing expenditure for equalization and decreasing efficiency, it is necessary first to change the allocation of legislative competence.

So what will actually happen in years to come? One thing is clear: there will be no fundamental overhaul of the federal system in its entirety. Germany will continue to adhere to the type of functional federalism that has evolved historically, and will not adopt the American type of jurisdictional federalism. In economic terms, this means that there will be no change from cooperative to competitive federalism. The radical changes which have been advocated by theoreticians of fiscal federalism stand no chance of winning over a political majority.

A reform should however provide for more efficiency in policy delivery, faster decision-making and more flexibility. One remedy for current problems would be to disentangle federal and Land governments in areas where they could easily pursue policies of their own. Co-financing should be reduced and simplified. The regulation of joint tasks and of various kinds of federal contributions to Länder tasks could also be freed of unnecessary complications, and reduced to one general rule which allows the federal government to support ailing Länder under specific circumstances. Notably, there can be no doubt that the East German Länder in particular will require further federal assistance for the next two years or so to come.

As far as the much debated devolution of the right to tax is concerned, however, we should not expect any change. To date, the federal government has not given any indication that is is ready to devolve tax-raising powers. The federal minister of finance argues that European tax harmonization will be the number one tax issue of future years, not 'parochialization'. Neither do the majority of the Länder have a real interest in acquiring tax-raising powers. Most fear that tax competition would provide undue advantages for the better-off Länder and that as a result, the gap between the better-off and poorer Länder would widen. Indeed, it is considered vital to preserve a functional federalism in which public tasks are predominantly defined by the federation, and supported by the individual Länder. Policy delivery, by contrast, should be financed by the Länder under competitive terms.

In the field of intergovernmental fiscal relations, new legislation is on the cards. Due to the ruling of the Federal Constitutional Court, the risks associated with failure are much higher for all concerned than the risks of controlled amendments. As this area of reform constitutes a no-win situation, however, a change which will minimize the fiscal impact on the status quo is likely. Looking at the positions the Länder governments have taken, it is quite clear that for the time being, ten out of sixteen Länder oppose any fundamental change. All Länder currently face a comparatively difficult budgetary situation, and none is in the position to support significant financial redistribution at their expense. Only a solution that minimizes divergence from the status quo will stand any chance of getting accepted by the necessary majorities of the federal legislature.

Federal finance reforms are tricky because they are connected with the issue of devolution of legislative powers to the Länder. Although in principle, a large number of politicians from all major parties agree on this issue, they behave quite differently in day-to-day practice. The 16 minister presidents created a working group in order to draft a proposal to realize the provision of Article 125a of the *Grundgesetz*, which states that federal law can under certain circumstances be transformed into Land law. The results were trivial. We have to accept that there is a huge difference between a general plea for the decentralization of political power, and finding majorities in order that competence on real issues can be devolved in practice.

It is not yet clear what objectives the federal government will pursue in this field. Generally speaking, it can have little interest in significant change. Any dramatic reform will lead to a loss of federal influence and power. The federal government is therefore not in favour of decentralizing regulation. This is partly based on an error of judgement. Devolution could avoid many damaging confrontations with the

Länder. Canada provides a good example for pacifying intergovernmental relations by a retreat of the federal government from interfering in provincial policies. Why fight over issues like closing hours for shops, regulations for civil servants or fees for universities when a retreat of the federal government would guarantee peace in federation-Länder relations?

A piecemeal, incremental development which tries to preserve the features of the German model which are worth preserving may well be the way to go. The buzzwords are successful coordination between the two tiers of government, uniform regulation when politically desirable, and policy implementation at the local levels, in touch with the citizen's practical concerns. There will be no cooperative decision-making leading to uniform national standards of policy delivery which has to be financed by the Länder governments under competitive terms.

By way of a conclusion, a reform proposal by Fritz Scharpf could indicate the direction of future change in the German federal system. Scharpf's recommendation resembles a procedure practised in Canada. He suggests that in the area of concurrent legislation, the Länder legislatures should be allowed to replace federal legislation by equivalent Land legislation. The federal legislature, however, could veto Land legislation within a certain period of time. Canada has successfully implemented this compromise with the introduction of an opt-out clause. In practice, it has seldom been necessary to use it. Rather, the function of a constitutional opt-out clause is to pacify the thorny and controversial debate on devolution of federal legislative powers. It could provide for conflict resolution in the field of federation-Länder relations. There would be a general federal rule, but for those Länder wishing to implement a different way, there would be an opportunity to do so. Such a clause would allow a kind of flexibility which is unknown to German federalism up to now, while preserving intergovernmental cooperation when desired. However, the main political parties seem to be rather reluctant to accept this kind of 'Sinatra' federalism.

Notes

1. Fritz W. Scharpf, Bernd Reissert, Fritz Schnabel, *Politikverflechtung: Theorie und Empire des kooperativen Föderalismus in der Bundesrepublik Deutschland* (Kronberg/Ts. 1976); Fritz W. Scharpf, Bernd Reissert, Fritz Schnabel, 'Policy Effectiveness and Conflict Avoidance in Intergovernmental Policy Formation' in Kenneth Hanf, ed., *Interorganizational Policy Making* (London 1978).
2. Fritz W. Scharpf, 'The Joint-Decision Trap: Lesson from German Federalism and European Integration', *Public Administration*, 66 (1988).

3. Gerhard Lehmbruch, *Parteienwettbewerb im Bundesstaat* (Stuttgart, Berlin, Cologne and Mainz 1976); Gerhard Lehmbruch, *Parteienwettbewerb im Bundesstaat: Regelsysteme und Spannungslagen im Institutionengefüge der Bundesrepublik Deutschland*, 2nd revised edn (Opladen 1998); Gerhard Lehmbruch, *Parteienwettbewerb im Bundesstaat: Regelsysteme und Spannungslagen im politischen System der Bundesrepublik Deutschland*, 3rd revised edn (Wiesbaden 2000).
4. Two examples. An official of the ministry of education and research in Brandenburg reported that the Land itself is hardly in a position to run the research institutes located in Brandenburg. Financial and administrative assistance of the federal government is required. Autonomy in this field would imply either 'parochialization' or centralization of research policies. Neither is wanted. An official of the Sachsen-Anhalt ministry of economic development spoke about coordination of waterways policies. Waterways are partly under federal, partly under Land jurisdiction. Extensive collaboration on a day-to-day base is in the interest of both sides involved.
5. Wolfgang Renzsch, 'Budgetäre Anpassung statt institutionellen Wandels. Zur finanziellen Bewältigung der Lasten des Beitritts der DDR zur Bundesrepublik', in Hellmut Wollmann, Hans-Ulrich Derlien, Klaus König, Wolfgang Renzsch and Wolfgang Seibel, eds, *Transformation der politisch-administrativen Strukturen in Ostdeutschland*, Beiträge zu den Berichten der Kommission für die Erforschung des sozialen und politischen Wandels in den neuen Ländern e.V. (KPSW) 3.1 (Opladen 1997); Wolfgang Renzsch, 'Financing German Unity: Fiscal Conflict Resolution in a Complex Federation', *Publius: The Journal of Federalism* (Fall 1998).
6. These and the following data are drawn from Statistisches Bundesamt, Fachserie 14, Steuern und Finanzen, Reihe 3.1.
7. Wolfgang Renzsch, 'Aufgabenschwerpunkte und –verschiebungen im Bund', in Thomas Ellwein, Everhard Holtmann, eds, *50 Jahre Bundesrepublik. Rahmenbedingungen – Entwicklungen – Perspektiven* (PVS – Sonderheft, Opladen 30/1999).
8. It is quite obvious that North Rhine-Westphalia has become the leader of the caucus of SPD-governed *Länder* while Bavarian has taken over this role for the CDU/CSU-governed ones.
9. BVerfGE 101, 158.
10. *Süddeutsche Zeitung*, 5 May 2000.
11. The PDS, the former Socialist Unity Party, returns roughly 20 per cent of East German votes. That is good for getting elected to the East German Land legislatures, but it does not make 5 per cent at federal level. Therefore, it is important for the party to gain 1 or 2 per cent in West Germany to overcome the 5 per cent hurdle to safely achieve representation in the Bundestag.
12. Wolfgang Renzsch, 'Parteien im Bundesstaat. Sand oder Öl im Getriebe?', in Ursula Männle, ed., *Föderalismus zwischen Konsens und Konkurrenz* (Baden-Baden 1998); Wolfgang Renzsch, 'Party Competition in the Federal State. New Variations on an Old Theme', *Federal and Regional Studies* 9, 3.
13. Bundesrats-Drucksache 280/98 [Beschluss]. See Wolfgang Renzsch, 'Konfliktlösung im parlamentarischen Bundesstaat: Zur Verfahrenssteuerung durch politische Parteien', in Tobias Dürr and Franz Walter, eds,

Solidargemeinschaft und fragmentierte Gesellschaft: Parteien, Milieus und Verbände im Vergleich. Festschrift zum 60. Geburtstag von Peter Lösche (Opladen 1999).
14. The fact that the Länder governments requesting the reintroduction of the property tax were the ones which would have gained less than average was quite remarkable. Their interest was to get a federally regulated tax and to profit from the revenues of the better-off Länder through fiscal equalization.
15. Entwurf Maßstäbegesetz, Bundesrats-Drucksache 161/01.

10
German Federalism in History: Some Afterthoughts

Anthony J. Nicholls

Why are the Germans more comfortable with federalism than the English? Is a Yorkshireman less proud of his regional heritage than a Bavarian? Is North Rhine-Westphalia less of an artificial construct than Wessex? This collection of essays on the background to and contemporary operation of German federalism provokes reflections on the role of history in the development of both political institutions and regional identities.

Several of the contributors mention the way in which German nationalists in the nineteenth century down-played the federal elements in their history and glorified the creation of a powerful nation-state. Yet the German Empire which Bismarck forged was itself an ambiguous construction. Its primary aim from his point of view was the aggrandisement of Prussia, which itself met the requirements of a centralized state. It did not, however, fulfil the National Liberal ideal of a unitary, national system organized along rational lines. Bismarck was careful to ensure that the seat of sovereignty in the new Reich remained in the Bundesrat, the forum for the representatives of the older, aristocratically dominated states which had been established by the Vienna settlement in 1815. With the exception of the unfortunate victims of Prussian rapacity, such as the Kingdom of Hanover, the old pre-imperial structures of administration remained in place, to the dismay of radical reformers, including those in Prussia itself.

From Bismarck's point of view this had many advantages. The maintenance of administrative autonomy in countries like Bavaria or Saxony dulled the edge of anti-Prussian feeling and encouraged the integration of otherwise reluctant regions into the Reich. The success of this policy was illustrated by the enthusiastic response to the outbreak of war in August 1914, even in such a particularist Land as

Bavaria. It was also useful for the Iron Chancellor to be able to play-off the Land parliaments and governments, including that of Prussia itself, against the Reichstag, the only possible instrument of democratization within the constitution.

Is it possible, however, to talk of 'federalism' when considering the Wilhelmine Empire? The 'federal' elements in the constitution of that body were legacies of the former Bund established after Napoleon's defeat, and that in turn was a modified and rather streamlined version of the Holy Roman Empire dissolved in 1806. The fascinating contributions by Joachim Whaley and Maiken Umbach in this volume demonstrate that there is much more to the Holy Roman Empire than its nationalist critics would have had us believe. Nevertheless, it is difficult not to agree with Karl Otmar von Aretin that there was no realistic chance of a reform of the Empire, or of its successor the Bund, which might have led to a viable federation of German states. Nor did the apparently federal elements built into the Wilhelmine Empire develop into an balanced and effective federal system.

The completely lopsided nature of the Reich, dominated as it was by Prussia, meant that even after the November revolution of 1918 no solution could be found to Germany's structural problem, despite the various, and contradictory, proposals for reform bruited about during the Weimar Republic. One reason for this was that two of the parties which supported the original 'Weimar coalition', the Democrats and the Social Democrats, were ideologically opposed to federalism anyhow, and tended to prefer a centralized Reich with democratized local government. The situation was further complicated by the fact that both those parties and the Roman Catholic Centre, itself more sympathetic to regional autonomy, found themselves in a stronger position politically in Prussia than they enjoyed elsewhere in the Reich. Despite Adenauer's desire to see a new West German Land created from the Rhineland provinces of Prussia, any attempt to weaken the Prussian state was regarded in Berlin as threatening the integrity of the Reich. Yet no rational solution for Germany's structural problems, either federal or centralized, could be found while Prussia retained such a disproportionate influence over Germany's administrative system.

It was not until after the total defeat of Germany and the abolition of Prussia in February 1947, one of the few war aims on which the Allied Powers were entirely agreed, that it was possible to set up a genuinely federal structure in Germany. Even then, as Mary Fulbrook points out, political developments in the GDR quickly proved incompatible with any form of federal decentralization there. In the Western zones the combination of conservative distaste for strong central governments, and the Allied desire to prevent Germany reappearing as a great power, meant that the founding fathers of the Federal Republic, meeting in the Parliamentary Council in Bonn, 1948–9, were encouraged to create a system which combined regional identity with effective central government. This enabled West Germany to emerge as an outstandingly successful democratic state.

What part did history play in all this? In a direct sense, that is to say in the sense that pre-1945 forms of government foreshadowed the creation of the Federal Republic, or that there was in Germany a powerful federalist movement which just needed the defeat of the Third Reich to reveal itself, the answer is probably not very much. But, as several of the contributions to this volume indicate, there was enough of a tradition of the 'other Germany', the Germany which had opposed unification by force in 1870 and which had tried to preserve certain autonomous features of the Reich under both the Wilhelmine Empire and the Weimar Republic, to enable a consensus to be found amongst the majority of the constitution-makers in 1948–9 in favour of a federal solution. The powerful advocacy of decentralization by the Bavarian government was one factor in this discussion, but it should be noted that even some Protestant liberal intellectuals had by that time come round to the view that Germany had taken a fateful wrong turning in the middle of the nineteenth century, and that Prussian hegemony had been disastrous for the country's political, social and economic development.

An interesting example of this was the neo-liberal economist Wilhelm Röpke who, in the summer of 1945, when the Big Three Allied powers at Potsdam were still committed to administering Germany as a unity, already argued that the best solution would be for the area East of the Elbe to be left to its Soviet occupiers so that a decentralized federal state could be created in the West. Needless to say, historical justifications were advanced for this, with reference to the flourishing medieval towns of Western Germany within the former *limes* of the Roman Empire. Similar visions of past occidental peace and prosperity were to be found in the writings of Roman Catholic Rhinelanders during the occupation.[1]

It is certainly worth noting that throughout most of the so-called modern period Germans were used to being administered in their daily lives by officials and politicians from their own regional area. There were, of course, exceptions to this after Bismarck's wars of conquest, and resentments resulted from them. The appearance of the Deutsche Partei after the Second World War attested to the longevity of Hanoverian sentiments after 1871, and Rhinelanders' commitment to the Prussian state was somewhat half-hearted. Particularism – not separatism – was a detectable characteristic in Germany throughout its modern history. As Jeremy Noakes demonstrates in his masterly study of the demise of any sort of federalism in the Third Reich, even Nazi Gauleiter found it convenient to adopt local patriotism when it offered them the chance to defend or extend their own authority.

The two dictatorships in recent German history, those of Hitler and Ulbricht, illustrate both the limitations and the tenacity of regionalism amongst the Germans. Neither Prussia nor Bavaria was able to withstand illegal centralization on the part of the enemies of democracy, in 1932–3. But the Bavarians did at least make a show of resistance, and were able to create a post-war myth of the nazi *Einmarsch* across the Main. So far as the GDR is concerned I wonder whether Mary Fulbrook does not underestimate the regional resentments caused by Ulbricht's relentlessly centralizing policy, a policy which had already become apparent in the economic sphere before the creation of the GDR itself. It is difficult otherwise to explain the subsequent political developments in Saxony, for example, a country of Protestant character in which the German socialist labour movement had a strong tradition stretching back to the beginnings of the Wilhelmine Empire. Yet it emerged from the ruins of the GDR as a stronghold of the Christian Democrats. In the *Landtag* elections of September 1999, the CDU led the poll in every constituency, which means that under a British first-past-the-post electoral system the Saxon parliament would at the time of writing consist only of Christian Democratic deputies. How did this transformation come about? Doubtless the skill of Kurt Biedenkopf should not be underestimated, but surely the widespread belief that the *Nomenklatura* in Berlin and Potsdam were being being favoured over the provincial populations in the GDR must have had a lot to do with it.

Indeed, one of the remarkable features of the development of the former GDR has been the rapidity with which the federal system has taken root; not only Saxony but also Thuringia has recreated its own identity, and in Brandenburg the figure of Manfred Stolpe can be seen as a typical *Landesvater*. As for the idea that the only regionalism in the former East Germany is the 'Ossie' mentality created by the GDR itself, one might argue that such solidarity hardly existed before the collapse of the Berlin Wall and was largely a reaction against insensitive behaviour by West Germans on the one hand, and the unexpected economic upheavals which accompanied the collapse of the command economy on the other. Already we are seeing differences appearing between the south and the north in the new Länder which may turn out to be just as important as the 'Ossie/Wessie' divide.

However, it should be noted that the success of federalism does not necessarily rest on its historical roots. With the clear exception of Bavaria, and the possible exception of Hesse and Hamburg, few West German Länder could be regarded as historical entities. Yet their inhabitants show no desire to see them amalgamated or emasculated. The rejection of the Berlin–Brandenburg merger indicated the concern of those East Germans involved to retain their newly minted regional identities.

Furthermore, the view which could be heard in the 1980s that German federalism was a busted flush and that, under the guise of 'cooperative federalism', Bonn was really taking over, has been at least put on hold since the appearance of Kohl as Chancellor in 1982, the intensification of European integration and the unification of Germany. As Charlie Jeffery points out, cooperative federalism is now being challenged by a harder-nosed version which stresses Land autonomy, and even though the practical experience of Wolfgang Rensch indicates that future reforms in the direction of decentralization may not be very drastic, there is little doubt that federalism seems here to stay as a characteristic of German governance.

Lastly, we should note that the German model of federalism is being imitated abroad, most notably in Spain, but even – to a limited extent – in the United Kingdom. Historical precedents for regional devolution can usually be found. But if, as some of us believe, federalism is a method of government which combines humane and democratic principles with effective fulfilment of popular wishes, it will be political commitment, and not historical tradition, which will ensure that it continues to develop and flourish.

Note

1. Compare Hans-Peter Schwarz, *Vom Reich zur Bundesrepublik: Deutschland im Widerstreit der Außenpolitischen Konzeptionen in den Jahren der Besatzungsherrschaft 1945–1949*, 2nd edn (Stuttgart 1980) Section VIII. See also Wilhelm Röpke, *Die deutsche Frage* (Erlenbach and Zurich 1945).

Index